# Create Your Own DTM Programs

## a Programmer's Guide to Do-It-Yourself Digital Terrain Modelling

by Giles Darling

## Book Two of Two

# What's inside these two books?

Book One and this book contain complete listings of C++ source code for a suite of programs that create and work with digital terrain models (DTMs). These programs are written for computers running the Microsoft Windows 7 (or above) operating system.

## Book One:

Chapters 1 to 3 introduce core components that are used in the rest of the chapters. These core components include:

- a text window that doesn't get full or run out of memory,
- a file importer and exporter that converts between a variety of text formats,
- a tool to manage time-intensive number-crunching tasks,
- a graphics window with in-built zoom, pan, and point- and rectangle-selection abilities that can also export images to JPEG files, and
- a range of shape classes that manage and interact with arrays of data for a variety of shapes including points, lines, triangles, slope or gradient arrows, and paths or polylines containing lines and arcs.

Chapter 4 details the code required to create a DTM from 3D points and optional breaklines and optional boundary lines. The code creates a DTM containing 3D triangles.

## Book Two (this book):

Chapters 5 to 14 use the triangles created in Chapter 4 for various purposes including:

- applying contours to your DTM,
- calculating z values, maximum slopes and slope directions,
- calculating areas and volumes under your DTM,
- identifying high and low points,
- calculating flow paths,
- identifying DTM boundaries,
- calculating the intersection and difference in z values or levels between two overlapping DTMs, and
- creating vertical sections or profiles through your DTM along paths or polylines.

Finally, the appendices at the end of Book Two include generic lisp routines to extract point, line, triangle and path data from your CAD drawings, and derivations and proofs of the geometric equations used in the two books.

The C++ source files (.cpp, .h and .rc), lisp routine files (.lsp), and sample data files (.txt) are all available from my website, as detailed at the end of Chapter 3 in Book One.

**Book One can be used on its own. However, Book Two assumes that you have access to the source code in Book One. Book Two cannot be used on its own.**

# Table of Contents

The Introduction and Chapters 1 to 4 are in Book One.

# Chapter 5

## Create Contours

Chapter 5 lists the source code for a program called **Chapter05** that creates contours from a DTM of 3D triangles. These 3D triangles could have been created by the code in Chapter 4, extracted from a CAD drawing using the lisp routine EXTRACTTRIAS (see Appendix A), or created by hand. The program uses two custom dialog boxes to enable the user to enter major and minor z intervals to create groups of contours, or to enter a single z value to create contours with a single z value. The contours created by the program can be exported as a text file, as a CAD script file, or as a JPEG file. The user can also get information about individual contour lines by left-clicking the mouse over the lines in the graphics window.

The following files are discussed in this chapter:

**Chapter05.h**          **Chapter05.rc**          **Chapter05.cpp**

## Chapter05 Source Files

The first file is the header file:

**CHAPTER05.H**

```
#ifndef CHAPTER05_H
#define CHAPTER05_H

#define IDM_IMPORTTRIANGLES           101
#define IDM_EXPORTSINGLECONTOURS      102
#define IDM_EXPORTCONTOURGROUPS       103
#define IDM_EXPORTSCREEN              104
#define IDM_EXPORTMODEL               105
#define IDM_EXIT                      106

#define IDM_CREATESINGLECONTOUR       201
#define IDM_CREATECONTOURGROUPS       202

#define IDN_SHOWMENU                  2

#define IDM_SHOWTRIANGLES             301
#define IDM_SHOWSINGLECONTOURS        302
#define IDM_SHOWCONTOURGROUPS         303
#define IDM_COLOURBACKGROUND          304
#define IDM_COLOURCOORDSTEXT          305
#define IDM_COLOURTRIANGLES           306
#define IDM_COLOURSINGLECONTOURS      307
#define IDM_COLOURMAJORCONTOURS       308
#define IDM_COLOURMINORCONTOURS       309
#define IDM_ZOOMEXTENTS               310
#define IDM_REDRAW                    311

#define IDN_MOUSEMENU                 3
```

```
#define IDM_MOUSEZOOM                      401
#define IDM_MOUSEPAN                       402
#define IDM_MOUSESINGLECONTOUR             403
#define IDM_MOUSEGROUPCONTOUR              404

#define IDM_LISTTRIANGLESSTATS             501
#define IDM_LISTSINGLECONTOURSSTATS        502
#define IDM_LISTCONTOURGROUPSSTATS         503
#define IDM_LISTTRIANGLES                  504
#define IDM_LISTSINGLECONTOURS             505
#define IDM_LISTCONTOURGROUPS              506

#define IDM_ESCAPEKEY                      901

#define IDD_MAJORCONTOUR                   1001
#define IDD_MINORCONTOUR                   1002

#define IDD_SINGLECONTOUR                  1011

#endif // CHAPTER05_H
```

As in previous chapters, **Chapter05.h** contains ID numbers for menu bar options, drop-down menus, accelerator keys and dialog box controls.

The second file is the resource script file:

**CHAPTER05.RC**

```
#include <windows.h>
#include "Chapter05.h"

Chapter05 MENU {
    POPUP "&File" {
        POPUP "&Import" {
            MENUITEM "&Triangles",            IDM_IMPORTTRIANGLES
        }
        POPUP "&Export" {
            MENUITEM "&Single Contours",      IDM_EXPORTSINGLECONTOURS
            MENUITEM "Contour &Groups",       IDM_EXPORTCONTOURGROUPS
            MENUITEM SEPARATOR
            MENUITEM "S&creen image",         IDM_EXPORTSCREEN
            MENUITEM "&Model image",          IDM_EXPORTMODEL
        }
        MENUITEM SEPARATOR
        MENUITEM "E&xit",                     IDM_EXIT
    }
    POPUP "&Edit" {
        MENUITEM "Create &single contour",    IDM_CREATESINGLECONTOUR
        MENUITEM "Create contour &groups",    IDM_CREATECONTOURGROUPS
    }
    POPUP "&Show" {
        MENUITEM "&Triangles",                IDM_SHOWTRIANGLES
        MENUITEM "&Single Contours",          IDM_SHOWSINGLECONTOURS
        MENUITEM "Contour &Groups",           IDM_SHOWCONTOURGROUPS
        MENUITEM SEPARATOR
        POPUP "&Colour" {
            MENUITEM "Back&ground",           IDM_COLOURBACKGROUND
            MENUITEM "&Coords text",          IDM_COLOURCOORDSTEXT
            MENUITEM SEPARATOR
            MENUITEM "&Triangles",            IDM_COLOURTRIANGLES
```

```
                    MENUITEM "&Single Contours",        IDM_COLOURSINGLECONTOURS
                    MENUITEM "&Major contours",         IDM_COLOURMAJORCONTOURS
                    MENUITEM "M&inor contours",         IDM_COLOURMINORCONTOURS
                }
            MENUITEM SEPARATOR
            MENUITEM "&Zoom extents",                   IDM_ZOOMEXTENTS
            MENUITEM "&Redraw",                         IDM_REDRAW
        }
        POPUP "&Mouse" {
            MENUITEM "&Zoom in/out",                    IDM_MOUSEZOOM
            MENUITEM "&Pan",                            IDM_MOUSEPAN
            MENUITEM SEPARATOR
            MENUITEM "Find &single contour",            IDM_MOUSESINGLECONTOUR
            MENUITEM "Find &group contour",             IDM_MOUSEGROUPCONTOUR
        }
        POPUP "&List" {
            POPUP "&Statistics" {
                    MENUITEM "&Triangles",              IDM_LISTTRIANGLESSTATS
                    MENUITEM "&Single Contours",        IDM_LISTSINGLECONTOURSSTATS
                    MENUITEM "Contour &Groups",         IDM_LISTCONTOURGROUPSSTATS
                }
            MENUITEM SEPARATOR
            MENUITEM "&Triangles",                      IDM_LISTTRIANGLES
            MENUITEM "&Single Contours",                IDM_LISTSINGLECONTOURS
            MENUITEM "Contour &Groups",                 IDM_LISTCONTOURGROUPS
        }
    }
}

Chapter05 ACCELERATORS {
    VK_ESCAPE,        IDM_ESCAPEKEY,         VIRTKEY, NOINVERT
}

ContourIntervals DIALOG 32, 32, 120, 70
STYLE DS_MODALFRAME | WS_POPUP | WS_CAPTION
CAPTION "Set contour intervals"
FONT 8, "MS Sans Serif" {
    LTEXT "Major interval", -1, 8, 10, 48, 10
    EDITTEXT IDD_MAJORCONTOUR, 64, 8, 48, 14
    LTEXT "Minor interval", -1, 8, 30, 48, 10
    EDITTEXT IDD_MINORCONTOUR, 64, 28, 48, 14
    DEFPUSHBUTTON "OK", IDOK, 8, 48, 48, 14
    PUSHBUTTON "Cancel", IDCANCEL, 64, 48, 48, 14
}

SingleContour DIALOG 32, 32, 120, 50
STYLE DS_MODALFRAME | WS_POPUP | WS_CAPTION
CAPTION "Set single contour"
FONT 8, "MS Sans Serif" {
    LTEXT "Contour z value", -1, 8, 10, 54, 10
    EDITTEXT IDD_SINGLECONTOUR, 64, 8, 48, 14
    DEFPUSHBUTTON "OK", IDOK, 8, 28, 48, 14
    PUSHBUTTON "Cancel", IDCANCEL, 64, 28, 48, 14
}
```

Like previous chapters, **Chapter05.rc** defines the contents of the program's menu bar, accelerator keys (or just one accelerator key in this case), and two custom dialog boxes called 'ContourIntervals' and 'SingleContour'.

The third file is the source code file, which includes function listings.

## CHAPTER05.CPP

```cpp
#ifndef UNICODE
#define UNICODE
#endif

#include <windows.h>
#include <gdiplus.h>
using namespace Gdiplus;
#include <math.h>
#include "Chapter05.h"
#include "BigTask.h"
#include "FileInOut.h"
#include "TextWnd.h"
#include "Graphics.h"
#include "Colours.h"
#include "Shapes.h"
#include "Common.h"

#define ID_TEXTWND                          1
#define ID_DISPLAYWND                       2
#define ID_IMAGEEXPORT                      3

#define IDT_IMPORTTRIANGLES                 11

#define IDT_EXPORTSINGLECONTOURS            21
#define IDT_EXPORTSINGLECONTOURSSCRIPT      22
#define IDT_EXPORTCONTOURGROUPS             23
#define IDT_EXPORTCONTOURGROUPSSCRIPT       24
#define IDT_EXPORTIMAGE                     25

#define IDT_CREATESINGLECONTOUR             31
#define IDT_CREATECONTOURGROUP              32

#define IDT_LISTTRIANGLES                   41
#define IDT_LISTSINGLECONTOURS              42
#define IDT_LISTCONTOURGROUPS               43

#define CREATETCONTOURS_STEPSIZE            20L

#define PENCOLOUR_TRIANGLES                 11
#define PENCOLOUR_SINGLECONTOURS            3
#define PENCOLOUR_MAJORCONTOURS             0
#define PENCOLOUR_MINORCONTOURS             10

HINSTANCE _hInst;
DTMTEXTWINDOW _dtmText;
DTMFILEDATA _dtmFile;
DTMBIGTASK _dtmTask, _dtmTaskDisplay;
DTMDISPLAY _dtmDisplay;
DTMCOLOURS _dtmColours;
DTMTRIAS _dtmTrias;
DTMLINES _dtmSingleContours, _dtmContourGroups;
DOUBLE _rSingleContour, _rMajorContourInterval, _rMinorContourInterval;

LRESULT CALLBACK WndProc (HWND, UINT, WPARAM, LPARAM);
BOOL CarryOutTasks (HWND);
WORD DrawModel (DTMFRAME *, DTMBIGTASK *);
void InitShowDropdownMenu (HMENU);
void InitMouseDropdownMenu (HMENU, BOOL);
BOOL CreateContoursStart (HWND, DTMLINES *, BOOL, UINT);
BOOL CALLBACK ContourIntervalsDlgProc (HWND, UINT, WPARAM, LPARAM);
```

```
BOOL CALLBACK SingleContourDlgProc (HWND, UINT, WPARAM, LPARAM);
WORD CreateContoursCont (DTMLINES *, BOOL);
BOOL AddContours (DTMLINES *, DTMTRIA *, DOUBLE, BOOL);
BOOL AddSingleContour (DTMLINES *, DTMTRIA *, DOUBLE, WORD);
void GetContourAtMousePosition (DTMLINES *);

int WINAPI WinMain (HINSTANCE hInst, HINSTANCE, PSTR, int nCmdShow) {
    return InitAndRunProgram (hInst, nCmdShow, TEXT ("Chapter05"),
        TEXT ("Chapter 5: Create Contours"));
}

LRESULT CALLBACK WndProc (HWND hwnd, UINT message, WPARAM wParam, LPARAM lParam) {
    static BOOL fFindSingleContour;

    switch (message) {
        case WM_CREATE :
            _hInst = ((LPCREATESTRUCT) lParam)->hInstance;
            _dtmText.Create (hwnd, ID_TEXTWND, _hInst);
            _dtmFile.Init (hwnd);
            _dtmDisplay.Init (hwnd, 0, ID_DISPLAYWND, _hInst,
                1.0, 4.0, 4.0, 4.0, 5.0, 1.0, 2.0, 0.5);
            _dtmColours.Init ();
            _dtmTrias.Init (TEXT ("triangles"), PENCOLOUR_TRIANGLES, 0, FALSE);
            _dtmSingleContours.Init (TEXT ("single contours"),
                PENCOLOUR_SINGLECONTOURS);
            _dtmContourGroups.Init (TEXT ("grouped contours"),
                PENCOLOUR_MINORCONTOURS);
            _rSingleContour = 0.0;
            _rMajorContourInterval = 1.0;
            _rMinorContourInterval = 0.2;
            fFindSingleContour = TRUE;
            return 0;
        case WM_ENTERSIZEMOVE :
            _dtmDisplay.StartResizing ();
            return 0;
        case WM_SIZE :
            ResizeChildWindows (lParam);
            return 0;
        case WM_EXITSIZEMOVE :
            _dtmDisplay.StopResizing ();
            return 0;
        case WM_INITMENUPOPUP :
            if (HIWORD (lParam) == FALSE) {
                switch (LOWORD (lParam)) {
                    case IDN_SHOWMENU :
                        InitShowDropdownMenu ((HMENU) wParam);
                        return 0;
                    case IDN_MOUSEMENU :
                        InitMouseDropdownMenu ((HMENU) wParam, fFindSingleContour);
                        return 0;
                    default : break;
                }
            }
            break;
        case WM_COMMAND :
            if (HIWORD (wParam) == 0) {
                switch (LOWORD (wParam)) {
                    case IDM_IMPORTTRIANGLES :
                        _dtmTrias.ImportStart (hwnd, IDT_IMPORTTRIANGLES);
                        return 0;
                    case IDM_EXPORTSINGLECONTOURS :
```

```
            _dtmSingleContours.ExportStart (IDT_EXPORTSINGLECONTOURS,
                IDT_EXPORTSINGLECONTOURSSCRIPT);
            return 0;
        case IDM_EXPORTCONTOURGROUPS :
            _dtmContourGroups.ExportStart (IDT_EXPORTCONTOURGROUPS,
                IDT_EXPORTCONTOURGROUPSSCRIPT);
            return 0;
        case IDM_EXPORTSCREEN :
            ExportImage (FALSE, ID_IMAGEEXPORT);
            return 0;
        case IDM_EXPORTMODEL :
            ExportImage (TRUE, ID_IMAGEEXPORT);
            return 0;
        case IDM_EXIT :
            SendMessage (hwnd, WM_CLOSE, 0, 0);
            return 0;
        case IDM_CREATESINGLECONTOUR :
            CreateContoursStart (hwnd, &_dtmSingleContours, FALSE,
                IDT_CREATESINGLECONTOUR);
            return 0;
        case IDM_CREATECONTOURGROUPS :
            CreateContoursStart (hwnd, &_dtmContourGroups, TRUE,
                IDT_CREATECONTOURGROUP);
            return 0;
        case IDM_SHOWTRIANGLES :
            _dtmTrias.FlipVisible ();
            _dtmTaskDisplay.Start ();
            return 0;
        case IDM_SHOWSINGLECONTOURS :
            _dtmSingleContours.FlipVisible ();
            _dtmTaskDisplay.Start ();
            return 0;
        case IDM_SHOWCONTOURGROUPS :
            _dtmContourGroups.FlipVisible ();
            _dtmTaskDisplay.Start ();
            return 0;
        case IDM_COLOURBACKGROUND :
            ChangeBackgroundColour (hwnd);
            return 0;
        case IDM_COLOURCOORDSTEXT :
            ChangeCoordsTextColour (hwnd);
            return 0;
        case IDM_COLOURTRIANGLES :
            ChangePenColour (hwnd, PENCOLOUR_TRIANGLES);
            return 0;
        case IDM_COLOURSINGLECONTOURS :
            ChangePenColour (hwnd, PENCOLOUR_SINGLECONTOURS);
            return 0;
        case IDM_COLOURMAJORCONTOURS :
            ChangePenColour (hwnd, PENCOLOUR_MAJORCONTOURS);
            return 0;
        case IDM_COLOURMINORCONTOURS :
            ChangePenColour (hwnd, PENCOLOUR_MINORCONTOURS);
            return 0;
        case IDM_ZOOMEXTENTS :
            _dtmDisplay.ZoomExtents ();
            _dtmTaskDisplay.Start ();
            return 0;
        case IDM_REDRAW :
            _dtmTaskDisplay.Start ();
            return 0;
```

```
                    case IDM_MOUSEZOOM :
                        _dtmDisplay.SetMouseAction (MOUSEACT_ZOOM);
                        return 0;
                    case IDM_MOUSEPAN :
                        _dtmDisplay.SetMouseAction (MOUSEACT_PAN);
                        return 0;
                    case IDM_MOUSESINGLECONTOUR :
                        _dtmDisplay.SetMouseAction (MOUSEACT_POINT);
                        fFindSingleContour = TRUE;
                        return 0;
                    case IDM_MOUSEGROUPCONTOUR :
                        _dtmDisplay.SetMouseAction (MOUSEACT_POINT);
                        fFindSingleContour = FALSE;
                        return 0;
                    case IDM_LISTTRIANGLESSTATS :
                        _dtmTrias.ListStats ();
                        return 0;
                    case IDM_LISTSINGLECONTOURSSTATS :
                        _dtmSingleContours.ListStats ();
                        return 0;
                    case IDM_LISTCONTOURGROUPSSTATS :
                        _dtmContourGroups.ListStats ();
                        return 0;
                    case IDM_LISTTRIANGLES :
                        _dtmTrias.ListStart (IDT_LISTTRIANGLES);
                        return 0;
                    case IDM_LISTSINGLECONTOURS :
                        _dtmSingleContours.ListStart (IDT_LISTSINGLECONTOURS);
                        return 0;
                    case IDM_LISTCONTOURGROUPS :
                        _dtmContourGroups.ListStart (IDT_LISTCONTOURGROUPS);
                        return 0;
                    default : break;
            }
        }
        else if (HIWORD (wParam) == 1) {
            if (LOWORD (wParam) == IDM_ESCAPEKEY) {
                _dtmTask.Quit (TRUE);
                _dtmTaskDisplay.Quit (TRUE);
                return 0;
            }
        }
        else if (LOWORD (wParam) == ID_DISPLAYWND) {
            switch (HIWORD (wParam)) {
                case DTM_REDRAW :
                    _dtmTaskDisplay.Start ();
                    return 0;
                case DTM_DRAW_STOPPED :
                case DTM_DRAW_COMPLETED :
                    _dtmDisplay.RepaintNow (REPAINT_ALL);
                    return 0;
                case DTM_SELPOINT :
                    if (fFindSingleContour) {
                        GetContourAtMousePosition (&_dtmSingleContours);
                    }
                    else {
                        GetContourAtMousePosition (&_dtmContourGroups);
                    }
                    return 0;
                default : return 0;
            }
```

```
            }
            else if (LOWORD (wParam) == ID_IMAGEEXPORT) {
                ProcessExportImageMessages (wParam, IDT_EXPORTIMAGE);
                return 0;
            }
            break;
        case WM_CLOSE :
            AskCloseWindowMessage (hwnd);
            return 0;
        case WM_DESTROY:
            _dtmDisplay.Free ();
            _dtmColours.Free ();
            _dtmText.Destroy ();
            _dtmFile.FreeImportBuffer ();
            _dtmTrias.Free ();
            _dtmSingleContours.Free ();
            _dtmContourGroups.Free ();
            PostQuitMessage (0);
            return 0;
        default : break;
    }
    return DefWindowProc (hwnd, message, wParam, lParam);
}

BOOL CarryOutTasks (HWND hwnd) {
    WORD wTaskStatus;

    if (!_dtmTask.IsBusy ()) {
        return FALSE;
    }
    if (_dtmTask.GetStage () == 0) {
        EnableMenuBar (hwnd, FALSE);
        _dtmDisplay.Enable (FALSE);
        _dtmTask.NextStage ();
    }
    switch (_dtmTask.GetID ()) {
        case IDT_IMPORTTRIANGLES :
            wTaskStatus = _dtmTrias.ImportCont (FALSE);
            break;
        case IDT_EXPORTSINGLECONTOURS :
            wTaskStatus = _dtmSingleContours.ExportCont (FALSE);
            break;
        case IDT_EXPORTSINGLECONTOURSSCRIPT :
            wTaskStatus = _dtmSingleContours.ExportCont (TRUE);
            break;
        case IDT_EXPORTCONTOURGROUPS :
            wTaskStatus = _dtmContourGroups.ExportCont (FALSE);
            break;
        case IDT_EXPORTCONTOURGROUPSSCRIPT :
            wTaskStatus = _dtmContourGroups.ExportCont (TRUE);
            break;
        case IDT_EXPORTIMAGE :
            wTaskStatus = DrawModel (_dtmDisplay.GetImageDtmPtr (), &_dtmTask);
            break;
        case IDT_CREATESINGLECONTOUR :
            wTaskStatus = CreateContoursCont (&_dtmSingleContours, FALSE);
            break;
        case IDT_CREATECONTOURGROUP :
            wTaskStatus = CreateContoursCont (&_dtmContourGroups, TRUE);
            break;
        case IDT_LISTTRIANGLES :
```

```
                wTaskStatus = _dtmTrias.ListCont ();
                break;
            case IDT_LISTSINGLECONTOURS :
                wTaskStatus = _dtmSingleContours.ListCont ();
                break;
            case IDT_LISTCONTOURGROUPS :
                wTaskStatus = _dtmContourGroups.ListCont ();
                break;
            default :
                wTaskStatus = TASK_STOPPED;
                break;
        }
        if ((wTaskStatus & TASK_STOPPED) || (wTaskStatus & TASK_COMPLETED)) {
            EnableMenuBar (hwnd, TRUE);
            _dtmDisplay.Enable (TRUE);
            _dtmTask.Stop ();
        }
        if (wTaskStatus & TASK_COMPLETED) {
            switch (_dtmTask.GetID ()) {
                case IDT_IMPORTTRIANGLES :
                    AddShapeToDisplay (&_dtmTrias);
                    break;
                default : break;
            }
        }
        if (wTaskStatus & TASK_REDRAW) {
            _dtmTaskDisplay.Start ();
        }
        return TRUE;
}

WORD DrawModel (DTMFRAME * pdtmFrame, DTMBIGTASK * pdtmTask) {
    if (pdtmFrame == NULL || !pdtmFrame->IsActive () ||
        !pdtmFrame->IsGdiOK () || pdtmTask == NULL) {
        return TASK_STOPPED;
    }
    if (pdtmTask->Quit ()) {
        pdtmFrame->NotifyParent (DTM_DRAW_STOPPED);
        return TASK_STOPPED;
    }
    switch (pdtmTask->GetStage ()) {
        case 1 :
            pdtmFrame->ClearBackground ();
            _dtmColours.SetPenWidths (pdtmFrame->GetPenWidth (),
                pdtmFrame->GetVertExag ());
            pdtmTask->NextStage ();
            break;
        case 2 :
            _dtmTrias.Draw (pdtmFrame, pdtmTask);
            break;
        case 3 :
            _dtmContourGroups.Draw (pdtmFrame, pdtmTask);
            break;
        case 4 :
            _dtmSingleContours.Draw (pdtmFrame, pdtmTask);
            break;
        default : break;
    }
    pdtmFrame->NotifyParent (DTM_DRAW_UPDATED);
    if (pdtmTask->GetStage () < 5) {
        return TASK_ONGOING;
```

```
        }
        pdtmFrame->NotifyParent (DTM_DRAW_COMPLETED);
        return TASK_COMPLETED;
}

void InitShowDropdownMenu (HMENU hMenu) {
        CheckMenuItem (hMenu, IDM_SHOWTRIANGLES, MF_BYCOMMAND |
                (_dtmTrias.IsVisible () ? MF_CHECKED : MF_UNCHECKED));
        CheckMenuItem (hMenu, IDM_SHOWSINGLECONTOURS, MF_BYCOMMAND |
                (_dtmSingleContours.IsVisible () ? MF_CHECKED : MF_UNCHECKED));
        CheckMenuItem (hMenu, IDM_SHOWCONTOURGROUPS, MF_BYCOMMAND |
                (_dtmContourGroups.IsVisible () ? MF_CHECKED : MF_UNCHECKED));
}

void InitMouseDropdownMenu (HMENU hMenu, BOOL fFindSingleContour) {
        DTMMOUSEACT mouseAction;

        mouseAction = _dtmDisplay.GetMouseAction ();
        CheckMenuItem (hMenu, IDM_MOUSEZOOM, MF_BYCOMMAND |
                (mouseAction == MOUSEACT_ZOOM ? MF_CHECKED : MF_UNCHECKED));
        CheckMenuItem (hMenu, IDM_MOUSEPAN, MF_BYCOMMAND |
                (mouseAction == MOUSEACT_PAN ? MF_CHECKED : MF_UNCHECKED));
        CheckMenuItem (hMenu, IDM_MOUSESINGLECONTOUR, MF_BYCOMMAND |
                ((mouseAction == MOUSEACT_POINT && fFindSingleContour) ?
                MF_CHECKED : MF_UNCHECKED));
        CheckMenuItem (hMenu, IDM_MOUSEGROUPCONTOUR, MF_BYCOMMAND |
                ((mouseAction == MOUSEACT_POINT && !fFindSingleContour) ?
                MF_CHECKED : MF_UNCHECKED));
}

BOOL CreateContoursStart (HWND hwnd, DTMLINES * pdtmContours, BOOL fGroup,
        UINT uTaskID) {
        if (_dtmTask.IsBusy ()) {
            _dtmText.Output (_szTaskBusyMessage);
            return FALSE;
        }
        if (_dtmTrias.GetTotal () == 0L) {
            _dtmText.Output (TEXT ("There are no %s available. Unable to create ") \
                TEXT ("contour(s)\r\n"), _dtmTrias.GetDescription ());
            return FALSE;
        }
        if (pdtmContours->GetTotal () != 0L) {
            int iMessage;

            iMessage = MessageBox (hwnd,
                TEXT ("Do you want to discard contours already created?"),
                TEXT ("Create contours"), MB_YESNOCANCEL | MB_ICONWARNING);
            if (iMessage == IDCANCEL) {
                return FALSE;
            }
            else if (iMessage == IDYES) {
                pdtmContours->Free ();
            }
        }
        if (fGroup) {
            if (!DialogBox (_hInst, TEXT ("ContourIntervals"), hwnd,
                ContourIntervalsDlgProc)) {
                return FALSE;
            }
        }
        else {
```

```
            if (!DialogBox (_hInst, TEXT ("SingleContour"), hwnd, SingleContourDlgProc)) {
                return FALSE;
            }
        }
    _dtmText.Output (TEXT ("Creating %s\r\n"), pdtmContours->GetDescription ());
    _dtmTask.Start (uTaskID, CREATETCONTOURS_STEPSIZE);
    return TRUE;
}

BOOL CALLBACK ContourIntervalsDlgProc (HWND hdlg, UINT message, WPARAM wParam,
    LPARAM lParam) {
    switch (message) {
        case WM_INITDIALOG :
            SetDlgItemNumber (hdlg, IDD_MAJORCONTOUR, _rMajorContourInterval);
            SetDlgItemNumber (hdlg, IDD_MINORCONTOUR, _rMinorContourInterval);
            return TRUE;
        case WM_COMMAND :
            switch (LOWORD (wParam)) {
                case IDOK :
                    _rMajorContourInterval = GetDlgItemNumber (hdlg, IDD_MAJORCONTOUR,
                        0.001, 99999.999);
                    _rMinorContourInterval = GetDlgItemNumber (hdlg, IDD_MINORCONTOUR,
                        0.001, 99999.999);
                    EndDialog (hdlg, TRUE);
                    return TRUE;
                case IDCANCEL :
                    EndDialog (hdlg, FALSE);
                    return TRUE;
                case IDD_MAJORCONTOUR :
                    if (HIWORD (wParam) == EN_KILLFOCUS) {
                        DOUBLE rValue;

                        rValue = GetDlgItemNumber (hdlg, IDD_MAJORCONTOUR,
                            0.001, 99999.999);
                        SetDlgItemNumber (hdlg, IDD_MAJORCONTOUR, rValue);
                        return TRUE;
                    }
                    break;
                case IDD_MINORCONTOUR :
                    if (HIWORD (wParam) == EN_KILLFOCUS) {
                        DOUBLE rValue;

                        rValue = GetDlgItemNumber (hdlg, IDD_MINORCONTOUR,
                            0.001, 99999.999);
                        SetDlgItemNumber (hdlg, IDD_MINORCONTOUR, rValue);
                        return TRUE;
                    }
                    break;
                default : break;
            }
        default : break;
    }
    return FALSE;
}

BOOL CALLBACK SingleContourDlgProc (HWND hdlg, UINT message, WPARAM wParam,
    LPARAM lParam) {
    switch (message) {
        case WM_INITDIALOG :
            SetDlgItemNumber (hdlg, IDD_SINGLECONTOUR, _rSingleContour);
            return TRUE;
```

```
            case WM_COMMAND :
                switch (LOWORD (wParam)) {
                    case IDOK :
                        _rSingleContour = GetDlgItemNumber (hdlg, IDD_SINGLECONTOUR,
                            -99999.999, 99999.999);
                        EndDialog (hdlg, TRUE);
                        return TRUE;
                    case IDCANCEL :
                        EndDialog (hdlg, FALSE);
                        return TRUE;
                    case IDD_SINGLECONTOUR :
                        if (HIWORD (wParam) == EN_KILLFOCUS) {
                            DOUBLE rValue;

                            rValue = GetDlgItemNumber (hdlg, IDD_SINGLECONTOUR,
                                -99999.999, 99999.999);
                            SetDlgItemNumber (hdlg, IDD_SINGLECONTOUR, rValue);
                            return TRUE;
                        }
                        break;
                    default : break;
                }
            default : break;
        }
    return FALSE;
}

WORD CreateContoursCont (DTMLINES * pdtmContours, BOOL fGroup) {
    static DWORD dwTotalAtStart;

    if (pdtmContours == NULL) {
        return TASK_STOPPED | TASK_REDRAW;
    }
    if (_dtmTask.AtStart ()) {
        dwTotalAtStart = pdtmContours->GetTotal ();
    }
    if (_dtmTask.Quit ()) {
        _dtmText.Output (TEXT ("\r\nCreating contours stopped\r\n"));
        return TASK_STOPPED | TASK_REDRAW;
    }
    _dtmTask.StartNewBatch ();
    while (!_dtmTask.NoMoreItems (_dtmTrias.GetTotal ()) && !_dtmTask.AtEndOfBatch ()) {
        DTMTRIA * pdtmTria;

        pdtmTria = _dtmTrias.GetPtr (_dtmTask.GetItemNumber ());
        if (pdtmTria->cdMax.rZ != pdtmTria->cdMin.rZ) {
            if (fGroup) {
                AddContours (pdtmContours, pdtmTria, _rMajorContourInterval, TRUE);
                AddContours (pdtmContours, pdtmTria, _rMinorContourInterval, FALSE);
            }
            else {
                AddSingleContour (pdtmContours, pdtmTria, _rSingleContour,
                    PENCOLOUR_SINGLECONTOURS);
            }
        }
        _dtmTask.NextItem ();
        _dtmTask.IncBatchCounter ();
    }
    _dtmText.ProgressDot ();
    if (!_dtmTask.NoMoreItems (_dtmTrias.GetTotal ())) {
        return TASK_ONGOING;
```

```
        }
        _dtmText.Output (TEXT ("\r\nNumber of contours created: %lu\r\n"),
            pdtmContours->GetTotal () - dwTotalAtStart);
        return TASK_COMPLETED | TASK_REDRAW;
}

BOOL AddContours (DTMLINES * pdtmContours, DTMTRIA * pdtmTria, DOUBLE rInterval,
    BOOL fMajor) {
    DOUBLE rZ;
    WORD wPenColour;

    if (pdtmContours == NULL || pdtmTria == NULL) {
        return FALSE;
    }
    rZ = rInterval * floor (pdtmTria->cdMin.rZ / rInterval);
    wPenColour = fMajor ? PENCOLOUR_MAJORCONTOURS : PENCOLOUR_MINORCONTOURS;
    while (rZ <= pdtmTria->cdMax.rZ) {
        if (fMajor) {
            AddSingleContour (pdtmContours, pdtmTria, rZ, wPenColour);
        }
        else {
            DOUBLE rFraction, rIgnore;

            rFraction = fabs (modf (rZ / _rMajorContourInterval, &rIgnore));
            if (rFraction > FUZZFACTOR) {
                AddSingleContour (pdtmContours, pdtmTria, rZ, wPenColour);
            }
        }
        rZ += rInterval;
    }
    return TRUE;
}

BOOL AddSingleContour (DTMLINES * pdtmContours, DTMTRIA * pdtmTria,
    DOUBLE rZ, WORD wPenColour) {
    WORD wLineEnd, wEdge;
    DTMLINE dtmLine;

    if (pdtmContours == NULL || pdtmTria == NULL) {
        return FALSE;
    }
    if (rZ < pdtmTria->cdMin.rZ || rZ > pdtmTria->cdMax.rZ) {
        return TRUE;
    }
    wLineEnd = 0;
    dtmLine.wColour = wPenColour;
    for (wEdge = 0; wEdge < TRIA_COORDS; wEdge ++) {
        DOUBLE rX1, rY1, rX2, rY2, rZ1, rZ2, rAlong;

        _dtmTrias.GetEdge (pdtmTria, wEdge, &rX1, &rY1, &rZ1, &rX2, &rY2, &rZ2);
        if (rZ2 - rZ1 == 0) {
            continue;
        }
        rAlong = (rZ - rZ1) / (rZ2 - rZ1);
        if (rAlong <= -FUZZFACTOR || (rAlong - 1.0) >= FUZZFACTOR) {
            continue;
        }
        if (wLineEnd < 2) {
            dtmLine.cdEnd [wLineEnd].rX = rX1 + rAlong * (rX2 - rX1);
            dtmLine.cdEnd [wLineEnd].rY = rY1 + rAlong * (rY2 - rY1);
            dtmLine.cdEnd [wLineEnd].rZ = rZ;
```

```
            if (wLineEnd == 0) {
                wLineEnd ++;
            }
            else if (wLineEnd == 1) {
                DOUBLE rHowCloseX, rHowCloseY;

                rHowCloseX = fabs (dtmLine.cdEnd [0].rX - dtmLine.cdEnd [1].rX);
                rHowCloseY = fabs (dtmLine.cdEnd [0].rY - dtmLine.cdEnd [1].rY);
                if (rHowCloseX >= FUZZFACTOR || rHowCloseY >= FUZZFACTOR) {
                    wLineEnd ++;
                }
            }
        }
    }
    if (wLineEnd == 2) {
        pdtmContours->AddNear (&dtmLine, FUZZFACTOR);
    }
    return TRUE;
}

void GetContourAtMousePosition (DTMLINES * pdtmContours) {
    DOUBLE rMouseX, rMouseY;
    DWORD dwContour;

    rMouseX = _dtmDisplay.GetSelFromX ();
    rMouseY = _dtmDisplay.GetSelFromY ();
    if (pdtmContours->Closest (rMouseX, rMouseY, &dwContour)) {
        DTMLINE * pdtmContour;

        pdtmContour = pdtmContours->GetPtr (dwContour);
        if (pdtmContour != NULL) {
            DOUBLE rX, rY, rZ;

            _dtmText.Output (TEXT ("Details of contour nearest to %.3f, %.3f:\r\n"),
                rMouseX, rMouseY);
            pdtmContours->GetEnd (pdtmContour, 0, &rX, &rY, &rZ);
            _dtmText.Output (TEXT (" From x, y, z:\r\n %.3f, %.3f, %.3f\r\n"),
                rX, rY, rZ);
            pdtmContours->GetEnd (pdtmContour, 1, &rX, &rY, &rZ);
            _dtmText.Output (TEXT (" To x, y, z:\r\n %.3f, %.3f, %.3f\r\n"),
                rX, rY, rZ);
        }
    }
    else {
        _dtmText.Output (TEXT ("No contour found near to %.3f, %.3f\r\n"),
            rMouseX, rMouseY);
    }
}
```

**Chapter05.cpp** has the same layout as Chapter03.cpp and Chapter04.cpp in Chapters 3 and 4. It starts with the header files, including <math.h> for the functions *fabs*, *floor* and *modf*, followed by child window IDs, task IDs, the task batch size constant CREATECONTOURS_STEPSIZE which is used when creating contours, and coloured pen numbers.

It then defines thirteen global variables, most of which are the same as in Chapter04.cpp. *_dtmSingleContours* is a lines array of contours at a single z value defined by *_rSingleContour*. *_dtmContourGroups* is a lines array of groups of contours at major and minor z intervals defined by *_rMajorContourInterval* and *_rMinorContourInterval*.

Twelve functions are then declared, followed by the C++ source code.

The functions *WinMain*, *WndProc*, *CarryOutTasks*, *DrawModel*, *InitShowDropdownMenu* and *InitMouseDropdownMenu* are similar to the equivalent functions in Chapter03.cpp and Chapter04.cpp. The static variable *fFindSingleContour* in *WndProc* determines if the user finds a contour line in *_dtmSingleContours* or in *_dtmContoursGroups* when left-clicking the mouse in the graphics window. After the message WM_CREATE in *WndProc*, the initial z value for contours at a single z value is set to 0.0 units, the major and minor z intervals for groups of contours are set as 1.0 and 0.2 units, and *fFindSingleContour* is initialised to find contour lines in *_dtmSingleContours*. This program does not display points, slope arrows or tangent marks. Therefore the values of the point arm length, slope arrow size and tangent mark size passed in the function *_dtmDisplay.Init* are arbitrary. However, they are set as 4.0 to maintain consistency with Chapter 4. No brush colour number is provided when initialising *_dtmTrias* because this program does not display filled triangles. The user can import 3D triangles, create contours (either at a single z value, or groups at z intervals), export contours and get information about contour lines in the graphics window. *DrawModel* draws the triangles first, followed by the contour groups and then the contours at a single z value.

The function *CreateContoursStart* starts the task that creates contours. *hwnd* is the handle of the parent window, *pdtmContours* points to the global lines array that contains the contours, *fGroup* is TRUE if groups of contours are to be created or FALSE if contours at a single z value are to be created, and *uTaskID* is the task ID number. If there are no triangles in the triangles array *_dtmTrias*, the function displays an error message. If the lines array already contains some contours, the function asks the user if they want to discard these contours. If the user selects 'Yes', the existing contours are discarded. Depending on the value of *fGroup*, *CreateContoursStart* displays the appropriate custom dialog box so that the user can enter either major and minor z intervals or a single z value. Finally, *CreateContoursStart* displays a message in the text window and starts the task. The function returns TRUE if successful, or FALSE if the user cancels the task or if an error occurs.

The functions *ContourIntervalsDlgProc* and *SingleContourDlgProc* activate custom dialog boxes that enable the user to enter values for *_rMajorContourInterval*, *_rMinorContourInterval*, or *_rSingleContour*. The existing values of these global variables are stored in the dialog boxes' edit controls when the dialog boxes are initialised with the message WM_INITDIALOG. The message WM_COMMAND is sent when the user clicks on the OK or Cancel buttons, or when the user interacts with one of the dialog boxes' edit controls. If the user clicks on the OK button, the new values in the edit controls are stored in the global variables. New z intervals are limited to be between 0.001 and 99999.999. The new single z value is limited to be between -99999.999 and 99999.999. If the user cancels either dialog box, the values in the edit controls are discarded and the global variables remain unchanged. If the user exits one of the edit controls, the value in the edit control is forced to be within the same limits as applied when the user clicks on the OK button.

The function *CreateContoursCont* carries out the task that creates contours. *pdtmContours* and *fGroup* are the same as in *CreateContoursStart*. *CreateContoursCont* follows the standard task manager template as discussed in Chapter 1, looking at each triangle in the triangles array *_dtmTrias* in batches. Within the while-loop, *CreateContoursCont* ignores flat triangles where the z values at each corner are the same because contours cannot be applied to these triangles. Otherwise it attempts to add contours at major and then minor z intervals, or contours at a single z value, to each triangle depending on the value of *fGroup*. The function returns the TASK_ constants as discussed in Chapter 1.

The function *AddContours* adds contours at z intervals, defined by *rInterval*, to the lines array pointed to by *pdtmContours*. The contours are based on the x,y,z coordinates at the corners of the triangle pointed to by *pdtmTria*. *fMajor* is TRUE if the contours are at major intervals, or FALSE if they are at minor intervals. *AddContours* starts by finding the z value at the nearest interval at or below the triangle's minimum z value. It uses the function *floor* which rounds a value down to the nearest whole number by removing the value's fractional part. It also sets the number of the coloured pen depending on whether the contours are major or minor. *AddContours* then enters a while-loop where it adds contours at increasing z values to the triangle until the z value is above the triangle's maximum z value. For minor contours, *AddContours* uses the function *modf*, which separates the fractional and whole parts of a number, to ensure that minor contours are only added when the z value does not equal a z value at a major z interval. *rIgnore* in *modf* is ignored. *AddContours* returns TRUE if successful, or FALSE if an error occurs.

The function *AddSingleContour* adds a single contour at the z value *rZ* to the lines array pointed to by *pdtmContours*, based on the triangle pointed to by *pdtmTria*. *wPenColour* is the number of the coloured pen to apply to the contour.

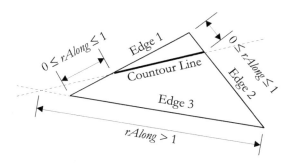

*AddSingleContour* exits if the z value is beyond the triangle's minimum or maximum z values. Otherwise it interpolates where the contour crosses each edge of the triangle. It uses the continue-statement to skip to the next edge if the z values at each end of the current edge are the same (in which case no contour can be applied) or if the contour crosses the edge, but beyond the ends of the edge. The following conditions exist if the contour crosses the edge beyond the ends of the edge:

```
rAlong < 0.0 or rAlong > 1.0
```

which, when using FUZZFACTOR (refer to Chapter 3), becomes:

```
rAlong <= -FUZZFACTOR or (rAlong - 1.0) >= FUZZFACTOR
```

*wLineEnd* defines which end of the contour line (0 or 1) to store the interpolated intersection position of the contour and the current edge. *wLineEnd* is initially 0 because the contour line is initially undefined. When storing the second end of the line, *AddSingleContour* checks that the contour line's ends are not the same or nearly the same. It doesn't use the function *DTMLINES::MatchingEnds* for this, because that function does not allow the use of FUZZFACTOR. If the ends are not the same, *wLineEnd* is increased to indicate that a contour line has been calculated. Outside the while loop, if *wLineEnd* equals 2, the contour line is added to the lines array.

*AddSingleContour* checks that the contour line's ends are not the same because it is possible for the contour line to cross all three triangle edges if the contour line goes through one of the triangle's corners, in which case two of the intersection points are the same. Also, if the contour crosses one corner only, the contour line has no length and therefore should not be added to the contour lines array. The following diagrams show these two situations.

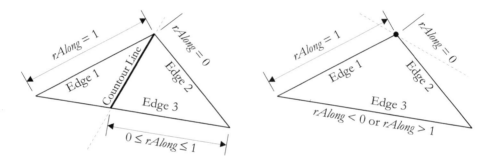

*AddSingleContour* returns TRUE if successful, or FALSE if an error occurs.

The function *GetContourAtMousePosition* displays information in the text window about the contour line closest to the mouse x,y coordinates in the graphics window. *pdtmContours* points to the lines array containing the contours. If the function successfully finds a line, it displays the x,y,z values at each end of the line. Otherwise it displays an error message.

## Running Chapter05

Before you can compile and run your program, you need to add the following nineteen source files to your Chapter05 project. Refer to Chapter 1 for how to do this:

| | |
|---|---|
| TextWnd.h | TextWnd.cpp |
| FileInOut.h | FileInOut.cpp |
| BigTask.h | BigTask.cpp |
| Graphics.h | Graphics.cpp |
| Colours.h | Colours.cpp |
| Shapes.h | Shapes.cpp |
| Lines.cpp | Triangles.cpp |

**Common.h**          **Common.cpp**

**Chapter05.h**       **Chapter05.cpp**          **Chapter05.rc**

You also need to add the Gdiplus.lib library file as an 'additional dependency' in your project's linker/input settings. Refer to Chapter 2 for how to do this. Finally, don't forget to set Chapter05 as your start-up project.

Otherwise, assuming you have compiled the code for Chapter05 successfully, and it is running, you can now test it out.

Start by importing your DTM of 3D triangles. Click on 'File' in the menu bar, then select 'Import' from the drop-down menu, and finally click on 'Triangles'. Next, select a file containing the triangles data. You can use the sample file Triangles.txt. If successful, the program's window should look something like this:

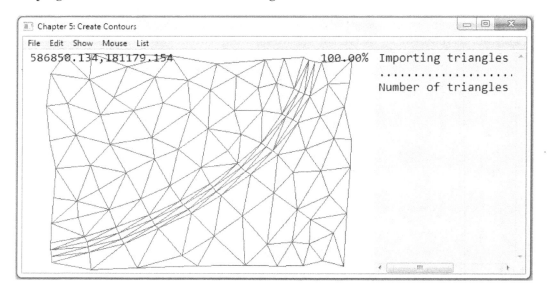

Next, you can add a contour, or set of contours, at a single z value. To do this, click on 'Edit' in the menu bar, and then select 'Create single contour' from the drop-down menu. A custom dialog box appears that allows you to enter the z value for the contour or contours. The default z value is 0.0.

If you click on OK the program attempts to add contours at this z value. However, no contours are added because the triangles in Triangles.cpp have z values between 3.35

and 8.7. You can check this by clicking on 'List' in the menu bar, then 'Statistics' from the drop-down menu and finally 'Triangles'. This displays the minimum and maximum x,y,z values for the triangles in the triangles array.

Therefore try a z value of 5.0 instead. If successful, the program's window should look like this (the colours of the triangles and contour lines have been adjusted to make the contour more prominent):

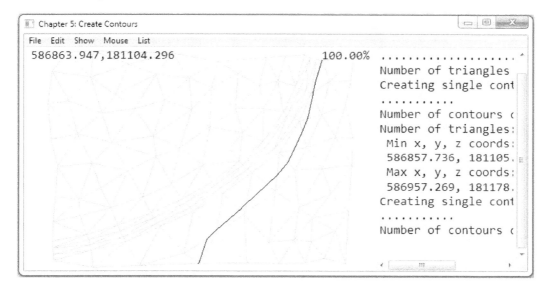

A contour, containing sixteen lines, is created. It runs from near to the top right-hand corner of the DTM down to the middle of the bottom edge of the DTM.

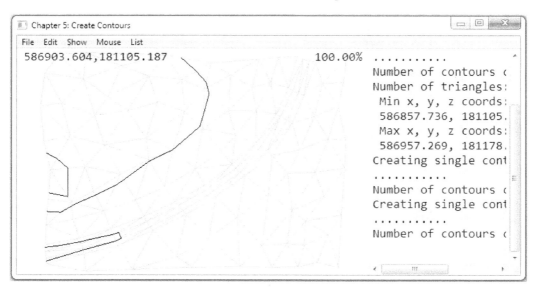

It is also possible to create more than one contour with a single z value, depending on the topography of the DTM. If you click on 'Edit', 'Create single contour' again and this time enter a z value of 7.4 (and select 'Yes' when the program asks if you want to discard existing contours), three contours are created, as shown in the previous image. These contours, containing thirty-three lines, are located on the left-hand side of the DTM and they all have the same single z value. You can add and keep contours at different z values by selecting 'No' each time the program asks if you want to discard existing contours.

To add groups of contours at major and minor z intervals, click on 'Edit' in the menu bar, and this time select 'Create contour groups'. A different custom dialog box appears that allows you to enter the major and minor z intervals. The default values are 1.0 and 0.2.

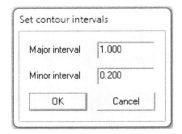

The minor interval is usually smaller than the major interval, and it usually equals the major interval divided by a whole number, for example 0.2 is 1.0 divided by five. In this case, this means that there are four minor contours between each major contour.

If you accept the default values and click on OK, the program's window should look like this, with major contours coloured red and minor contours coloured orange:

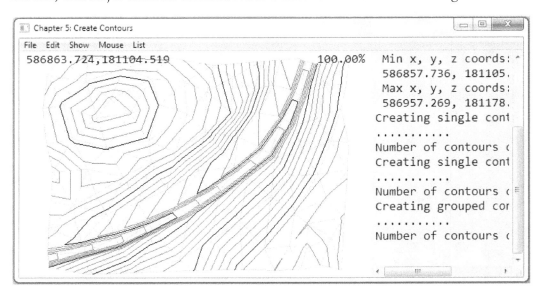

The contours at single z values have been hidden in the last image by using 'Show' in the menu bar. Because contours at single z values are in a separate lines array to groups of contours, they can duplicate the contours in the groups of contours that they overlap.

Contours at single z values and groups of contours at major and minor z intervals can be exported as a CAD script file or as a text file by selecting 'File' from the menu bar, then 'Export' from the drop-down menu, and finally selecting either 'Single Contours' or 'Contour Groups'. The data in the exported text files includes coloured pen numbers, so you can identify which contours are at major intervals and which are at minor intervals.

As in Chapters 2, 3 and 4, you can export an image of the program's graphics window, or an image of the whole model, to a JPEG file by selecting 'Screen image' or 'Model image' from the 'File', 'Export' menu.

Finally, if you click on 'Mouse' in the menu bar and select either 'Find single contour' or 'Find group contour' from the drop-down menu, then when you left-click the mouse over, or near to, a contour line in the graphics window, x,y,z information about that contour line is displayed in the text window.

As in previous chapters, to exit the program click on 'File' in the menu bar, select 'Exit' and then choose 'Yes' in the message box that appears.

# Chapter 6

## Calculate Z Values

Chapter 6 lists the source code for a program called **Chapter06** that calculates z values for a set of imported points based on the 3D triangles in a DTM. The points are separated into two points arrays: one for points inside the DTM and the other for points outside the DTM. The contents of the two points arrays can be exported as text files, as CAD script files, or as JPEG files. The user can also obtain z values by left-clicking the mouse in the graphics window. These on-the-fly z values cannot be exported directly by the program.

The following files are discussed in this chapter:

**Chapter06.h**          **Chapter06.rc**          **Chapter06.cpp**

## Chapter06 Source Files

The first file is the header file:

**CHAPTER06.H**

```
#ifndef CHAPTER06_H
#define CHAPTER06_H

#define IDM_IMPORTPOINTS          101
#define IDM_IMPORTTRIANGLES       102
#define IDM_EXPORTPOINTSINSIDE    103
#define IDM_EXPORTPOINTSOUTSIDE   104
#define IDM_EXPORTSCREEN          105
#define IDM_EXPORTMODEL           106
#define IDM_EXIT                  107

#define IDM_GETZVALUES            201

#define IDN_SHOWMENU              2

#define IDM_SHOWPOINTSINSIDE      301
#define IDM_SHOWPOINTSOUTSIDE     302
#define IDM_SHOWTRIANGLES         303
#define IDM_COLOURBACKGROUND      304
#define IDM_COLOURCOORDSTEXT      305
#define IDM_COLOURPOINTSINSIDE    306
#define IDM_COLOURPOINTSOUTSIDE   307
#define IDM_COLOURTRIANGLES       308
#define IDM_ZOOMEXTENTS           309
#define IDM_REDRAW                310

#define IDN_MOUSEMENU             3

#define IDM_MOUSEZOOM             401
#define IDM_MOUSEPAN              402
#define IDM_MOUSEZVALUE           403
```

```
#define IDM_LISTPOINTSINSIDESTATS      501
#define IDM_LISTPOINTSOUTSIDESTATS     502
#define IDM_LISTTRIANGLESSTATS         503
#define IDM_LISTPOINTSINSIDE           504
#define IDM_LISTPOINTSOUTSIDE          505
#define IDM_LISTTRIANGLES              506

#define IDM_ESCAPEKEY                  901

#endif // CHAPTER06_H
```

As in previous chapters, **Chapter06.h** contains ID numbers for menu bar options, drop-down menus and accelerator keys.

The second file is the resource script file:

**CHAPTER06.RC**

```
#include <windows.h>
#include "Chapter06.h"

Chapter06 MENU {
    POPUP "&File" {
        POPUP "&Import" {
            MENUITEM "&Points",         IDM_IMPORTPOINTS
            MENUITEM "&Triangles",      IDM_IMPORTTRIANGLES
        }
        POPUP "&Export" {
            MENUITEM "&Points inside",  IDM_EXPORTPOINTSINSIDE
            MENUITEM "Points &outside", IDM_EXPORTPOINTSOUTSIDE
            MENUITEM SEPARATOR
            MENUITEM "S&creen image",   IDM_EXPORTSCREEN
            MENUITEM "&Model image",    IDM_EXPORTMODEL
        }
        MENUITEM SEPARATOR
        MENUITEM "E&xit",               IDM_EXIT
    }
    POPUP "&Edit" {
        MENUITEM "&Calculate Z values", IDM_GETZVALUES
    }
    POPUP "&Show" {
        MENUITEM "&Points inside",      IDM_SHOWPOINTSINSIDE
        MENUITEM "Points &outside",     IDM_SHOWPOINTSOUTSIDE
        MENUITEM "&Triangles",          IDM_SHOWTRIANGLES
        MENUITEM SEPARATOR
        POPUP "&Colour" {
            MENUITEM "Back&ground",     IDM_COLOURBACKGROUND
            MENUITEM "&Coords text",    IDM_COLOURCOORDSTEXT
            MENUITEM SEPARATOR
            MENUITEM "&Points inside",  IDM_COLOURPOINTSINSIDE
            MENUITEM "Points &outside", IDM_COLOURPOINTSOUTSIDE
            MENUITEM "&Triangles",      IDM_COLOURTRIANGLES
        }
        MENUITEM SEPARATOR
        MENUITEM "&Zoom extents",       IDM_ZOOMEXTENTS
        MENUITEM "&Redraw",             IDM_REDRAW
    }
    POPUP "&Mouse" {
        MENUITEM "&Zoom in/out",        IDM_MOUSEZOOM
        MENUITEM "&Pan",                IDM_MOUSEPAN
```

```
            MENUITEM SEPARATOR
            MENUITEM "&Z value",                 IDM_MOUSEZVALUE
        }
        POPUP "&List" {
            POPUP "&Statistics" {
                MENUITEM "&Points inside",       IDM_LISTPOINTSINSIDESTATS
                MENUITEM "Points &outside",      IDM_LISTPOINTSOUTSIDESTATS
                MENUITEM "&Triangles",           IDM_LISTTRIANGLESSTATS
            }
            MENUITEM SEPARATOR
            MENUITEM "&Points inside",           IDM_LISTPOINTSINSIDE
            MENUITEM "Points &outside",          IDM_LISTPOINTSOUTSIDE
            MENUITEM "&Triangles",               IDM_LISTTRIANGLES
        }
    }
}

Chapter06 ACCELERATORS {
    VK_ESCAPE,          IDM_ESCAPEKEY,          VIRTKEY, NOINVERT
}
```

Like previous chapters, **Chapter06.rc** defines the contents of the program's menu bar and accelerator keys (or key). Unlike Chapter 5, there are no custom dialog boxes in this program.

The third file is the source code file, which includes function listings.

## CHAPTER06.CPP

```cpp
#ifndef UNICODE
#define UNICODE
#endif

#include <windows.h>
#include <gdiplus.h>
using namespace Gdiplus;
#include "Chapter06.h"
#include "BigTask.h"
#include "FileInOut.h"
#include "TextWnd.h"
#include "Graphics.h"
#include "Colours.h"
#include "Shapes.h"
#include "Common.h"

#define ID_TEXTWND                      1
#define ID_DISPLAYWND                   2
#define ID_IMAGEEXPORT                  3

#define IDT_IMPORTPOINTS                11
#define IDT_IMPORTTRIANGLES             12

#define IDT_EXPORTPOINTSINSIDE          21
#define IDT_EXPORTPOINTSINSIDESCRIPT    22
#define IDT_EXPORTPOINTSOUTSIDE         23
#define IDT_EXPORTPOINTSOUTSIDESCRIPT   24
#define IDT_EXPORTIMAGE                 25

#define IDT_GETZVALUES                  31
```

```
#define IDT_LISTPOINTS                    41
#define IDT_LISTPOINTSOUTSIDE             42
#define IDT_LISTTRIANGLES                 43

#define GETZVALUES_STEPSIZE               20L

#define PENCOLOUR_POINTS                  4
#define PENCOLOUR_POINTSOUTSIDE           0
#define PENCOLOUR_TRIANGLES               11

DTMTEXTWINDOW _dtmText;
DTMFILEDATA _dtmFile;
DTMBIGTASK _dtmTask, _dtmTaskDisplay;
DTMDISPLAY _dtmDisplay;
DTMCOLOURS _dtmColours;
DTMPOINTS _dtmPointsInside, _dtmPointsOutside;
DTMTRIAS _dtmTrias;

LRESULT CALLBACK WndProc (HWND, UINT, WPARAM, LPARAM);
BOOL CarryOutTasks (HWND);
WORD DrawModel (DTMFRAME *, DTMBIGTASK *);
void InitShowDropdownMenu (HMENU);
void InitMouseDropdownMenu (HMENU);
BOOL GetZValuesStart (UINT);
WORD GetZValuesCont (void);
void GetZValueAtMousePosition (void);

int WINAPI WinMain (HINSTANCE hInst, HINSTANCE, PSTR, int nCmdShow) {
    return InitAndRunProgram (hInst, nCmdShow, TEXT ("Chapter06"),
        TEXT ("Chapter 6: Calculate Z Values"));
}

LRESULT CALLBACK WndProc (HWND hwnd, UINT message, WPARAM wParam, LPARAM lParam) {
    switch (message) {
        case WM_CREATE : {
            HINSTANCE hInst;

            hInst = ((LPCREATESTRUCT) lParam)->hInstance;
            _dtmText.Create (hwnd, ID_TEXTWND, hInst);
            _dtmFile.Init (hwnd);
            _dtmDisplay.Init (hwnd, 0, ID_DISPLAYWND, hInst,
                1.0, 4.0, 4.0, 4.0, 5.0, 1.0, 2.0, 0.5);
            _dtmColours.Init ();
            _dtmPointsInside.Init (TEXT ("points inside"), PENCOLOUR_POINTS,
                POINTSTYLE_PLUS);
            _dtmPointsOutside.Init (TEXT ("points outside"), PENCOLOUR_POINTSOUTSIDE,
                POINTSTYLE_CROSS);
            _dtmTrias.Init (TEXT ("triangles"), PENCOLOUR_TRIANGLES, 0, FALSE);
            return 0;
        }
        case WM_ENTERSIZEMOVE :
            _dtmDisplay.StartResizing ();
            return 0;
        case WM_SIZE :
            ResizeChildWindows (lParam);
            return 0;
        case WM_EXITSIZEMOVE :
            _dtmDisplay.StopResizing ();
            return 0;
        case WM_INITMENUPOPUP :
            if (HIWORD (lParam) == FALSE) {
```

```
                    switch (LOWORD (lParam)) {
                    case IDN_SHOWMENU :
                        InitShowDropdownMenu ((HMENU) wParam);
                        return 0;
                    case IDN_MOUSEMENU :
                        InitMouseDropdownMenu ((HMENU) wParam);
                        return 0;
                    default : break;
                    }
                }
                break;
        case WM_COMMAND :
            if (HIWORD (wParam) == 0) {
                switch (LOWORD (wParam)) {
                    case IDM_IMPORTPOINTS :
                        if (_dtmPointsOutside.GetTotal () != 0L) {
                            _dtmPointsInside.TransferAll (&_dtmPointsOutside,
                                PENCOLOUR_POINTS);
                            _dtmTaskDisplay.Start ();
                        }
                        _dtmPointsInside.ImportStart (hwnd, IDT_IMPORTPOINTS);
                        return 0;
                    case IDM_IMPORTTRIANGLES :
                        _dtmTrias.ImportStart (hwnd, IDT_IMPORTTRIANGLES);
                        return 0;
                    case IDM_EXPORTPOINTSINSIDE :
                        _dtmPointsInside.ExportStart (IDT_EXPORTPOINTSINSIDE,
                            IDT_EXPORTPOINTSINSIDESCRIPT);
                        return 0;
                    case IDM_EXPORTPOINTSOUTSIDE :
                        _dtmPointsOutside.ExportStart (IDT_EXPORTPOINTSOUTSIDE,
                            IDT_EXPORTPOINTSOUTSIDESCRIPT);
                        return 0;
                    case IDM_EXPORTSCREEN :
                        ExportImage (FALSE, ID_IMAGEEXPORT);
                        return 0;
                    case IDM_EXPORTMODEL :
                        ExportImage (TRUE, ID_IMAGEEXPORT);
                        return 0;
                    case IDM_EXIT :
                        SendMessage (hwnd, WM_CLOSE, 0, 0);
                        return 0;
                    case IDM_GETZVALUES :
                        GetZValuesStart (IDT_GETZVALUES);
                        return 0;
                    case IDM_SHOWPOINTSINSIDE :
                        _dtmPointsInside.FlipVisible ();
                        _dtmTaskDisplay.Start ();
                        return 0;
                    case IDM_SHOWPOINTSOUTSIDE :
                        _dtmPointsOutside.FlipVisible ();
                        _dtmTaskDisplay.Start ();
                        return 0;
                    case IDM_SHOWTRIANGLES :
                        _dtmTrias.FlipVisible ();
                        _dtmTaskDisplay.Start ();
                        return 0;
                    case IDM_COLOURBACKGROUND :
                        ChangeBackgroundColour (hwnd);
                        return 0;
                    case IDM_COLOURCOORDSTEXT :
```

```
                    ChangeCoordsTextColour (hwnd);
                    return 0;
                case IDM_COLOURPOINTSINSIDE :
                    ChangePenColour (hwnd, PENCOLOUR_POINTS);
                    return 0;
                case IDM_COLOURPOINTSOUTSIDE :
                    ChangePenColour (hwnd, PENCOLOUR_POINTSOUTSIDE);
                    return 0;
                case IDM_COLOURTRIANGLES :
                    ChangePenColour (hwnd, PENCOLOUR_TRIANGLES);
                    return 0;
                case IDM_ZOOMEXTENTS :
                    _dtmDisplay.ZoomExtents ();
                    _dtmTaskDisplay.Start ();
                    return 0;
                case IDM_REDRAW :
                    _dtmTaskDisplay.Start ();
                    return 0;
                case IDM_MOUSEZOOM :
                    _dtmDisplay.SetMouseAction (MOUSEACT_ZOOM);
                    return 0;
                case IDM_MOUSEPAN :
                    _dtmDisplay.SetMouseAction (MOUSEACT_PAN);
                    return 0;
                case IDM_MOUSEZVALUE :
                    _dtmDisplay.SetMouseAction (MOUSEACT_POINT);
                    return 0;
                case IDM_LISTPOINTSINSIDESTATS :
                    _dtmPointsInside.ListStats ();
                    return 0;
                case IDM_LISTPOINTSOUTSIDESTATS :
                    _dtmPointsOutside.ListStats ();
                    return 0;
                case IDM_LISTTRIANGLESSTATS :
                    _dtmTrias.ListStats ();
                    return 0;
                case IDM_LISTPOINTSINSIDE :
                    _dtmPointsInside.ListStart (IDT_LISTPOINTS);
                    return 0;
                case IDM_LISTPOINTSOUTSIDE :
                    _dtmPointsOutside.ListStart (IDT_LISTPOINTSOUTSIDE);
                    return 0;
                case IDM_LISTTRIANGLES :
                    _dtmTrias.ListStart (IDT_LISTTRIANGLES);
                    return 0;
                default : break;
            }
        }
        else if (HIWORD (wParam) == 1) {
            if (LOWORD (wParam) == IDM_ESCAPEKEY) {
                _dtmTask.Quit (TRUE);
                _dtmTaskDisplay.Quit (TRUE);
                return 0;
            }
        }
        else if (LOWORD (wParam) == ID_DISPLAYWND) {
            switch (HIWORD (wParam)) {
                case DTM_REDRAW :
                    _dtmTaskDisplay.Start ();
                    return 0;
                case DTM_DRAW_STOPPED :
```

```
                           case DTM_DRAW_COMPLETED :
                               _dtmDisplay.RepaintNow (REPAINT_ALL);
                               return 0;
                           case DTM_SELPOINT :
                               GetZValueAtMousePosition ();
                               return 0;
                           default : return 0;
                       }
                   }
                   else if (LOWORD (wParam) == ID_IMAGEEXPORT) {
                       ProcessExportImageMessages (wParam, IDT_EXPORTIMAGE);
                       return 0;
                   }
                   break;
              case WM_CLOSE :
                  AskCloseWindowMessage (hwnd);
                  return 0;
              case WM_DESTROY:
                  _dtmDisplay.Free ();
                  _dtmColours.Free ();
                  _dtmText.Destroy ();
                  _dtmFile.FreeImportBuffer ();
                  _dtmPointsInside.Free ();
                  _dtmPointsOutside.Free ();
                  _dtmTrias.Free ();
                  PostQuitMessage (0);
                  return 0;
              default : break;
         }
         return DefWindowProc (hwnd, message, wParam, lParam);
}

BOOL CarryOutTasks (HWND hwnd) {
    WORD wTaskStatus;

    if (!_dtmTask.IsBusy ()) {
        return FALSE;
    }
    if (_dtmTask.GetStage () == 0) {
        EnableMenuBar (hwnd, FALSE);
        _dtmDisplay.Enable (FALSE);
        _dtmTask.NextStage ();
    }
    switch (_dtmTask.GetID ()) {
        case IDT_IMPORTPOINTS :
            wTaskStatus = _dtmPointsInside.ImportCont (FALSE);
            break;
        case IDT_IMPORTTRIANGLES :
            wTaskStatus = _dtmTrias.ImportCont (FALSE);
            break;
        case IDT_EXPORTPOINTSINSIDE :
            wTaskStatus = _dtmPointsInside.ExportCont (FALSE);
            break;
        case IDT_EXPORTPOINTSINSIDESCRIPT :
            wTaskStatus = _dtmPointsInside.ExportCont (TRUE);
            break;
        case IDT_EXPORTPOINTSOUTSIDE :
            wTaskStatus = _dtmPointsOutside.ExportCont (FALSE);
            break;
        case IDT_EXPORTPOINTSOUTSIDESCRIPT :
            wTaskStatus = _dtmPointsOutside.ExportCont (TRUE);
```

```
                break;
            case IDT_EXPORTIMAGE :
                wTaskStatus = DrawModel (_dtmDisplay.GetImageDtmPtr (), &_dtmTask);
                break;
            case IDT_GETZVALUES :
                wTaskStatus = GetZValuesCont ();
                break;
            case IDT_LISTPOINTS :
                wTaskStatus = _dtmPointsInside.ListCont ();
                break;
            case IDT_LISTPOINTSOUTSIDE :
                wTaskStatus = _dtmPointsOutside.ListCont ();
                break;
            case IDT_LISTTRIANGLES :
                wTaskStatus = _dtmTrias.ListCont ();
                break;
            default :
                wTaskStatus = TASK_STOPPED;
                break;
        }
        if ((wTaskStatus & TASK_STOPPED) || (wTaskStatus & TASK_COMPLETED)) {
            EnableMenuBar (hwnd, TRUE);
            _dtmDisplay.Enable (TRUE);
            _dtmTask.Stop ();
        }
        if (wTaskStatus & TASK_COMPLETED) {
            switch (_dtmTask.GetID ()) {
                case IDT_IMPORTPOINTS :
                    AddShapeToDisplay (&_dtmPointsInside);
                    break;
                case IDT_IMPORTTRIANGLES :
                    AddShapeToDisplay (&_dtmTrias);
                    break;
                default : break;
            }
        }
        if (wTaskStatus & TASK_REDRAW) {
            _dtmTaskDisplay.Start ();
        }
        return TRUE;
}

WORD DrawModel (DTMFRAME * pdtmFrame, DTMBIGTASK * pdtmTask) {
    if (pdtmFrame == NULL || !pdtmFrame->IsActive () ||
        !pdtmFrame->IsGdiOK () || pdtmTask == NULL) {
        return TASK_STOPPED;
    }
    if (pdtmTask->Quit ()) {
        pdtmFrame->NotifyParent (DTM_DRAW_STOPPED);
        return TASK_STOPPED;
    }
    switch (pdtmTask->GetStage ()) {
        case 1 :
            pdtmFrame->ClearBackground ();
            _dtmColours.SetPenWidths (pdtmFrame->GetPenWidth (),
                pdtmFrame->GetVertExag ());
            pdtmTask->NextStage ();
            break;
        case 2 :
            _dtmTrias.Draw (pdtmFrame, pdtmTask);
            break;
```

```
            case 3 :
                _dtmPointsOutside.Draw (pdtmFrame, pdtmTask);
                break;
            case 4 :
                _dtmPointsInside.Draw (pdtmFrame, pdtmTask);
                break;
            default : break;
    }
    pdtmFrame->NotifyParent (DTM_DRAW_UPDATED);
    if (pdtmTask->GetStage () < 5) {
        return TASK_ONGOING;
    }
    pdtmFrame->NotifyParent (DTM_DRAW_COMPLETED);
    return TASK_COMPLETED;
}

void InitShowDropdownMenu (HMENU hMenu) {
    CheckMenuItem (hMenu, IDM_SHOWPOINTSINSIDE, MF_BYCOMMAND |
        (_dtmPointsInside.IsVisible () ? MF_CHECKED : MF_UNCHECKED));
    CheckMenuItem (hMenu, IDM_SHOWPOINTSOUTSIDE, MF_BYCOMMAND |
        (_dtmPointsOutside.IsVisible () ? MF_CHECKED : MF_UNCHECKED));
    CheckMenuItem (hMenu, IDM_SHOWTRIANGLES, MF_BYCOMMAND |
        (_dtmTrias.IsVisible () ? MF_CHECKED : MF_UNCHECKED));
}

void InitMouseDropdownMenu (HMENU hMenu) {
    DTMMOUSEACT mouseAction;

    mouseAction = _dtmDisplay.GetMouseAction ();
    CheckMenuItem (hMenu, IDM_MOUSEZOOM, MF_BYCOMMAND |
        (mouseAction == MOUSEACT_ZOOM ? MF_CHECKED : MF_UNCHECKED));
    CheckMenuItem (hMenu, IDM_MOUSEPAN, MF_BYCOMMAND |
        (mouseAction == MOUSEACT_PAN ? MF_CHECKED : MF_UNCHECKED));
    CheckMenuItem (hMenu, IDM_MOUSEZVALUE, MF_BYCOMMAND |
        (mouseAction == MOUSEACT_POINT ? MF_CHECKED : MF_UNCHECKED));
}

BOOL GetZValuesStart (UINT uTaskID) {
    if (_dtmTask.IsBusy ()) {
        _dtmText.Output (_szTaskBusyMessage);
        return FALSE;
    }
    if (_dtmPointsOutside.GetTotal () != 0L) {
        _dtmPointsInside.TransferAll (&_dtmPointsOutside, PENCOLOUR_POINTS);
        _dtmTaskDisplay.Start ();
    }
    if (_dtmPointsInside.GetTotal () == 0L) {
        _dtmText.Output (TEXT ("There are no %s available. Unable to calculate ") \
            TEXT ("spot levels\r\n"), _dtmPointsInside.GetDescription ());
        return FALSE;
    }
    if (_dtmTrias.GetTotal () == 0L) {
        _dtmText.Output (TEXT ("There are no %s available. Unable to ") \
            TEXT ("calculate z values\r\n"), _dtmTrias.GetDescription ());
        return FALSE;
    }
    _dtmText.Output (TEXT ("Calculating z values\r\n"));
    _dtmTask.Start (uTaskID, GETZVALUES_STEPSIZE);
    return TRUE;
}
```

```
WORD GetZValuesCont (void) {
    if (_dtmTask.Quit ()) {
        _dtmText.Output (TEXT ("\r\nCalculating spot levels stopped\r\n"));
        return TASK_STOPPED | TASK_REDRAW;
    }
    _dtmTask.StartNewBatch ();
    while (!_dtmTask.NoMoreItems (_dtmPointsInside.GetTotal ()) &&
        !_dtmTask.AtEndOfBatch ()) {
        DTMPOINT * pdtmPoint;
        DOUBLE rZValue;

        pdtmPoint = _dtmPointsInside.GetPtr (_dtmTask.GetItemNumber ());
        if (_dtmTrias.GetZ (&(pdtmPoint->cdPoint), & rZValue)) {
            pdtmPoint->cdPoint.rZ = rZValue;
            _dtmTask.NextItem ();
        }
        else {
            pdtmPoint->cdPoint.rZ = 0.0;
            _dtmPointsOutside.Transfer (&_dtmPointsInside,
                _dtmTask.GetItemNumber (), PENCOLOUR_POINTSOUTSIDE);
        }
        _dtmTask.IncBatchCounter ();
    }
    _dtmText.ProgressDot ();
    if (!_dtmTask.NoMoreItems (_dtmPointsInside.GetTotal ())) {
        return TASK_ONGOING;
    }
    _dtmPointsInside.ResetLimits ();
    _dtmPointsOutside.ResetLimits ();
    _dtmText.Output (TEXT ("\r\nNumber of %s calculated: %lu\r\n"),
        _dtmPointsInside.GetDescription (), _dtmPointsInside.GetTotal ());
    _dtmText.Output (TEXT ("Number of %s triangles: %lu\r\n"),
        _dtmPointsOutside.GetDescription (), _dtmPointsOutside.GetTotal ());
    return TASK_COMPLETED | TASK_REDRAW;
}

void GetZValueAtMousePosition (void) {
    DTMCOORD dtmMouse;
    DOUBLE rZValue;

    dtmMouse.rX = _dtmDisplay.GetSelFromX ();
    dtmMouse.rY = _dtmDisplay.GetSelFromY ();
    if (_dtmTrias.GetZ (&dtmMouse, & rZValue)) {
        _dtmText.Output (TEXT ("x, y, z:\r\n %.3f, %.3f, %.3f\r\n"),
            dtmMouse.rX, dtmMouse.rY, rZValue);
    }
    else {
        _dtmText.Output (TEXT ("No z value found at %.3f, %.3f\r\n"),
            dtmMouse.rX, dtmMouse.rY);
    }
}
```

**Chapter06.cpp** has the same layout as Chapter05.cpp in Chapter 5. It starts with the header files, not including <math.h> this time, followed by child window IDs, task IDs, the task batch size constant GETZVALUES_STEPSIZE which is used when calculating z values, and coloured pen numbers.

It then defines nine global variables, most of which are the same as in Chapter05.cpp. *_dtmPointsInside* is a points array that contains imported points and, once their z values have been calculated, it contains points that are inside the DTM. _dtmPointsOutside is a points array that contains points formerly in _dtmPointsInside, but for which it is not possible to calculate their z values because they are outside the DTM.

Eight functions are then declared, followed by the C++ source code.

The functions *WinMain*, *WndProc*, *CarryOutTasks*, *DrawModel*, *InitShowDropdownMenu* and *InitMouseDropdownMenu* are similar to the equivalent functions in Chapter05.cpp. The points array _dtmPointsOutside is initialised to display its points as x-shaped crosses instead of plus signs. When the user imports points (IDM_IMPORTPOINTS) any points in _dtmPointsOutside are transferred to _dtmPointsInside to avoid new imported points duplicating existing points, and the graphics window updates its contents so that the changes are displayed even if the user cancels the import task. The user can import points and triangles, calculate the points' z values, and export the points. The user can set the mouse (IDM_MOUSEZVALUE) to calculate z values on the fly, as well as standard zoom and pan options. *DrawModel* draws the triangles first, followed by the points outside the DTM, and then the points inside the DTM. *InitMouseDropdownMenu* contains a third mouse action option (MOUSEACT_POINT) for calculating z values when the user left-clicks the mouse in the graphics window.

The function *GetZValuesStart* starts the task to calculate z values for points in the points array _dtmPointsInside. *uTaskID* is the task's ID number. If there are any points in _dtmPointsOutside, they are transferred to _dtmPointsInside and the graphics window is set to update its contents to reflect this change in case the task does not start. If there are no points in _dtmPointsInside or triangles in _dtmTrias, *GetZValuesStart* displays an error message. Otherwise it starts the task. The function returns TRUE if successful, or FALSE if an error occurs.

The function *GetZValuesCont* carries out the task that calculates z values for the points in _dtmPointsInside. *GetZValuesCont* follows the standard task manager template as discussed in Chapter 1, looking at each point in _dtmPointsInside in batches. There is no need to store static variables when the task starts, as in previous chapters, because this task does not add any new points to the model. It just transfers existing points between two arrays. Within the while-loop, *GetZValuesCont* gets z values for each point and stores that z value in the point. If it cannot get a z value, for example because the point is outside the DTM, the point's z value is set to 0.0 and the point is transferred to _dtmPointsOutside. When this occurs *GetZValuesCont* does not call the function _dtmTask.NextItem because the next point now occupies the space in _dtmPointsInside previously occupied by the point that has just been transferred to _dtmPointsOutside. When all the points have been processed, *GetZValuesCont* resets each points array's minimum and maximum x,y,z values, and then displays in the text window how many points there are in each points array. The function returns the TASK_ constants as discussed in Chapter 1.

The function *GetZValueAtMousePosition* displays the z value in the DTM where the user has left-clicked the mouse in the graphics window. The function displays the x,y,z values in the text window, or an error message if the z value cannot be calculated because the mouse's position is outside the DTM.

# Running Chapter06

Before you can compile and run your program, you need to add the following nineteen source files to your Chapter06 project. Refer to Chapter 1 for how to do this:

| | | |
|---|---|---|
| TextWnd.h | TextWnd.cpp | |
| FileInOut.h | FileInOut.cpp | |
| BigTask.h | BigTask.cpp | |
| Graphics.h | Graphics.cpp | |
| Colours.h | Colours.cpp | |
| Shapes.h | Shapes.cpp | |
| Points.cpp | Triangles.cpp | |
| Common.h | Common.cpp | |
| Chapter06.h | Chapter06.cpp | Chapter06.rc |

You also need to add the Gdiplus.lib library file as an 'additional dependency' in your project's linker/input settings. Refer to Chapter 2 for how to do this. Finally, don't forget to set Chapter06 as your start-up project.

Otherwise, assuming you have compiled the code for Chapter06 successfully, and it is running, you can now test it out.

Start by importing the points for which you want to calculate z values. Click on 'File' in the menu bar, then select 'Import' in the drop-down menu, and finally click on 'Points'. Next, select a file containing the points data. You can use the sample file Points_Ch06.txt. Note that this file must contain x,y,z values to be imported successfully, not just x,y values. Initially, the z values can be any value. Next, import your DTM triangles, again via 'File' in the menu bar and 'Import'. You can use the sample file Triangles.txt. If successful, the program's window should look something like this:

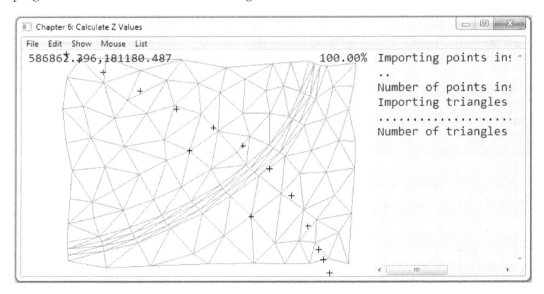

There are fifteen points, most of which follow the path used in Chapter 14. Two of the fifteen points are on corners of triangles in the body of the DTM.

Next, click on 'Edit' in the menu bar and select 'Calculate Z values' from the drop-down menu. You should see three of the points convert to red crosses and the rest remain unchanged. This indicates that three of the points are outside the DTM while the rest are inside, or on the edge of, the DTM. These point totals are shown in the text window.

In the bottom right-hand corner of the model, note that the point on the edge of the DTM has been identified by the program as being outside the DTM, as shown in the following image where the model has also been zoomed and panned (refer to Chapter 2).

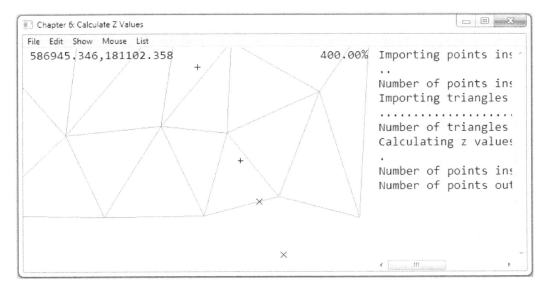

This is because of rounding errors, as the point's coordinates are expressed to three decimal places. Adjusting the x,y coordinates of this point by ±0.001 units will enable the program to identify this point as being inside the DTM.

You can confirm the number of points and the range of values in each points array by clicking on 'List' in the menu bar and then either selecting 'Statistics' from the drop-down menu to list ranges of values, or selecting 'Points inside' or 'Points outside' to list the points' x,y,z values in the text window. As in previous chapters, pressing the escape key, as the list unfolds, halts the list.

You can also export the points data, including the z values, by clicking on 'File' in the menu bar, selecting 'Export' from the drop-down menu, and then 'Points inside'. If you select 'Points outside' this exports the list of points outside the DTM where z values could not be calculated. Data can be exported as a CAD script file or as a text file.

Next, you can test obtaining z values from the DTM via the graphics window. To do this, click on 'Mouse' in the menu bar, then select 'Z value' from the drop-down menu. Now, when you left-click the mouse over the graphics window the x,y,z values at the mouse's position are displayed in the text window. These x,y,z values cannot be exported directly. However, depending on the version of Windows you're running, you may be able to copy and paste these values from the text window by left-clicking the mouse in the text window and dragging the mouse's cursor over some text to highlight it. Then either press Control and C, or right-click the mouse to display a pop-up menu and select 'Copy', to copy the highlighted text to the Windows clipboard. You can then paste this text into a separate program, such as Windows Notepad, and edit and save it from there. This copy and paste function is provided by the standard Windows edit control. It is not part of the source code in Chapter06.cpp.

When calculating z values via the graphics window, if you left-click the mouse outside the DTM, a message telling you that the z value cannot be calculated at that position is displayed in the text window.

---

A nice-to-have feature to add to your DTM programs would be the ability to import and display an image from a JPEG file in the background of the graphics window behind your DTM triangles, points and other shapes. This image could be a cropped screen capture of your CAD program showing a base survey of the site covered by your DTM, for example including building outlines, locations of trees and other vegetation, and edges of ditches and kerb lines etc. The image would pan and zoom with the rest of your DTM, and it would enable the user, when left-clicking the mouse in the graphics window, to position the mouse more meaningfully and accurately.

To implement this feature would require (i) some GDI+ code to load the JPEG file into a GDI+ Image or Bitmap class object, (ii) code to attribute coordinates to the image (at least two coordinates to calculate translation, rotation and scale) either dynamically or via custom dialog boxes, and (iii) code to display the image. Such code has not been included in this book or in Book One because, while it would provide a useful feature, it is not vital to the processes and outcomes of the programs in this book and in Book One.

---

As in previous chapters, to exit the program click on 'File' in the menu bar, select 'Exit' and then choose 'Yes' in the message box that appears.

# Chapter 7

## Calculate Maximum Slopes and Fill Triangles with Colour

Chapter 7 lists the source code for a program called **Chapter07** that calculates the maximum slope and slope direction for each 3D triangle in a DTM, and fills the triangles with colour depending on their slopes. The program creates an array of slope arrows that show the slope direction in the graphics window. The slope values can be exported as a text file or as a CAD script file. The user can also obtain slope values for individual triangles by left-clicking the mouse in the graphics window over each triangle. These on-the-fly slope values cannot be exported directly by the program. The colour that fills the triangles depends on which band, or range, of slope values each triangle's slope falls within. The program uses a custom dialog box to enable the user to enter the slope values that define each band, or range, of slopes. These coloured triangles can be exported as a text file, a CAD script file, or also as a JPEG file.

The following files are discussed in this chapter:

**Chapter07.h**          **Chapter07.rc**          **Chapter07.cpp**

## Chapter07 Source Files

The first file is the header file:

**CHAPTER07.H**

```
#ifndef CHAPTER07_H
#define CHAPTER07_H

#define IDM_IMPORTTRIANGLES      101
#define IDM_EXPORTTRIANGLES      102
#define IDM_EXPORTSLOPES         103
#define IDM_EXPORTSCREEN         104
#define IDM_EXPORTMODEL          105
#define IDM_EXIT                 106

#define IDM_GETSLOPES            201
#define IDM_APPLYCOLOURS         202

#define IDN_SHOWMENU             2

#define IDM_SHOWTRIANGLES        301
#define IDM_SHOWSLOPES           302
#define IDM_SHOWSLOPECOLOURS     303
#define IDM_COLOURBACKGROUND     304
#define IDM_COLOURCOORDSTEXT     305
#define IDM_COLOURTRIANGLES      306
#define IDM_COLOURSLOPES         307
#define IDM_COLOURFILL1          308
#define IDM_COLOURFILL2          309
#define IDM_COLOURFILL3          310
#define IDM_COLOURFILL4          311
```

```
#define IDM_COLOURFILL5          312
#define IDM_ZOOMEXTENTS          313
#define IDM_REDRAW               314

#define IDN_MOUSEMENU            3

#define IDM_MOUSEZOOM            401
#define IDM_MOUSEPAN             402
#define IDM_MOUSEGETSLOPE        403

#define IDM_LISTTRIANGLESSTATS   501
#define IDM_LISTSLOPESSTATS      502
#define IDM_LISTTRIANGLES        503
#define IDM_LISTSLOPES           504

#define IDM_ESCAPEKEY            901

#define IDD_BAND1                1001
#define IDD_BAND2                1002
#define IDD_BAND3                1003
#define IDD_BAND4                1004
#define IDD_BAND5                1005

#endif // CHAPTER07_H
```

As in previous chapters, **Chapter07.h** contains ID numbers for menu bar options, drop-down menus, accelerator keys and dialog box controls.

The second file is the resource script file:

**CHAPTER07.RC**

```
#include <windows.h>
#include "Chapter07.h"

Chapter07 MENU {
    POPUP "&File" {
        POPUP "&Import" {
            MENUITEM "&Triangles",         IDM_IMPORTTRIANGLES
        }
        POPUP "&Export" {
            MENUITEM "&Triangles",         IDM_EXPORTTRIANGLES
            MENUITEM "&Slopes",            IDM_EXPORTSLOPES
            MENUITEM SEPARATOR
            MENUITEM "S&creen image",      IDM_EXPORTSCREEN
            MENUITEM "&Model image",       IDM_EXPORTMODEL
        }
        MENUITEM SEPARATOR
        MENUITEM "E&xit",                  IDM_EXIT
    }
    POPUP "&Edit" {
        MENUITEM "&Get slopes",            IDM_GETSLOPES
        MENUITEM "&Colour slopes",         IDM_APPLYCOLOURS
    }
    POPUP "&Show" {
        MENUITEM "&Triangles",             IDM_SHOWTRIANGLES
        MENUITEM "&Slopes",                IDM_SHOWSLOPES
        MENUITEM "S&lope colours",         IDM_SHOWSLOPECOLOURS
        MENUITEM SEPARATOR
        POPUP "&Colour" {
```

```
                MENUITEM "Back&ground",        IDM_COLOURBACKGROUND
                MENUITEM "&Coords text",        IDM_COLOURCOORDSTEXT
                MENUITEM SEPARATOR
                MENUITEM "&Triangles",          IDM_COLOURTRIANGLES
                MENUITEM "&Slopes",             IDM_COLOURSLOPES
                POPUP "S&lope colours" {
                    MENUITEM "&Flat",           IDM_COLOURFILL1
                    MENUITEM "&Slight",         IDM_COLOURFILL2
                    MENUITEM "&Moderate",       IDM_COLOURFILL3
                    MENUITEM "S&teep",          IDM_COLOURFILL4
                    MENUITEM "&Extreme",        IDM_COLOURFILL5
                }
            }
            MENUITEM SEPARATOR
            MENUITEM "&Zoom extents",           IDM_ZOOMEXTENTS
            MENUITEM "&Redraw",                 IDM_REDRAW
        }
        POPUP "&Mouse" {
            MENUITEM "&Zoom in/out",            IDM_MOUSEZOOM
            MENUITEM "&Pan",                    IDM_MOUSEPAN
            MENUITEM SEPARATOR
            MENUITEM "&Slope values",           IDM_MOUSEGETSLOPE
        }
        POPUP "&List" {
            POPUP "&Statistics" {
                MENUITEM "&Triangles",          IDM_LISTTRIANGLESSTATS
                MENUITEM "&Slopes",             IDM_LISTSLOPESSTATS
            }
            MENUITEM SEPARATOR
            MENUITEM "&Triangles",              IDM_LISTTRIANGLES
            MENUITEM "S&lopes",                 IDM_LISTSLOPES
        }
    }
}

Chapter07 ACCELERATORS {
    VK_ESCAPE,       IDM_ESCAPEKEY,         VIRTKEY, NOINVERT
}

SetSlopeBands DIALOG 32, 32, 184, 128
STYLE DS_MODALFRAME | WS_POPUP | WS_CAPTION
CAPTION "Set slope band intervals"
FONT 8, "MS Sans Serif" {
    LTEXT "Band 1 (flat) less than", -1, 8, 10, 104, 10
    EDITTEXT IDD_BAND1, 120, 8, 48, 14
    LTEXT "%", -1, 172, 10, 10, 10
    LTEXT "Band 2 (slight) less than", -1, 8, 30, 104, 10
    EDITTEXT IDD_BAND2, 120, 28, 48, 14
    LTEXT "%", -1, 172, 30, 10, 10
    LTEXT "Band 3 (moderate) less than", -1, 8, 50, 104, 10
    EDITTEXT IDD_BAND3, 120, 48, 48, 14
    LTEXT "%", -1, 172, 50, 10, 10
    LTEXT "Band 4 (steep) less than", -1, 8, 70, 104, 10
    EDITTEXT IDD_BAND4, 120, 68, 48, 14
    LTEXT "%", -1, 172, 70, 10, 10
    LTEXT "Band 5 (extreme) at and beyond", -1, 8, 90, 104, 10
    EDITTEXT IDD_BAND5, 120, 88, 48, 14, WS_DISABLED
    LTEXT "%", -1, 172, 90, 10, 10
    DEFPUSHBUTTON "OK", IDOK, 72, 108, 48, 14
    PUSHBUTTON "Cancel", IDCANCEL, 128, 108, 48, 14
}
```

Like previous chapters, **Chapter07.rc** defines the contents of the program's menu bar, accelerator keys (or key), and a custom dialog box called 'SetSlopeBands'. Note that the final EditText control in SetSlopeBands (IDD_BAND5) is disabled (WS_DISABLED) so that the user cannot enter a value into this edit control directly.

The third file is the source code file, which includes function listings.

**CHAPTER07.CPP**

```
#ifndef UNICODE
#define UNICODE
#endif

#include <windows.h>
#include <gdiplus.h>
using namespace Gdiplus;
#include "Chapter07.h"
#include "BigTask.h"
#include "FileInOut.h"
#include "TextWnd.h"
#include "Graphics.h"
#include "Colours.h"
#include "Shapes.h"
#include "Common.h"

#define ID_TEXTWND                      1
#define ID_DISPLAYWND                   2
#define ID_IMAGEEXPORT                  3

#define IDT_IMPORTTRIANGLES             11

#define IDT_EXPORTTRIANGLES             21
#define IDT_EXPORTTRIANGLESSCRIPT       22
#define IDT_EXPORTSLOPES                23
#define IDT_EXPORTSLOPESSCRIPT          24
#define IDT_EXPORTIMAGE                 25

#define IDT_GETSLOPES                   31
#define IDT_APPLYCOLOURS                32

#define IDT_LISTTRIANGLES               41
#define IDT_LISTSLOPES                  42

#define GETSLOPES_STEPSIZE              20L
#define APPLYCOLOURS_STEPSIZE           20L

#define PENCOLOUR_TRIANGLES             11
#define PENCOLOUR_SLOPES                5

#define BRUSHCOLOUR_TRIANGLES           2

#define SLOPEBANDS_TOTAL                4

HINSTANCE _hInst;
DTMTEXTWINDOW _dtmText;
DTMFILEDATA _dtmFile;
DTMBIGTASK _dtmTask, _dtmTaskDisplay;
DTMDISPLAY _dtmDisplay;
DTMCOLOURS _dtmColours;
DTMTRIAS _dtmTrias;
```

```
DTMSLOPES _dtmSlopes;
DOUBLE _rSlopeBands [SLOPEBANDS_TOTAL];

LRESULT CALLBACK WndProc (HWND, UINT, WPARAM, LPARAM);
BOOL CarryOutTasks (HWND);
WORD DrawModel (DTMFRAME *, DTMBIGTASK *);
void InitShowDropdownMenu (HMENU);
void InitMouseDropdownMenu (HMENU);
BOOL GetSlopesStart (HWND, UINT);
WORD GetSlopesCont (WORD);
BOOL ApplyColoursStart (HWND, UINT);
BOOL CALLBACK SetSlopeBandsDlgProc (HWND, UINT, WPARAM, LPARAM);
WORD ApplyColoursCont (void);
void GetSlopeAtMousePosition (void);

int WINAPI WinMain (HINSTANCE hInst, HINSTANCE, PSTR, int nCmdShow) {
    return InitAndRunProgram (hInst, nCmdShow, TEXT ("Chapter07"),
        TEXT ("Chapter 7: Calculate Slopes and Fill Colours"));
}

LRESULT CALLBACK WndProc (HWND hwnd, UINT message, WPARAM wParam, LPARAM lParam) {
    switch (message) {
        case WM_CREATE :
            _hInst = ((LPCREATESTRUCT) lParam)->hInstance;
            _dtmText.Create (hwnd, ID_TEXTWND, _hInst);
            _dtmFile.Init (hwnd);
            _dtmDisplay.Init (hwnd, 0, ID_DISPLAYWND, _hInst,
                1.0, 10.0, 4.0, 4.0, 11.0, 1.0, 2.0, 0.5);
            _dtmColours.Init ();
            _dtmTrias.Init (TEXT ("triangles"), PENCOLOUR_TRIANGLES,
                BRUSHCOLOUR_TRIANGLES, FALSE);
            _dtmSlopes.Init (TEXT ("slopes"), PENCOLOUR_SLOPES);
            _rSlopeBands [0] = 0.8;
            _rSlopeBands [1] = 2.5;
            _rSlopeBands [2] = 5.0;
            _rSlopeBands [3] = 20.0;
            return 0;
        case WM_ENTERSIZEMOVE :
            _dtmDisplay.StartResizing ();
            return 0;
        case WM_SIZE :
            ResizeChildWindows (lParam);
            return 0;
        case WM_EXITSIZEMOVE :
            _dtmDisplay.StopResizing ();
            return 0;
        case WM_INITMENUPOPUP :
            if (HIWORD (lParam) == FALSE) {
                switch (LOWORD (lParam)) {
                case IDN_SHOWMENU :
                    InitShowDropdownMenu ((HMENU) wParam);
                    return 0;
                case IDN_MOUSEMENU :
                    InitMouseDropdownMenu ((HMENU) wParam);
                    return 0;
                default : break;
                }
            }
            break;
        case WM_COMMAND :
            if (HIWORD (wParam) == 0) {
```

```
switch (LOWORD (wParam)) {
    case IDM_IMPORTTRIANGLES :
        _dtmTrias.ImportStart (hwnd, IDT_IMPORTTRIANGLES);
        return 0;
    case IDM_EXPORTTRIANGLES :
        _dtmTrias.ExportStart (IDT_EXPORTTRIANGLES,
            IDT_EXPORTTRIANGLESSCRIPT);
        return 0;
    case IDM_EXPORTSLOPES :
        _dtmSlopes.ExportStart (IDT_EXPORTSLOPES,
            IDT_EXPORTSLOPESSCRIPT);
        return 0;
    case IDM_EXPORTSCREEN :
        ExportImage (FALSE, ID_IMAGEEXPORT);
        return 0;
    case IDM_EXPORTMODEL :
        ExportImage (TRUE, ID_IMAGEEXPORT);
        return 0;
    case IDM_EXIT :
        SendMessage (hwnd, WM_CLOSE, 0, 0);
        return 0;
    case IDM_GETSLOPES :
        GetSlopesStart (hwnd, IDT_GETSLOPES);
        return 0;
    case IDM_APPLYCOLOURS :
        ApplyColoursStart (hwnd, IDT_APPLYCOLOURS);
        return 0;
    case IDM_SHOWTRIANGLES :
        _dtmTrias.FlipVisible ();
        _dtmTaskDisplay.Start ();
        return 0;
    case IDM_SHOWSLOPES :
        _dtmSlopes.FlipVisible ();
        _dtmTaskDisplay.Start ();
        return 0;
    case IDM_SHOWSLOPECOLOURS :
        _dtmTrias.FlipFillVisible ();
        _dtmTaskDisplay.Start ();
        return 0;
    case IDM_COLOURBACKGROUND :
        ChangeBackgroundColour (hwnd);
        return 0;
    case IDM_COLOURCOORDSTEXT :
        ChangeCoordsTextColour (hwnd);
        return 0;
    case IDM_COLOURTRIANGLES :
        ChangePenColour (hwnd, PENCOLOUR_TRIANGLES);
        return 0;
    case IDM_COLOURSLOPES :
        ChangePenColour (hwnd, PENCOLOUR_SLOPES);
        return 0;
    case IDM_COLOURFILL1 :
    case IDM_COLOURFILL2 :
    case IDM_COLOURFILL3 :
    case IDM_COLOURFILL4 :
    case IDM_COLOURFILL5 :
        ChangeBrushColour (hwnd, LOWORD (wParam) - IDM_COLOURFILL1);
        return 0;
    case IDM_ZOOMEXTENTS :
        _dtmDisplay.ZoomExtents ();
        _dtmTaskDisplay.Start ();
```

```
                            return 0;
                  case IDM_REDRAW :
                      _dtmTaskDisplay.Start ();
                      return 0;
                  case IDM_MOUSEZOOM :
                      _dtmDisplay.SetMouseAction (MOUSEACT_ZOOM);
                      return 0;
                  case IDM_MOUSEPAN :
                      _dtmDisplay.SetMouseAction (MOUSEACT_PAN);
                      return 0;
                  case IDM_MOUSEGETSLOPE :
                      _dtmDisplay.SetMouseAction (MOUSEACT_POINT);
                      return 0;
                  case IDM_LISTTRIANGLESSTATS :
                      _dtmTrias.ListStats ();
                      return 0;
                  case IDM_LISTSLOPESSTATS :
                      _dtmSlopes.ListStats ();
                      return 0;
                  case IDM_LISTTRIANGLES :
                      _dtmTrias.ListStart (IDT_LISTTRIANGLES);
                      return 0;
                  case IDM_LISTSLOPES :
                      _dtmSlopes.ListStart (IDT_LISTSLOPES);
                      return 0;
                  default : break;
              }
          }
          else if (HIWORD (wParam) == 1) {
              if (LOWORD (wParam) == IDM_ESCAPEKEY) {
                  _dtmTask.Quit (TRUE);
                  _dtmTaskDisplay.Quit (TRUE);
                  return 0;
              }
          }
          else if (LOWORD (wParam) == ID_DISPLAYWND) {
              switch (HIWORD (wParam)) {
                  case DTM_REDRAW :
                      _dtmTaskDisplay.Start ();
                      return 0;
                  case DTM_DRAW_STOPPED :
                  case DTM_DRAW_COMPLETED :
                      _dtmDisplay.RepaintNow (REPAINT_ALL);
                      return 0;
                  case DTM_SELPOINT :
                      GetSlopeAtMousePosition ();
                      return 0;
                  default : return 0;
              }
          }
          else if (LOWORD (wParam) == ID_IMAGEEXPORT) {
              ProcessExportImageMessages (wParam, IDT_EXPORTIMAGE);
              return 0;
          }
          break;
      case WM_CLOSE :
          AskCloseWindowMessage (hwnd);
          return 0;
      case WM_DESTROY:
          _dtmDisplay.Free ();
          _dtmColours.Free ();
```

```
            _dtmText.Destroy ();
            _dtmFile.FreeImportBuffer ();
            _dtmTrias.Free ();
            _dtmSlopes.Free ();
            PostQuitMessage (0);
            return 0;
        default : break;
    }
    return DefWindowProc (hwnd, message, wParam, lParam);
}

BOOL CarryOutTasks (HWND hwnd) {
    WORD wTaskStatus;

    if (!_dtmTask.IsBusy ()) {
        return FALSE;
    }
    if (_dtmTask.GetStage () == 0) {
        EnableMenuBar (hwnd, FALSE);
        _dtmDisplay.Enable (FALSE);
        _dtmTask.NextStage ();
    }
    switch (_dtmTask.GetID ()) {
        case IDT_IMPORTTRIANGLES :
            wTaskStatus = _dtmTrias.ImportCont (FALSE);
            break;
        case IDT_EXPORTTRIANGLES :
            wTaskStatus = _dtmTrias.ExportCont (FALSE);
            break;
        case IDT_EXPORTTRIANGLESSCRIPT :
            wTaskStatus = _dtmTrias.ExportCont (TRUE);
            break;
        case IDT_EXPORTSLOPES :
            wTaskStatus = _dtmSlopes.ExportCont (FALSE);
            break;
        case IDT_EXPORTSLOPESSCRIPT :
            wTaskStatus = _dtmSlopes.ExportCont (TRUE);
            break;
        case IDT_EXPORTIMAGE :
            wTaskStatus = DrawModel (_dtmDisplay.GetImageDtmPtr (), &_dtmTask);
            break;
        case IDT_GETSLOPES :
            wTaskStatus = GetSlopesCont (PENCOLOUR_SLOPES);
            break;
        case IDT_APPLYCOLOURS :
            wTaskStatus = ApplyColoursCont ();
            break;
        case IDT_LISTTRIANGLES :
            wTaskStatus = _dtmTrias.ListCont ();
            break;
        case IDT_LISTSLOPES :
            wTaskStatus = _dtmSlopes.ListCont ();
            break;
        default :
            wTaskStatus = TASK_STOPPED;
            break;
    }
    if ((wTaskStatus & TASK_STOPPED) || (wTaskStatus & TASK_COMPLETED)) {
        EnableMenuBar (hwnd, TRUE);
        _dtmDisplay.Enable (TRUE);
        _dtmTask.Stop ();
```

```
        }
    if (wTaskStatus & TASK_COMPLETED) {
        switch (_dtmTask.GetID ()) {
            case IDT_IMPORTTRIANGLES :
                AddShapeToDisplay (&_dtmTrias);
                break;
            default : break;
        }
    }
    if (wTaskStatus & TASK_REDRAW) {
        _dtmTaskDisplay.Start ();
    }
    return TRUE;
}

WORD DrawModel (DTMFRAME * pdtmFrame, DTMBIGTASK * pdtmTask) {
    if (pdtmFrame == NULL || !pdtmFrame->IsActive () ||
        !pdtmFrame->IsGdiOK () || pdtmTask == NULL) {
        return TASK_STOPPED;
    }
    if (pdtmTask->Quit ()) {
        pdtmFrame->NotifyParent (DTM_DRAW_STOPPED);
        return TASK_STOPPED;
    }
    switch (pdtmTask->GetStage ()) {
        case 1 :
            pdtmFrame->ClearBackground ();
            _dtmColours.SetPenWidths (pdtmFrame->GetPenWidth (),
                pdtmFrame->GetVertExag ());
            pdtmTask->NextStage ();
            break;
        case 2 :
            _dtmTrias.DrawFill (pdtmFrame, pdtmTask);
            break;
        case 3 :
            _dtmTrias.Draw (pdtmFrame, pdtmTask);
            break;
        case 4 :
            _dtmSlopes.Draw (pdtmFrame, pdtmTask);
            break;
        default : break;
    }
    pdtmFrame->NotifyParent (DTM_DRAW_UPDATED);
    if (pdtmTask->GetStage () < 5) {
        return TASK_ONGOING;
    }
    pdtmFrame->NotifyParent (DTM_DRAW_COMPLETED);
    return TASK_COMPLETED;
}

void InitShowDropdownMenu (HMENU hMenu) {
    CheckMenuItem (hMenu, IDM_SHOWTRIANGLES, MF_BYCOMMAND |
        (_dtmTrias.IsVisible () ? MF_CHECKED : MF_UNCHECKED));
    CheckMenuItem (hMenu, IDM_SHOWSLOPES, MF_BYCOMMAND |
        (_dtmSlopes.IsVisible () ? MF_CHECKED : MF_UNCHECKED));
    CheckMenuItem (hMenu, IDM_SHOWSLOPECOLOURS, MF_BYCOMMAND |
        (_dtmTrias.IsFillVisible () ? MF_CHECKED : MF_UNCHECKED));
}
```

```
void InitMouseDropdownMenu (HMENU hMenu) {
    DTMMOUSEACT mouseAction;

    mouseAction = _dtmDisplay.GetMouseAction ();
    CheckMenuItem (hMenu, IDM_MOUSEZOOM, MF_BYCOMMAND |
        (mouseAction == MOUSEACT_ZOOM ? MF_CHECKED : MF_UNCHECKED));
    CheckMenuItem (hMenu, IDM_MOUSEPAN, MF_BYCOMMAND |
        (mouseAction == MOUSEACT_PAN ? MF_CHECKED : MF_UNCHECKED));
    CheckMenuItem (hMenu, IDM_MOUSEGETSLOPE, MF_BYCOMMAND |
        (mouseAction == MOUSEACT_POINT ? MF_CHECKED : MF_UNCHECKED));
}

BOOL GetSlopesStart (HWND hwnd, UINT uTaskID) {
    if (_dtmTask.IsBusy ()) {
        _dtmText.Output (_szTaskBusyMessage);
        return FALSE;
    }
    if (_dtmTrias.GetTotal () == 0L) {
        _dtmText.Output (TEXT ("There are no %s available. Unable to ") \
            TEXT ("calculate slope values\r\n"), _dtmTrias.GetDescription ());
        return FALSE;
    }
    if (_dtmSlopes.GetTotal () != 0L) {
        int iMessage;

        iMessage = MessageBox (hwnd,
            TEXT ("Do you want to discard all slopes already created?"),
            TEXT ("Calculate slopes"), MB_YESNOCANCEL | MB_ICONWARNING);
        if (iMessage == IDCANCEL) {
            return FALSE;
        }
        else if (iMessage == IDYES) {
            _dtmSlopes.Free ();
        }
    }
    _dtmText.Output (TEXT ("Calculating slope values\r\n"));
    _dtmTask.Start (uTaskID, GETSLOPES_STEPSIZE);
    return TRUE;
}

WORD GetSlopesCont (WORD wSlopeColour) {
    static DWORD dwTotalAtStart;

    if (_dtmTask.AtStart ()) {
        dwTotalAtStart = _dtmSlopes.GetTotal ();
    }
    if (_dtmTask.Quit ()) {
        _dtmText.Output (TEXT ("\r\nCalculating %s stopped\r\n"),
            _dtmSlopes.GetDescription ());
        return TASK_STOPPED | TASK_REDRAW;
    }
    _dtmTask.StartNewBatch ();
    while (!_dtmTask.NoMoreItems (_dtmTrias.GetTotal ()) && !_dtmTask.AtEndOfBatch ()) {
        DTMTRIA * pdtmTria;
        DTMSLOPE dtmSlopeAdd;
        DOUBLE rSlope, rAngle;

        pdtmTria = _dtmTrias.GetPtr (_dtmTask.GetItemNumber ());
        _dtmTrias.Average (&(dtmSlopeAdd.cdSlope), pdtmTria->cdCorner);
        if (_dtmTrias.GetSlope (pdtmTria, &rSlope, &rAngle)) {
            dtmSlopeAdd.wColour = wSlopeColour;
```

```
                    dtmSlopeAdd.cdSlope.rZ = rSlope;
                    dtmSlopeAdd.rAngle = rAngle;
                    _dtmSlopes.Add (&dtmSlopeAdd);
                }
            _dtmTask.NextItem ();
            _dtmTask.IncBatchCounter ();
        }
        _dtmText.ProgressDot ();
        if (!_dtmTask.NoMoreItems (_dtmTrias.GetTotal ())) {
            return TASK_ONGOING;
        }
        _dtmText.Output (TEXT ("\r\nNumber of %s created: %lu\r\n"),
            _dtmSlopes.GetDescription (), _dtmSlopes.GetTotal () - dwTotalAtStart);
        return TASK_COMPLETED | TASK_REDRAW;
}

BOOL ApplyColoursStart (HWND hwnd, UINT uTaskID) {
        if (_dtmTask.IsBusy ()) {
            _dtmText.Output (_szTaskBusyMessage);
            return FALSE;
        }
        if (_dtmTrias.GetTotal () == 0L) {
            _dtmText.Output (TEXT ("There are no %s available. Unable to ") \
                TEXT ("apply slope colours\r\n"), _dtmTrias.GetDescription ());
            return FALSE;
        }
        if (!DialogBox (_hInst, TEXT ("SetSlopeBands"), hwnd, SetSlopeBandsDlgProc)) {
            return FALSE;
        }
        _dtmText.Output (TEXT ("Applying slope colours to triangles\r\n"));
        _dtmTask.Start (uTaskID, APPLYCOLOURS_STEPSIZE);
        return TRUE;
}

BOOL CALLBACK SetSlopeBandsDlgProc (HWND hdlg, UINT message, WPARAM wParam,
        LPARAM lParam) {
        switch (message) {
            case WM_INITDIALOG : {
                WORD wBand;

                for (wBand = 0; wBand < SLOPEBANDS_TOTAL; wBand ++) {
                    SetDlgItemNumber (hdlg, IDD_BAND1 + wBand, _rSlopeBands [wBand]);
                }
                SetDlgItemNumber (hdlg, IDD_BAND5, _rSlopeBands [3]);
                return TRUE;
            }
            case WM_COMMAND :
                switch (LOWORD (wParam)) {
                    case IDOK : {
                        WORD wBand;
                        DOUBLE rValues [SLOPEBANDS_TOTAL];
                        BOOL fError;

                        for (wBand = 0; wBand < SLOPEBANDS_TOTAL; wBand ++) {
                            rValues [wBand] = GetDlgItemNumber (hdlg,
                                IDD_BAND1 + wBand, 0.001, 99999.999);
                        }
                        fError = FALSE;
                        for (wBand = 0; wBand < SLOPEBANDS_TOTAL - 1; wBand ++) {
                            if (rValues [wBand] >= rValues [wBand + 1]) {
                                fError = TRUE;
```

```
                    }
                }
                if (fError) {
                    MessageBox (hdlg,
                        TEXT ("Slopes must be in increasing order"),
                        TEXT ("Slope band intervals error"),
                        MB_ICONWARNING | MB_OK);
                }
                else {
                    for (wBand = 0; wBand < SLOPEBANDS_TOTAL; wBand ++) {
                        _rSlopeBands [wBand] = rValues [wBand];
                    }
                    EndDialog (hdlg, TRUE);
                }
                return TRUE;
            }
            case IDCANCEL :
                EndDialog (hdlg, FALSE);
                return TRUE;
            case IDD_BAND1 :
            case IDD_BAND2 :
            case IDD_BAND3 :
            case IDD_BAND4 :
                if (HIWORD (wParam) == EN_KILLFOCUS) {
                    DOUBLE rValue;

                    rValue = GetDlgItemNumber (hdlg, LOWORD (wParam),
                        0.001, 99999.999);
                    SetDlgItemNumber (hdlg, LOWORD (wParam), rValue);
                    if (LOWORD (wParam) == IDD_BAND4) {
                        SetDlgItemNumber (hdlg, IDD_BAND5, rValue);
                    }
                    return TRUE;
                }
                break;
            default : break;
            }
        }
        default : break;
    }
    return FALSE;
}

WORD ApplyColoursCont (void) {
    if (_dtmTask.Quit ()) {
        _dtmText.Output (TEXT ("\r\nApplying slope colours stopped\r\n"));
        return TASK_STOPPED | TASK_REDRAW;
    }
    _dtmTask.StartNewBatch ();
    while (!_dtmTask.NoMoreItems (_dtmTrias.GetTotal ()) && !_dtmTask.AtEndOfBatch ()) {
        DTMTRIA * pdtmTria;
        BOOL fColourApplied;
        DOUBLE rSlope, rAngle;

        pdtmTria = _dtmTrias.GetPtr (_dtmTask.GetItemNumber ());
        fColourApplied = FALSE;
        if (_dtmTrias.GetSlope (pdtmTria, &rSlope, &rAngle)) {
            WORD wBand;

            wBand = 0;
            while (wBand < SLOPEBANDS_TOTAL && !fColourApplied) {
                if (rSlope < _rSlopeBands [wBand]) {
```

```
                        pdtmTria->wFillColour = wBand;
                        fColourApplied = TRUE;
                    }
                    wBand ++;
                }
            }
        }
        if (!fColourApplied) {
            pdtmTria->wFillColour = SLOPEBANDS_TOTAL;
        }
        _dtmTask.NextItem ();
        _dtmTask.IncBatchCounter ();
    }
    _dtmText.ProgressDot ();
    if (!_dtmTask.NoMoreItems (_dtmTrias.GetTotal ())) {
        return TASK_ONGOING;
    }
    _dtmText.Output (TEXT ("\r\nFinished applying slope colours\r\n"));
    if (!_dtmTrias.IsFillVisible ()) {
        _dtmTrias.FlipFillVisible ();
    }
    return TASK_COMPLETED | TASK_REDRAW;
}

void GetSlopeAtMousePosition (void) {
    DTMCOORD dtmMouse;
    DWORD dwTria;
    DOUBLE rSlope, rAngle;

    dtmMouse.rX = _dtmDisplay.GetSelFromX ();
    dtmMouse.rY = _dtmDisplay.GetSelFromY ();
    dwTria = _dtmTrias.FromCoords (&dtmMouse);
    if (_dtmTrias.GetSlope (dwTria, &rSlope, &rAngle)) {
        _dtmText.Output (TEXT ("x, y, slope, angle:\r\n %.3f, %.3f, %.3f%%, ") \
            TEXT ("%.3f\260\r\n"), dtmMouse.rX, dtmMouse.rY, rSlope, rAngle);
    }
    else {
        _dtmText.Output (TEXT ("No slope found at %.3f, %.3f\r\n"),
            dtmMouse.rX, dtmMouse.rY);
    }
}
```

**Chapter07.cpp** has the same layout as Chapter05.cpp and Chapter06.cpp in Chapters 5 and 6. It starts with the header files followed by child window IDs, task IDs, the task batch size constants GETSLOPES_STEPSIZE and APPLYCOLOURS_STEPSIZE which are used when calculating slopes and applying fill colours to triangles, and coloured pen and brush numbers. The constant SLOPEBANDS_TOTAL is the size of an array that contains slopes values that define bands, or ranges, of slopes. The array contains four values, but there are five bands because the last band is 'anything beyond' the fourth band.

Chapter07.cpp then defines ten global variables, most of which are the same as in Chapter05.cpp and Chapter06.cpp. _dtmSlopes is a slopes array that contains the slope arrows. _rSlopeBands is the array of slopes values that define bands, or ranges, of slopes. These bands, or ranges, determine which brush colour to fill triangles with, based on which band, or range, each triangle's slope falls within.

Eleven functions are then declared, followed by the C++ source code.

The functions *WinMain*, *WndProc*, *CarryOutTasks*, *DrawModel*, *InitShowDropdownMenu* and *InitMouseDropdownMenu* are similar to the equivalent functions in Chapter05.cpp and Chapter06.cpp. After the message WM_CREATE in *WndProc*, the array of slope band, or range, values is initialised as follows:

| Band | Lower limit | Upper limit |
|------|-------------|-------------|
| 0 (Flat) | None | < 0.8% (1 in 125) |
| 1 (Slight) | ≤ 0.8% | < 2.5% (1 in 40) |
| 2 (Moderate) | ≤ 2.5% | < 5.0% (1 in 20) |
| 3 (Steep) | ≤5.0% | < 20.0% (1 in 5) |
| 4 (Extreme) | ≤ 20.0% | None |

In these functions the user can import triangles, calculate maximum slopes and slope directions, fill triangles with colour depending on their slope, and export slope values and coloured triangles. The user can set the mouse (IDM_MOUSEGETSLOPE) to calculate slope values on the fly, as well as standard zoom and pan options. *DrawModel* draws the filled triangles first so that they do not overwrite other shapes, followed by the triangle outlines, and then the slope arrows. *InitMouseDropdownMenu* contains a third mouse action option (MOUSEACT_POINT) for calculating slope values when the user left-clicks the mouse in the graphics window.

The function *GetSlopesStart* starts the task that calculates maximum slopes and slope directions. *hwnd* is the handle of the parent window and *uTaskID* is the task ID number. If there are no triangles in the triangles array *_dtmTrias*, the function displays an error message. If the slopes array *_dtmSlopes* already contains some slope arrows, the function asks the user if they want to discard these slope arrows. If the user selects 'Yes', the existing slope arrows are discarded. Finally, *GetSlopesStart* displays a message in the text window and starts the task. The function returns TRUE if successful, or FALSE if the user cancels the task or if an error occurs.

The function *GetSlopesCont* carries out the task of calculating the maximum slopes and slope directions. *wSlopeColour* is the number of the coloured pen to apply to new slope arrows. *GetSlopesCont* follows the standard task manager template as discussed in Chapter 1, looking at each triangle in the triangles array *_dtmTrias* in batches. Within the while-loop, the x,y coordinates of each slope arrow are set as the centroid of each triangle, and if the slope values are calculated successfully they are copied to the slope arrow. The slope arrow's *rZ* member variable contains the maximum slope, not a z value. The function returns the TASK_ constants as discussed in Chapter 1.

The function *ApplyColoursStart* starts the task of applying fill colours to the triangles in *_dtmTrias* based on each triangle's slope. *hwnd* is the handle of the parent window and *uTaskID* is the task ID number. If there are no triangles in *_dtmTrias*, the function displays an error message. Otherwise it activates the custom dialog box 'SetSlopeBands' that enables the user to change the slopes values in the array *_rSlopeBands*. Finally, it displays a message in the text window and starts the task. *ApplyColoursStart* returns TRUE if successful, or FALSE if the user cancels the task or if an error occurs.

The function *SetSlopeBandsDlgProc* activates a custom dialog box that enables the user to enter slopes values that define the bands, or ranges, in the array *_rSlopeBands*. The existing slopes values are stored in the dialog box's edit controls when the dialog box is initialised with the message WM_INITDIALOG. The message WM_COMMAND is sent when the user clicks on the OK or Cancel buttons, or when the user interacts with one of the dialog box's edit controls. If the user clicks on the OK button, the new slope values in the edit controls are limited to be between 0.001 and 99999.999 and their order is checked. If the slopes are not in ascending order, a message box appears displaying an error message. Otherwise the slopes are stored in *_rSlopeBands*, and the dialog box closes. If the user cancels the dialog box, the values in the edit controls are discarded and *_rSlopeBands* remains unchanged. If the user exits one of the edit controls, the slope value in the edit control is forced to be between 0.001 and 99999.999. If exiting the fourth edit control (IDD_BAND4), its slope value is copied to edit control IDD_BAND5, which the user cannot edit because it is disabled (see the resource script file earlier in this chapter).

The function *ApplyColoursCont* carries out the task of applying fill brush colours to the triangles based on each triangle's slope. *ApplyColoursCont* follows the standard task manager template as discussed in Chapter 1, looking at each triangle in the triangles array *_dtmTrias* in batches. Within the while-loop, *ApplyColoursCont* gets each triangle's slope and steps through the array *_rSlopeBands* until it finds a band, or range, that the slope is within. Then it applies that band's number as the triangle's coloured brush number. If no band is found, normally because the triangle's slope is beyond the slope values in *_rSlopeBands*, the triangle's coloured brush number is set to the highest band (SLOPEBANDS_TOTAL). *ApplyColoursCont* returns the TASK_ constants as discussed in Chapter 1.

The function *GetSlopeAtMousePosition* displays the maximum slope and slope direction in the DTM where the user has left-clicked the mouse in the graphics window. For flat triangles with no slope, the maximum slope and slope direction are both zero. The function displays the slope values in the text window, or an error message if the slope values cannot be calculated because the mouse's position is outside the DTM.

## Running Chapter07

Before you can compile and run your program, you need to add the following nineteen source files to your Chapter07 project. Refer to Chapter 1 for how to do this:

| | | |
|---|---|---|
| TextWnd.h | TextWnd.cpp | |
| FileInOut.h | FileInOut.cpp | |
| BigTask.h | BigTask.cpp | |
| Graphics.h | Graphics.cpp | |
| Colours.h | Colours.cpp | |
| Shapes.h | Shapes.cpp | |
| Slopes.cpp | Triangles.cpp | |
| Common.h | Common.cpp | |
| Chapter07.h | Chapter07.cpp | Chapter07.rc |

You also need to add the Gdiplus.lib library file as an 'additional dependency' in your project's linker/input settings. Refer to Chapter 2 for how to do this. Finally, don't forget to set Chapter07 as your start-up project.

Otherwise, assuming you have compiled the code for Chapter07 successfully, and it is running, you can now test it out.

Start by importing your DTM of 3D triangles. Click on 'File' in the menu bar, then select 'Import' from the drop-down menu, and finally click on 'Triangles'. Next, select a file containing the triangles data. You can use the sample file Triangles.txt. To calculate slopes and display slope arrows, click on 'Edit' in the menu bar and select 'Get slopes' from the drop-down menu. If successful, the program's window should look something like this:

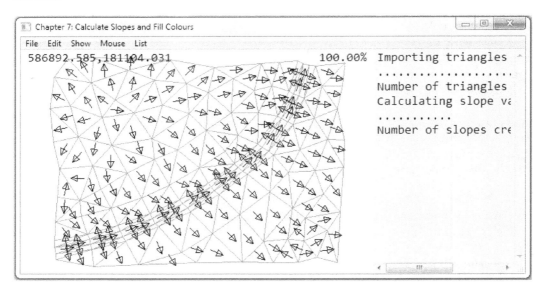

The arrows point downhill. Therefore you can see from the image above that there is a peak near the top left-hand corner of the DTM with arrows pointing downhill towards the bottom right-hand corner. A raised path runs downhill diagonally across the DTM from the bottom left-hand corner to the top right-hand corner. This sample data does not include any flat triangles without a slope (i.e. triangles where each corner has the same z value). Chapter07.cpp displays circles, instead of arrows, in such triangles because these triangles do not have a slope direction (Refer to the function *DTMSLOPES::_DrawItem* in Chapter 3).

Slope values can be exported as a CAD script file or a text file by clicking on 'File' in the menu bar, selecting 'Export' from the drop-down menu and then selecting 'Slopes' before entering a filename in the dialog box that appears.

You can also test obtaining slope values from the DTM via the graphics window. To do this, click on 'Mouse' in the menu bar, and then select 'Slope values' from the drop-down menu. Now, when you left-click the mouse over the graphics window the x,y coordinates at the mouse's position are displayed in the text window along with the maximum slope and slope direction at that location. For flat triangles with no slope (i.e. each corner has the same z value), the maximum slope and slope direction are both displayed as zero. As discussed in Chapter 6, these values cannot be exported directly, but they can be copied to the clipboard, depending on the version of Windows you're running. If you left-click the mouse outside the DTM in the graphics window, a message telling you that the slope value and slope direction cannot be calculated at that location is displayed in the text window.

To list slope values or slope statistics click on 'List' in the menu bar and then either select 'Statistics' then 'Slope' to list maximum and minimum x,y values and slopes for the array of slope arrows, or select 'Slope' to list the values for each slope arrow individually. Values displayed for each slope arrow are the x,y coordinates, the maximum slope, and the slope direction or angle measured in degrees anticlockwise from the positive x axis.

Next, you can test applying fill brush colours to the triangles, based on their slopes. First, click on 'Show' in the menu bar, and then 'Slopes' to untick, or hide, the slope arrows. Now click on 'Edit' in the menu bar, and select 'Colour slopes'. The following dialog box should appear, listing the slope values for each band, or range, of slopes. The fifth edit control is read-only and always contains the same value as the fourth edit control.

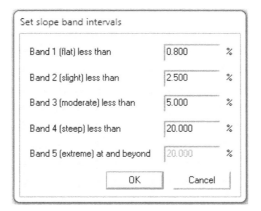

If you accept the default values and click on OK, colours will be applied to your DTM triangles and the program's window should look something like the image over the page.

The image shows one 'flat' (dark blue) triangle near the top left-hand corner. The sides of the raised path are 'extreme' (red) triangles. The rest of the DTM is a mix of 'slight', 'moderate' and mostly 'steep' (yellow) triangles. This tool can be very useful for quickly identifying parts of the DTM where slopes are too flat, for example for drainage purposes if you are designing a car park, or too steep, for example for pedestrians if you're designing ramped access to a building.

The colours displayed can be changed by clicking on 'Show' in the menu bar, then 'Colour' from the drop-down menu, then 'Slope colours' from the next menu and finally one of the five options: 'Flat', 'Slight', 'Moderate', 'Steep' or 'Extreme'.

You might also wish to experiment with different slope values in the custom dialog box, for example changing Band 1 to 1% and Band 4 to 10%. Make sure the slopes are in ascending order, otherwise an error message is displayed when you click on OK.

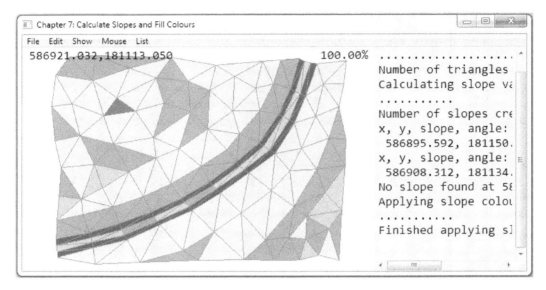

When triangles filled with colour are exported to a CAD script file (via 'File', 'Export', 'Triangles') the colours are applied to the outlines of the triangles because triangles in the CAD script file do not contain any fill. Triangles can also be exported as a text file, in which case the number of the fill colour is the last column of data, or as a JPEG file (via 'File', 'Export', 'Screen image' or 'Model image').

As in previous chapters, to exit the program click on 'File' in the menu bar, select 'Exit' and then choose 'Yes' in the message box that appears.

# Chapter 8

## Calculate Areas and Volumes

Chapter 8 lists the source code for a program called **Chapter08** that calculates the total area, in the x,y plane, and the total volume under a DTM. The user can also obtain area and volume information for individual triangles by left-clicking the mouse in the graphics window over each triangle. The results cannot be exported directly by the program. However, depending on the version of Windows you're running, you may be able to copy the results from the program's text window to the Windows clipboard, as mentioned in Chapters 6 and 7.

The following files are discussed in this chapter:

    **Chapter08.h**             **Chapter08.rc**             **Chapter08.cpp**

## Chapter08 Source Files

The first file is the header file:

**CHAPTER08.H**

```
#ifndef CHAPTER08_H
#define CHAPTER08_H

#define IDM_IMPORTTRIANGLES          101
#define IDM_EXIT                     102

#define IDM_TOTALAREAANDVOLUME       201

#define IDN_SHOWMENU                 2

#define IDM_SHOWTRIANGLES            301
#define IDM_COLOURBACKGROUND         302
#define IDM_COLOURCOORDSTEXT         303
#define IDM_COLOURTRIANGLES          304
#define IDM_ZOOMEXTENTS              305
#define IDM_REDRAW                   306

#define IDN_MOUSEMENU                3

#define IDM_MOUSEZOOM                401
#define IDM_MOUSEPAN                 402
#define IDM_MOUSEAREAANDVOLUME       403

#define IDM_LISTTRIANGLESSTATS       501
#define IDM_LISTTRIANGLES            502

#define IDM_ESCAPEKEY                901

#endif // CHAPTER08_H
```

As in previous chapters, **Chapter08.h** contains ID numbers for menu bar options, drop-down menus and accelerator keys.

The second file is the resource script file:

**CHAPTER08.RC**

```
#include <windows.h>
#include "Chapter08.h"

Chapter08 MENU {
    POPUP "&File" {
        POPUP "&Import" {
            MENUITEM "&Triangles",          IDM_IMPORTTRIANGLES
        }
        MENUITEM SEPARATOR
        MENUITEM "E&xit",                   IDM_EXIT
    }
    POPUP "&Edit" {
        MENUITEM "&Total area and volume",  IDM_TOTALAREAANDVOLUME
    }
    POPUP "&Show" {
        MENUITEM "&Triangles",              IDM_SHOWTRIANGLES
        MENUITEM SEPARATOR
        POPUP "&Colour" {
            MENUITEM "Back&ground",         IDM_COLOURBACKGROUND
            MENUITEM "&Coords text",        IDM_COLOURCOORDSTEXT
            MENUITEM SEPARATOR
            MENUITEM "&Triangles",          IDM_COLOURTRIANGLES
        }
        MENUITEM SEPARATOR
        MENUITEM "&Zoom extents",           IDM_ZOOMEXTENTS
        MENUITEM "&Redraw",                 IDM_REDRAW
    }
    POPUP "&Mouse" {
        MENUITEM "&Zoom in/out",            IDM_MOUSEZOOM
        MENUITEM "&Pan",                    IDM_MOUSEPAN
        MENUITEM SEPARATOR
        MENUITEM "&Area and volume",        IDM_MOUSEAREAANDVOLUME
    }
    POPUP "&List" {
        POPUP "&Statistics" {
            MENUITEM "&Triangles",          IDM_LISTTRIANGLESSTATS
        }
        MENUITEM SEPARATOR
        MENUITEM "&Triangles",              IDM_LISTTRIANGLES
    }
}

Chapter08 ACCELERATORS {
    VK_ESCAPE,      IDM_ESCAPEKEY,      VIRTKEY, NOINVERT
}
```

Like previous chapters, **Chapter08.rc** defines the contents of the program's menu bar and accelerator keys (or key). There is no custom dialog box in this program.

The third file is the source code file, which includes function listings.

## CHAPTER08.CPP

```cpp
#ifndef UNICODE
#define UNICODE
#endif

#include <windows.h>
#include <gdiplus.h>
using namespace Gdiplus;
#include "Chapter08.h"
#include "BigTask.h"
#include "FileInOut.h"
#include "TextWnd.h"
#include "Graphics.h"
#include "Colours.h"
#include "Shapes.h"
#include "Common.h"

#define ID_TEXTWND                  1
#define ID_DISPLAYWND               2

#define IDT_IMPORTTRIANGLES         11

#define IDT_TOTALAREAANDVOLUME      21

#define IDT_LISTTRIANGLES           31

#define TOTALAREAANDVOL_STEPSIZE    20L

#define PENCOLOUR_TRIANGLES         11

DTMTEXTWINDOW _dtmText;
DTMFILEDATA _dtmFile;
DTMBIGTASK _dtmTask, _dtmTaskDisplay;
DTMDISPLAY _dtmDisplay;
DTMCOLOURS _dtmColours;
DTMTRIAS _dtmTrias;

LRESULT CALLBACK WndProc (HWND, UINT, WPARAM, LPARAM);
BOOL CarryOutTasks (HWND);
WORD DrawModel (DTMFRAME *, DTMBIGTASK *);
void InitShowDropdownMenu (HMENU);
void InitMouseDropdownMenu (HMENU);
BOOL TotalAreasAndVolumesStart (UINT);
WORD TotalAreasAndVolumesCont (void);
void AreaAndVolumeAtMouse (void);

int WINAPI WinMain (HINSTANCE hInst, HINSTANCE, PSTR, int nCmdShow) {
    return InitAndRunProgram (hInst, nCmdShow, TEXT ("Chapter08"),
        TEXT ("Chapter 8: Calculate Areas and Volumes"));
}

LRESULT CALLBACK WndProc (HWND hwnd, UINT message, WPARAM wParam, LPARAM lParam) {
    switch (message) {
        case WM_CREATE : {
            HINSTANCE hInst;

            hInst = ((LPCREATESTRUCT) lParam)->hInstance;
            _dtmText.Create (hwnd, ID_TEXTWND, hInst);
            _dtmFile.Init (hwnd);
            _dtmDisplay.Init (hwnd, 0, ID_DISPLAYWND, hInst,
                1.0, 4.0, 4.0, 4.0, 5.0, 1.0, 2.0, 0.5);
```

```
            _dtmColours.Init ();
            _dtmTrias.Init (TEXT ("triangles"), PENCOLOUR_TRIANGLES, 0, FALSE);
            return 0;
    }
    case WM_ENTERSIZEMOVE :
        _dtmDisplay.StartResizing ();
        return 0;
    case WM_SIZE :
        ResizeChildWindows (lParam);
        return 0;
    case WM_EXITSIZEMOVE :
        _dtmDisplay.StopResizing ();
        return 0;
    case WM_INITMENUPOPUP :
        if (HIWORD (lParam) == FALSE) {
            switch (LOWORD (lParam)) {
            case IDN_SHOWMENU :
                InitShowDropdownMenu ((HMENU) wParam);
                return 0;
            case IDN_MOUSEMENU :
                InitMouseDropdownMenu ((HMENU) wParam);
                return 0;
            default : break;
            }
        }
        break;
    case WM_COMMAND :
        if (HIWORD (wParam) == 0) {
            switch (LOWORD (wParam)) {
                case IDM_IMPORTTRIANGLES :
                    _dtmTrias.ImportStart (hwnd, IDT_IMPORTTRIANGLES);
                    return 0;
                case IDM_EXIT :
                    SendMessage (hwnd, WM_CLOSE, 0, 0);
                    return 0;
                case IDM_TOTALAREAANDVOLUME :
                    TotalAreasAndVolumesStart (IDT_TOTALAREAANDVOLUME);
                    return 0;
                case IDM_SHOWTRIANGLES :
                    _dtmTrias.FlipVisible ();
                    _dtmTaskDisplay.Start ();
                    return 0;
                case IDM_COLOURBACKGROUND :
                    ChangeBackgroundColour (hwnd);
                    return 0;
                case IDM_COLOURCOORDSTEXT :
                    ChangeCoordsTextColour (hwnd);
                    return 0;
                case IDM_COLOURTRIANGLES :
                    ChangePenColour (hwnd, PENCOLOUR_TRIANGLES);
                    return 0;
                case IDM_ZOOMEXTENTS :
                    _dtmDisplay.ZoomExtents ();
                    _dtmTaskDisplay.Start ();
                    return 0;
                case IDM_REDRAW :
                    _dtmTaskDisplay.Start ();
                    return 0;
                case IDM_MOUSEZOOM :
                    _dtmDisplay.SetMouseAction (MOUSEACT_ZOOM);
                    return 0;
```

```
                        case IDM_MOUSEPAN :
                            _dtmDisplay.SetMouseAction (MOUSEACT_PAN);
                            return 0;
                        case IDM_MOUSEAREAANDVOLUME :
                            _dtmDisplay.SetMouseAction (MOUSEACT_POINT);
                            return 0;
                        case IDM_LISTTRIANGLESSTATS :
                            _dtmTrias.ListStats ();
                            return 0;
                        case IDM_LISTTRIANGLES :
                            _dtmTrias.ListStart (IDT_LISTTRIANGLES);
                            return 0;
                        default : break;
                    }
                }
                else if (HIWORD (wParam) == 1) {
                    if (LOWORD (wParam) == IDM_ESCAPEKEY) {
                        _dtmTask.Quit (TRUE);
                        _dtmTaskDisplay.Quit (TRUE);
                        return 0;
                    }
                }
                else if (LOWORD (wParam) == ID_DISPLAYWND) {
                    switch (HIWORD (wParam)) {
                        case DTM_REDRAW :
                            _dtmTaskDisplay.Start ();
                            return 0;
                        case DTM_DRAW_STOPPED :
                        case DTM_DRAW_COMPLETED :
                            _dtmDisplay.RepaintNow (REPAINT_ALL);
                            return 0;
                        case DTM_SELPOINT :
                            AreaAndVolumeAtMouse ();
                            return 0;
                        default : return 0;
                    }
                }
                break;
            case WM_CLOSE :
                AskCloseWindowMessage (hwnd);
                return 0;
            case WM_DESTROY:
                _dtmDisplay.Free ();
                _dtmColours.Free ();
                _dtmText.Destroy ();
                _dtmFile.FreeImportBuffer ();
                _dtmTrias.Free ();
                PostQuitMessage (0);
                return 0;
            default : break;
        }
        return DefWindowProc (hwnd, message, wParam, lParam);
}

BOOL CarryOutTasks (HWND hwnd) {
    WORD wTaskStatus;

    if (!_dtmTask.IsBusy ()) {
        return FALSE;
    }
    if (_dtmTask.GetStage () == 0) {
```

```
            EnableMenuBar (hwnd, FALSE);
            _dtmDisplay.Enable (FALSE);
            _dtmTask.NextStage ();
        }
    switch (_dtmTask.GetID ()) {
        case IDT_IMPORTTRIANGLES :
            wTaskStatus = _dtmTrias.ImportCont (FALSE);
            break;
        case IDT_TOTALAREAANDVOLUME :
            wTaskStatus = TotalAreasAndVolumesCont ();
            break;
        case IDT_LISTTRIANGLES :
            wTaskStatus = _dtmTrias.ListCont ();
            break;
        default :
            wTaskStatus = TASK_STOPPED;
            break;
    }
    if ((wTaskStatus & TASK_STOPPED) || (wTaskStatus & TASK_COMPLETED)) {
        EnableMenuBar (hwnd, TRUE);
        _dtmDisplay.Enable (TRUE);
        _dtmTask.Stop ();
    }
    if (wTaskStatus & TASK_COMPLETED) {
        switch (_dtmTask.GetID ()) {
            case IDT_IMPORTTRIANGLES :
                AddShapeToDisplay (&_dtmTrias);
                break;
            default : break;
        }
    }
    if (wTaskStatus & TASK_REDRAW) {
        _dtmTaskDisplay.Start ();
    }
    return TRUE;
}

WORD DrawModel (DTMFRAME * pdtmFrame, DTMBIGTASK * pdtmTask) {
    if (pdtmFrame == NULL || !pdtmFrame->IsActive () ||
        !pdtmFrame->IsGdiOK () || pdtmTask == NULL) {
        return TASK_STOPPED;
    }
    if (pdtmTask->Quit ()) {
        pdtmFrame->NotifyParent (DTM_DRAW_STOPPED);
        return TASK_STOPPED;
    }
    switch (pdtmTask->GetStage ()) {
        case 1 :
            pdtmFrame->ClearBackground ();
            _dtmColours.SetPenWidths (pdtmFrame->GetPenWidth (),
                pdtmFrame->GetVertExag ());
            pdtmTask->NextStage ();
            break;
        case 2 :
            _dtmTrias.Draw (pdtmFrame, pdtmTask);
            break;
        default : break;
    }
    pdtmFrame->NotifyParent (DTM_DRAW_UPDATED);
    if (pdtmTask->GetStage () < 3) {
        return TASK_ONGOING;
```

```
        }
        pdtmFrame->NotifyParent (DTM_DRAW_COMPLETED);
        return TASK_COMPLETED;
}

void InitShowDropdownMenu (HMENU hMenu) {
        CheckMenuItem (hMenu, IDM_SHOWTRIANGLES, MF_BYCOMMAND |
                (_dtmTrias.IsVisible () ? MF_CHECKED : MF_UNCHECKED));
}

void InitMouseDropdownMenu (HMENU hMenu) {
        DTMMOUSEACT mouseAction;

        mouseAction = _dtmDisplay.GetMouseAction ();
        CheckMenuItem (hMenu, IDM_MOUSEZOOM, MF_BYCOMMAND |
                (mouseAction == MOUSEACT_ZOOM ? MF_CHECKED : MF_UNCHECKED));
        CheckMenuItem (hMenu, IDM_MOUSEPAN, MF_BYCOMMAND |
                (mouseAction == MOUSEACT_PAN ? MF_CHECKED : MF_UNCHECKED));
        CheckMenuItem (hMenu, IDM_MOUSEAREAANDVOLUME, MF_BYCOMMAND |
                (mouseAction == MOUSEACT_POINT ? MF_CHECKED : MF_UNCHECKED));
}

BOOL TotalAreasAndVolumesStart (UINT uTaskID) {
        if (_dtmTask.IsBusy ()) {
                _dtmText.Output (_szTaskBusyMessage);
                return FALSE;
        }
        if (_dtmTrias.GetTotal () == 0L) {
                _dtmText.Output (TEXT ("There are no %s available. Unable to ") \
                        TEXT ("calculate total area and volume\r\n"),
                        _dtmTrias.GetDescription ());
                return FALSE;
        }
        _dtmText.Output (TEXT ("Calculating total area and volume\r\n"));
        _dtmTask.Start (uTaskID, TOTALAREAANDVOL_STEPSIZE);
        return TRUE;
}

WORD TotalAreasAndVolumesCont (void) {
        static DOUBLE rTotalArea, rTotalVolume;

        if (_dtmTask.AtStart ()) {
                rTotalArea = 0.0;
                rTotalVolume = 0.0;
        }
        if (_dtmTask.Quit ()) {
                _dtmText.Output (TEXT ("\r\nCalculating area and volume stopped\r\n"));
                return TASK_STOPPED;
        }
        _dtmTask.StartNewBatch ();
        while (!_dtmTask.NoMoreItems (_dtmTrias.GetTotal ()) && !_dtmTask.AtEndOfBatch ()) {
                DWORD dwTria;
                DOUBLE rArea, rVolume;

                dwTria = _dtmTask.GetItemNumber ();
                _dtmTrias.GetArea (dwTria, &rArea);
                _dtmTrias.GetVolume (dwTria, &rVolume);
                rTotalArea += rArea;
                rTotalVolume += rVolume;
                _dtmTask.NextItem ();
                _dtmTask.IncBatchCounter ();
```

```
    }
    _dtmText.ProgressDot ();
    if (!_dtmTask.NoMoreItems (_dtmTrias.GetTotal ())) {
        return TASK_ONGOING;
    }
    _dtmText.Output (TEXT ("\r\nTotal area is %.3f\r\n"), rTotalArea);
    _dtmText.Output (TEXT ("Total volume is %.3f\r\n"), rTotalVolume);
    return TASK_COMPLETED;
}

void AreaAndVolumeAtMouse (void) {
    DTMCOORD dtmMouse;
    DWORD dwTria;

    dtmMouse.rX = _dtmDisplay.GetSelFromX ();
    dtmMouse.rY = _dtmDisplay.GetSelFromY ();
    dwTria = _dtmTrias.FromCoords (&dtmMouse);
    if (dwTria < _dtmTrias.GetTotal ()) {
        DOUBLE rArea, rVolume;

        _dtmTrias.GetArea (dwTria, &rArea);
        _dtmTrias.GetVolume (dwTria, &rVolume);
        _dtmText.Output (TEXT ("Triangle at x, y: area, volume:\r\n") \
            TEXT (" %.3f, %.3f: %.3f, %.3f\r\n"),
            dtmMouse.rX, dtmMouse.rY, rArea, rVolume);
    }
    else {
        _dtmText.Output (TEXT ("No triangle found at %.3f, %.3f\r\n"),
            dtmMouse.rX, dtmMouse.rY);
    }
}
```

**Chapter08.cpp** has the same layout as source code files in earlier chapters in this book. It starts with the header files followed by child window IDs, task IDs, the task batch size constant TOTALAREAANDVOL_STEPSIZE which is used when calculating the DTM's total area and volume, and a coloured pen number.

It then defines seven global variables, most of which are the same as in earlier chapters. This program contains just one shapes array: *_dtmTrias* which is a triangles array.

Eight functions are then declared, followed by the C++ source code.

The functions *WinMain*, *WndProc*, *CarryOutTasks*, *DrawModel*, *InitShowDropdownMenu* and *InitMouseDropdownMenu* are similar to the equivalent functions in earlier chapters. The user can import triangles and calculate areas and volumes based on those triangles. The user can also set the mouse (IDM_MOUSEAREAANDVOLUME) to calculate areas and volumes on the fly, as well as standard zoom and pan options.

The function *TotalAreasAndVolumesStart* starts the task of calculating the total area, in the x,y plane, of the DTM and the total volume under the DTM. *uTaskID* is the task ID number. If there are no triangles in the triangles array *_dtmTrias*, the function displays an error message. Otherwise, *TotalAreasAndVolumesStart* displays a task-starting message in the text window and starts the task. The function returns TRUE if successful, or FALSE if an error occurs.

The function *TotalAreasAndVolumesCont* carries out the task of calculating the total area, in the x,y plane, of the DTM and the total volume under the DTM. *TotalAreasAndVolumesCont* follows the standard task manager template as discussed in Chapter 1, looking at each triangle in the triangles array *_dtmTrias* in batches. If at the start of the task, two static variables *_rTotalArea* and *_rTotalVolume* are set to zero. Within the while-loop, the area and volume of each triangle are added to *_rTotalArea* and *_rTotalVolume*. Note that if the DTM straddles the x,y plane at z equals zero, the total volume will not be a meaningful result, unless the DTM is a cut-and-fill DTM (refer to Chapter 13). The function returns the TASK_ constants as discussed in Chapter 1.

The function *AreaAndVolumeAtMouse* displays the area, in the x,y plane, and the volume under the triangle where the user has left-clicked the mouse in the graphics window. The function displays the values in the text window, or an error message if the area and volume cannot be calculated because the mouse's position is not inside a triangle in the DTM.

## Running Chapter08

Before you can compile and run your program, you need to add the following eighteen source files to your Chapter08 project. Refer to Chapter 1 for how to do this:

| | | |
|---|---|---|
| TextWnd.h | TextWnd.cpp | |
| FileInOut.h | FileInOut.cpp | |
| BigTask.h | BigTask.cpp | |
| Graphics.h | Graphics.cpp | |
| Colours.h | Colours.cpp | |
| Shapes.h | Shapes.cpp | Triangles.cpp |
| Common.h | Common.cpp | |
| Chapter08.h | Chapter08.cpp | Chapter08.rc |

You also need to add the Gdiplus.lib library file as an 'additional dependency' in your project's linker/input settings. Refer to Chapter 2 for how to do this. Finally, don't forget to set Chapter08 as your start-up project.

Otherwise, assuming you have compiled the code for Chapter08 successfully, and it is running, you can now test it out.

Start by importing your DTM of 3D triangles. Click on 'File' in the menu bar, then select 'Import' from the drop-down menu, and finally click on 'Triangles'. Next, select a file containing the triangles data. You can use the sample file Triangles.txt. Dark green triangles should appear in the graphics window. Then click on 'Edit' in the menu bar, and select 'Total area and volume' from the drop-down menu. After a moment, the program should display the following results in the text window:

```
Total area is 6759.443
Total volume is 41929.471
```

Next, test obtaining areas and volumes for individual triangles via the graphics window. Click on 'Mouse' in the menu bar, and then select 'Area and volume' from the drop-down menu. Now, when you left-click the mouse over the graphics window the area and volume of the triangle at the mouse's x,y position are displayed in the text window. If you left-click the mouse outside the DTM, a message telling you that the area and volume cannot be calculated at that location is displayed in the text window.

As in previous chapters, to exit the program click on 'File' in the menu bar, select 'Exit' and then choose 'Yes' in the message box that appears.

# Chapter 9

## Find High, Flat and Low Points

Chapter 9 lists the source code for a program called **Chapter09** that finds high points (or peaks), 'flat' points (which are the corners of 'flat' triangles where the z value at each corner is the same), and low points within a DTM. The user can export the three groups of points as CAD script files, as text files or as JPEG files.

The following files are discussed in this chapter:

**Chapter09.h**             **Chapter09.rc**             **Chapter09.cpp**

## Chapter09 Source Files

The first file is the header file:

**CHAPTER09.H**

```
#ifndef CHAPTER09_H
#define CHAPTER09_H

#define IDM_IMPORTTRIANGLES        101
#define IDM_EXPORTHIGHPOINTS       102
#define IDM_EXPORTFLATPOINTS       103
#define IDM_EXPORTLOWPOINTS        104
#define IDM_EXPORTSCREEN           105
#define IDM_EXPORTMODEL            106
#define IDM_EXIT                   107

#define IDM_FINDPOINTS             201

#define IDN_SHOWMENU               2

#define IDM_SHOWHIGHPOINTS         301
#define IDM_SHOWFLATPOINTS         302
#define IDM_SHOWLOWPOINTS          303
#define IDM_SHOWTRIANGLES          304
#define IDM_COLOURBACKGROUND       305
#define IDM_COLOURCOORDSTEXT       306
#define IDM_COLOURHIGHPOINTS       307
#define IDM_COLOURFLATPOINTS       308
#define IDM_COLOURLOWPOINTS        309
#define IDM_COLOURTRIANGLES        310
#define IDM_ZOOMEXTENTS            311
#define IDM_REDRAW                 312

#define IDN_MOUSEMENU              3

#define IDM_MOUSEZOOM              401
#define IDM_MOUSEPAN               402

#define IDM_LISTHIGHPOINTSSTATS    501
#define IDM_LISTFLATPOINTSSTATS    502
#define IDM_LISTLOWPOINTSSTATS     503
```

```
#define IDM_LISTTRIANGLESSTATS      504
#define IDM_LISTHIGHPOINTS          505
#define IDM_LISTFLATPOINTS          506
#define IDM_LISTLOWPOINTS           507
#define IDM_LISTTRIANGLES           508

#define IDM_ESCAPEKEY               901

#endif // CHAPTER09_H
```

As in previous chapters, **Chapter09.h** contains ID numbers for menu bar options, drop-down menus and accelerator keys.

The second file is the resource script file:

**CHAPTER09.RC**

```
#include <windows.h>
#include "Chapter09.h"

Chapter09 MENU {
    POPUP "&File" {
        POPUP "&Import" {
            MENUITEM "&Triangles",          IDM_IMPORTTRIANGLES
        }
        POPUP "&Export" {
            MENUITEM "&High points",        IDM_EXPORTHIGHPOINTS
            MENUITEM "&Flat points",        IDM_EXPORTFLATPOINTS
            MENUITEM "&Low points",         IDM_EXPORTLOWPOINTS
            MENUITEM SEPARATOR
            MENUITEM "S&creen image",       IDM_EXPORTSCREEN
            MENUITEM "&Model image",        IDM_EXPORTMODEL
        }
        MENUITEM SEPARATOR
        MENUITEM "E&xit",                   IDM_EXIT
    }
    POPUP "&Edit" {
        MENUITEM "&Find points",            IDM_FINDPOINTS
    }
    POPUP "&Show" {
        MENUITEM "&High points",            IDM_SHOWHIGHPOINTS
        MENUITEM "&Flat points",            IDM_SHOWFLATPOINTS
        MENUITEM "&Low points",             IDM_SHOWLOWPOINTS
        MENUITEM "&Triangles",              IDM_SHOWTRIANGLES
        MENUITEM SEPARATOR
        POPUP "&Colour" {
            MENUITEM "Back&ground",         IDM_COLOURBACKGROUND
            MENUITEM "&Coords text",        IDM_COLOURCOORDSTEXT
            MENUITEM SEPARATOR
            MENUITEM "&High points",        IDM_COLOURHIGHPOINTS
            MENUITEM "&Flat points",        IDM_COLOURFLATPOINTS
            MENUITEM "&Low points",         IDM_COLOURLOWPOINTS
            MENUITEM "&Triangles",          IDM_COLOURTRIANGLES
        }
        MENUITEM SEPARATOR
        MENUITEM "&Zoom extents",           IDM_ZOOMEXTENTS
        MENUITEM "&Redraw",                 IDM_REDRAW
    }
    POPUP "&Mouse" {
        MENUITEM "&Zoom in/out",            IDM_MOUSEZOOM
```

```
            MENUITEM "&Pan",                    IDM_MOUSEPAN
        }
    POPUP "&List" {
        POPUP "&Statistics" {
            MENUITEM "&High points",          IDM_LISTHIGHPOINTSSTATS
            MENUITEM "&Flat points",          IDM_LISTFLATPOINTSSTATS
            MENUITEM "&Low points",           IDM_LISTLOWPOINTSSTATS
            MENUITEM "&Triangles",            IDM_LISTTRIANGLESSTATS
        }
        MENUITEM SEPARATOR
        MENUITEM "&High points",              IDM_LISTHIGHPOINTS
        MENUITEM "&Flat points",              IDM_LISTFLATPOINTS
        MENUITEM "&Low points",               IDM_LISTLOWPOINTS
        MENUITEM "&Triangles",                IDM_LISTTRIANGLES
    }
}

Chapter09 ACCELERATORS {
    VK_ESCAPE,        IDM_ESCAPEKEY,        VIRTKEY, NOINVERT
}
```

Like previous chapters, **Chapter09.rc** defines the contents of the program's menu bar and accelerator keys (or key). There is no custom dialog box in this program.

The third file is the source code file, which includes function listings.

## CHAPTER09.CPP

```cpp
#ifndef UNICODE
#define UNICODE
#endif

#include <windows.h>
#include <gdiplus.h>
using namespace Gdiplus;
#include "Chapter09.h"
#include "BigTask.h"
#include "FileInOut.h"
#include "TextWnd.h"
#include "Graphics.h"
#include "Colours.h"
#include "Shapes.h"
#include "Common.h"

#define ID_TEXTWND                      1
#define ID_DISPLAYWND                   2
#define ID_IMAGEEXPORT                  3

#define IDT_IMPORTTRIANGLES             11

#define IDT_EXPORTHIGHPOINTS            21
#define IDT_EXPORTHIGHPOINTSSCRIPT      22
#define IDT_EXPORTFLATPOINTS            23
#define IDT_EXPORTFLATPOINTSSCRIPT      24
#define IDT_EXPORTLOWPOINTS             25
#define IDT_EXPORTLOWPOINTSSCRIPT       26
#define IDT_EXPORTIMAGE                 27

#define IDT_FINDPOINTS                  31
```

```
#define IDT_LISTHIGHPOINTS              41
#define IDT_LISTFLATPOINTS              42
#define IDT_LISTLOWPOINTS               43
#define IDT_LISTTRIANGLES               44

#define FINDPOINTS_STEPSIZE             20L

#define PENCOLOUR_HIGHPOINTS            0
#define PENCOLOUR_FLATPOINTS            3
#define PENCOLOUR_LOWPOINTS             4
#define PENCOLOUR_TRIANGLES             11

DTMTEXTWINDOW _dtmText;
DTMFILEDATA _dtmFile;
DTMBIGTASK _dtmTask, _dtmTaskDisplay;
DTMDISPLAY _dtmDisplay;
DTMCOLOURS _dtmColours;
DTMPOINTS _dtmHighPoints, _dtmFlatPoints, _dtmLowPoints;
DTMTRIAS _dtmTrias;

LRESULT CALLBACK WndProc (HWND, UINT, WPARAM, LPARAM);
BOOL CarryOutTasks (HWND);
WORD DrawModel (DTMFRAME *, DTMBIGTASK *);
void InitShowDropdownMenu (HMENU);
void InitMouseDropdownMenu (HMENU);
BOOL FindPointsStart (HWND, UINT);
WORD FindPointsCont (void);

int WINAPI WinMain (HINSTANCE hInst, HINSTANCE, PSTR, int nCmdShow) {
    return InitAndRunProgram (hInst, nCmdShow, TEXT ("Chapter09"),
        TEXT ("Chapter 9: Find High, Flat and Low Points"));
}

LRESULT CALLBACK WndProc (HWND hwnd, UINT message, WPARAM wParam, LPARAM lParam) {
    switch (message) {
        case WM_CREATE : {
            HINSTANCE hInst;

            hInst = ((LPCREATESTRUCT) lParam)->hInstance;
            _dtmText.Create (hwnd, ID_TEXTWND, hInst);
            _dtmFile.Init (hwnd);
            _dtmDisplay.Init (hwnd, 0, ID_DISPLAYWND, hInst,
                1.0, 4.0, 4.0, 4.0, 5.0, 1.0, 2.0, 0.5);
            _dtmColours.Init ();
            _dtmHighPoints.Init (TEXT ("high points"), PENCOLOUR_HIGHPOINTS,
                POINTSTYLE_PLUS);
            _dtmFlatPoints.Init (TEXT ("flat points"), PENCOLOUR_FLATPOINTS,
                POINTSTYLE_CIRCLE);
            _dtmLowPoints.Init (TEXT ("low points"), PENCOLOUR_LOWPOINTS,
                POINTSTYLE_CROSS);
            _dtmTrias.Init (TEXT ("triangles"), PENCOLOUR_TRIANGLES, 0, FALSE);
            return 0;
        }
        case WM_ENTERSIZEMOVE :
            _dtmDisplay.StartResizing ();
            return 0;
        case WM_SIZE :
            ResizeChildWindows (lParam);
            return 0;
        case WM_EXITSIZEMOVE :
            _dtmDisplay.StopResizing ();
```

```
        return 0;
    case WM_INITMENUPOPUP :
        if (HIWORD (lParam) == FALSE) {
            switch (LOWORD (lParam)) {
            case IDN_SHOWMENU :
                InitShowDropdownMenu ((HMENU) wParam);
                return 0;
            case IDN_MOUSEMENU :
                InitMouseDropdownMenu ((HMENU) wParam);
                return 0;
            default : break;
            }
        }
        break;
    case WM_COMMAND :
        if (HIWORD (wParam) == 0) {
            switch (LOWORD (wParam)) {
                case IDM_IMPORTTRIANGLES :
                    _dtmTrias.ImportStart (hwnd, IDT_IMPORTTRIANGLES);
                    return 0;
                case IDM_EXPORTHIGHPOINTS :
                    _dtmHighPoints.ExportStart (IDT_EXPORTHIGHPOINTS,
                        IDT_EXPORTHIGHPOINTSSCRIPT);
                    return 0;
                case IDM_EXPORTFLATPOINTS :
                    _dtmFlatPoints.ExportStart (IDT_EXPORTFLATPOINTS,
                        IDT_EXPORTFLATPOINTSSCRIPT);
                    return 0;
                case IDM_EXPORTLOWPOINTS :
                    _dtmLowPoints.ExportStart (IDT_EXPORTLOWPOINTS,
                        IDT_EXPORTLOWPOINTSSCRIPT);
                    return 0;
                case IDM_EXPORTSCREEN :
                    ExportImage (FALSE, ID_IMAGEEXPORT);
                    return 0;
                case IDM_EXPORTMODEL :
                    ExportImage (TRUE, ID_IMAGEEXPORT);
                    return 0;
                case IDM_EXIT :
                    SendMessage (hwnd, WM_CLOSE, 0, 0);
                    return 0;
                case IDM_FINDPOINTS :
                    FindPointsStart (hwnd, IDT_FINDPOINTS);
                    return 0;
                case IDM_SHOWHIGHPOINTS :
                    _dtmHighPoints.FlipVisible ();
                    _dtmTaskDisplay.Start ();
                    return 0;
                case IDM_SHOWFLATPOINTS :
                    _dtmFlatPoints.FlipVisible ();
                    _dtmTaskDisplay.Start ();
                    return 0;
                case IDM_SHOWLOWPOINTS :
                    _dtmLowPoints.FlipVisible ();
                    _dtmTaskDisplay.Start ();
                    return 0;
                case IDM_SHOWTRIANGLES :
                    _dtmTrias.FlipVisible ();
                    _dtmTaskDisplay.Start ();
                    return 0;
                case IDM_COLOURBACKGROUND :
```

```
                ChangeBackgroundColour (hwnd);
                return 0;
            case IDM_COLOURCOORDSTEXT :
                ChangeCoordsTextColour (hwnd);
                return 0;
            case IDM_COLOURTRIANGLES :
                ChangePenColour (hwnd, PENCOLOUR_TRIANGLES);
                return 0;
            case IDM_COLOURHIGHPOINTS :
                ChangePenColour (hwnd, PENCOLOUR_HIGHPOINTS);
                return 0;
            case IDM_COLOURFLATPOINTS :
                ChangePenColour (hwnd, PENCOLOUR_FLATPOINTS);
                return 0;
            case IDM_COLOURLOWPOINTS :
                ChangePenColour (hwnd, PENCOLOUR_LOWPOINTS);
                return 0;
            case IDM_ZOOMEXTENTS :
                _dtmDisplay.ZoomExtents ();
                _dtmTaskDisplay.Start ();
                return 0;
            case IDM_REDRAW :
                _dtmTaskDisplay.Start ();
                return 0;
            case IDM_MOUSEZOOM :
                _dtmDisplay.SetMouseAction (MOUSEACT_ZOOM);
                return 0;
            case IDM_MOUSEPAN :
                _dtmDisplay.SetMouseAction (MOUSEACT_PAN);
                return 0;
            case IDM_LISTHIGHPOINTSSTATS :
                _dtmHighPoints.ListStats ();
                return 0;
            case IDM_LISTFLATPOINTSSTATS :
                _dtmFlatPoints.ListStats ();
                return 0;
            case IDM_LISTLOWPOINTSSTATS :
                _dtmLowPoints.ListStats ();
                return 0;
            case IDM_LISTTRIANGLESSTATS :
                _dtmTrias.ListStats ();
                return 0;
            case IDM_LISTHIGHPOINTS :
                _dtmHighPoints.ListStart (IDT_LISTHIGHPOINTS);
                return 0;
            case IDM_LISTFLATPOINTS :
                _dtmFlatPoints.ListStart (IDT_LISTFLATPOINTS);
                return 0;
            case IDM_LISTLOWPOINTS :
                _dtmLowPoints.ListStart (IDT_LISTLOWPOINTS);
                return 0;
            case IDM_LISTTRIANGLES :
                _dtmTrias.ListStart (IDT_LISTTRIANGLES);
                return 0;
            default : break;
        }
    }
}
else if (HIWORD (wParam) == 1) {
    if (LOWORD (wParam) == IDM_ESCAPEKEY) {
        _dtmTask.Quit (TRUE);
        _dtmTaskDisplay.Quit (TRUE);
```

```
                                    return 0;
                            }
                    }
                else if (LOWORD (wParam) == ID_DISPLAYWND) {
                    switch (HIWORD (wParam)) {
                        case DTM_REDRAW :
                            _dtmTaskDisplay.Start ();
                            return 0;
                        case DTM_DRAW_STOPPED :
                        case DTM_DRAW_COMPLETED :
                            _dtmDisplay.RepaintNow (REPAINT_ALL);
                            return 0;
                        default : return 0;
                    }
                }
                else if (LOWORD (wParam) == ID_IMAGEEXPORT) {
                    ProcessExportImageMessages (wParam, IDT_EXPORTIMAGE);
                    return 0;
                }
                break;
            case WM_CLOSE :
                AskCloseWindowMessage (hwnd);
                return 0;
            case WM_DESTROY:
                _dtmDisplay.Free ();
                _dtmColours.Free ();
                _dtmText.Destroy ();
                _dtmFile.FreeImportBuffer ();
                _dtmHighPoints.Free ();
                _dtmFlatPoints.Free ();
                _dtmLowPoints.Free ();
                _dtmTrias.Free ();
                PostQuitMessage (0);
                return 0;
            default : break;
    }
    return DefWindowProc (hwnd, message, wParam, lParam);
}

BOOL CarryOutTasks (HWND hwnd) {
    WORD wTaskStatus;

    if (!_dtmTask.IsBusy ()) {
        return FALSE;
    }
    if (_dtmTask.GetStage () == 0) {
        EnableMenuBar (hwnd, FALSE);
        _dtmDisplay.Enable (FALSE);
        _dtmTask.NextStage ();
    }
    switch (_dtmTask.GetID ()) {
        case IDT_IMPORTTRIANGLES :
            wTaskStatus = _dtmTrias.ImportCont (FALSE);
            break;
        case IDT_EXPORTHIGHPOINTS :
            wTaskStatus = _dtmHighPoints.ExportCont (FALSE);
            break;
        case IDT_EXPORTHIGHPOINTSSCRIPT :
            wTaskStatus = _dtmHighPoints.ExportCont (TRUE);
            break;
        case IDT_EXPORTFLATPOINTS :
```

```
                    wTaskStatus = _dtmFlatPoints.ExportCont (FALSE);
                    break;
                case IDT_EXPORTFLATPOINTSSCRIPT :
                    wTaskStatus = _dtmFlatPoints.ExportCont (TRUE);
                    break;
                case IDT_EXPORTLOWPOINTS :
                    wTaskStatus = _dtmLowPoints.ExportCont (FALSE);
                    break;
                case IDT_EXPORTLOWPOINTSSCRIPT :
                    wTaskStatus = _dtmLowPoints.ExportCont (TRUE);
                    break;
                case IDT_EXPORTIMAGE :
                    wTaskStatus = DrawModel (_dtmDisplay.GetImageDtmPtr (), &_dtmTask);
                    break;
                case IDT_FINDPOINTS :
                    wTaskStatus = FindPointsCont ();
                    break;
                case IDT_LISTHIGHPOINTS :
                    wTaskStatus = _dtmHighPoints.ListCont ();
                    break;
                case IDT_LISTFLATPOINTS :
                    wTaskStatus = _dtmFlatPoints.ListCont ();
                    break;
                case IDT_LISTLOWPOINTS :
                    wTaskStatus = _dtmLowPoints.ListCont ();
                    break;
                case IDT_LISTTRIANGLES :
                    wTaskStatus = _dtmTrias.ListCont ();
                    break;
                default :
                    wTaskStatus = TASK_STOPPED;
                    break;
        }
        if ((wTaskStatus & TASK_STOPPED) || (wTaskStatus & TASK_COMPLETED)) {
            EnableMenuBar (hwnd, TRUE);
            _dtmDisplay.Enable (TRUE);
            _dtmTask.Stop ();
        }
        if (wTaskStatus & TASK_COMPLETED) {
            switch (_dtmTask.GetID ()) {
                case IDT_IMPORTTRIANGLES :
                    AddShapeToDisplay (&_dtmTrias);
                    break;
                case IDT_FINDPOINTS :
                    AddShapeToDisplay (&_dtmHighPoints);
                    AddShapeToDisplay (&_dtmFlatPoints);
                    AddShapeToDisplay (&_dtmLowPoints);
                    break;
                default : break;
            }
        }
        if (wTaskStatus & TASK_REDRAW) {
            _dtmTaskDisplay.Start ();
        }
        return TRUE;
}

WORD DrawModel (DTMFRAME * pdtmFrame, DTMBIGTASK * pdtmTask) {
    if (pdtmFrame == NULL || !pdtmFrame->IsActive () ||
        !pdtmFrame->IsGdiOK () || pdtmTask == NULL) {
        return TASK_STOPPED;
```

```
    }
    if (pdtmTask->Quit ()) {
        pdtmFrame->NotifyParent (DTM_DRAW_STOPPED);
        return TASK_STOPPED;
    }
    switch (pdtmTask->GetStage ()) {
        case 1 :
            pdtmFrame->ClearBackground ();
            _dtmColours.SetPenWidths (pdtmFrame->GetPenWidth (),
                pdtmFrame->GetVertExag ());
            pdtmTask->NextStage ();
            break;
        case 2 :
            _dtmTrias.Draw (pdtmFrame, pdtmTask);
            break;
        case 3 :
            _dtmHighPoints.Draw (pdtmFrame, pdtmTask);
            break;
        case 4 :
            _dtmFlatPoints.Draw (pdtmFrame, pdtmTask);
            break;
        case 5 :
            _dtmLowPoints.Draw (pdtmFrame, pdtmTask);
            break;
        default : break;
    }
    pdtmFrame->NotifyParent (DTM_DRAW_UPDATED);
    if (pdtmTask->GetStage () < 6) {
        return TASK_ONGOING;
    }
    pdtmFrame->NotifyParent (DTM_DRAW_COMPLETED);
    return TASK_COMPLETED;
}


void InitShowDropdownMenu (HMENU hMenu) {
    CheckMenuItem (hMenu, IDM_SHOWTRIANGLES, MF_BYCOMMAND |
        (_dtmTrias.IsVisible () ? MF_CHECKED : MF_UNCHECKED));
    CheckMenuItem (hMenu, IDM_SHOWHIGHPOINTS, MF_BYCOMMAND |
        (_dtmHighPoints.IsVisible () ? MF_CHECKED : MF_UNCHECKED));
    CheckMenuItem (hMenu, IDM_SHOWFLATPOINTS, MF_BYCOMMAND |
        (_dtmFlatPoints.IsVisible () ? MF_CHECKED : MF_UNCHECKED));
    CheckMenuItem (hMenu, IDM_SHOWLOWPOINTS, MF_BYCOMMAND |
        (_dtmLowPoints.IsVisible () ? MF_CHECKED : MF_UNCHECKED));
}


void InitMouseDropdownMenu (HMENU hMenu) {
    DTMMOUSEACT mouseAction;

    mouseAction = _dtmDisplay.GetMouseAction ();
    CheckMenuItem (hMenu, IDM_MOUSEZOOM, MF_BYCOMMAND |
        (mouseAction == MOUSEACT_ZOOM ? MF_CHECKED : MF_UNCHECKED));
    CheckMenuItem (hMenu, IDM_MOUSEPAN, MF_BYCOMMAND |
        (mouseAction == MOUSEACT_PAN ? MF_CHECKED : MF_UNCHECKED));
}


BOOL FindPointsStart (HWND hwnd, UINT uTaskID) {
    if (_dtmTask.IsBusy ()) {
        _dtmText.Output (_szTaskBusyMessage);
        return FALSE;
    }
    if (_dtmTrias.GetTotal () == 0L) {
```

```
        _dtmText.Output (TEXT ("There are no %s available. Unable to ") \
            TEXT ("find high, flat and low points\r\n"),
            _dtmTrias.GetDescription ());
        return FALSE;
    }
    if (_dtmHighPoints.GetTotal () != 0L || _dtmFlatPoints.GetTotal () != 0L ||
        _dtmLowPoints.GetTotal () != 0L) {
        int iMessage;

        iMessage = MessageBox (hwnd,
            TEXT ("Do you want to discard all points already created?"),
            TEXT ("Finding points"), MB_YESNOCANCEL | MB_ICONWARNING);
        if (iMessage == IDCANCEL) {
            return FALSE;
        }
        else if (iMessage == IDYES) {
            _dtmHighPoints.Free ();
            _dtmFlatPoints.Free ();
            _dtmLowPoints.Free ();
        }
    }
    _dtmText.Output (TEXT ("Finding high, flat and low points\r\n"));
    _dtmTask.Start (uTaskID, FINDPOINTS_STEPSIZE);
    return TRUE;
}

WORD FindPointsCont (void) {
    static DWORD dwHighAtStart, dwFlatAtStart, dwLowAtStart;
    static DTMPOINTS dtmMidPoints;

    if (_dtmTask.AtStart ()) {
        dwHighAtStart = _dtmHighPoints.GetTotal ();
        dwFlatAtStart = _dtmFlatPoints.GetTotal ();
        dwLowAtStart = _dtmLowPoints.GetTotal ();
        dtmMidPoints.Init (NULL, 0, POINTSTYLE_PLUS);
    }
    if (_dtmTask.Quit ()) {
        _dtmText.Output (TEXT ("\r\nFinding high, flat and low points stopped\r\n"));
        dtmMidPoints.Free ();
        return TASK_STOPPED | TASK_REDRAW;
    }
    _dtmTask.StartNewBatch ();
    while (!_dtmTask.NoMoreItems (_dtmTrias.GetTotal ()) && !_dtmTask.AtEndOfBatch ()) {
        DTMTRIA * pdtmTria;
        WORD wCorner1, wCorner2, wCorner3;

        pdtmTria = _dtmTrias.GetPtr (_dtmTask.GetItemNumber ());
        wCorner1 = 0;
        wCorner2 = 1;
        wCorner3 = 2;
        while (wCorner1 < TRIA_COORDS) {
            DTMPOINT dtmCorner;
            DOUBLE z1, z2, z3;

            CopyCoords (&(dtmCorner.cdPoint), &(pdtmTria->cdCorner [wCorner1]));
            z1 = pdtmTria->cdCorner [wCorner1].rZ;
            z2 = pdtmTria->cdCorner [wCorner2].rZ;
            z3 = pdtmTria->cdCorner [wCorner3].rZ;
            if (z1 > z2 && z1 > z3) {
                if (_dtmLowPoints.Match (&dtmCorner)) {
                    _dtmLowPoints.Remove (&dtmCorner);
```

```
                                dtmMidPoints.Add (&dtmCorner);
                            }
                        else if (!_dtmFlatPoints.Match (&dtmCorner) &&
                            !dtmMidPoints.Match (&dtmCorner)) {
                            dtmCorner.wColour = PENCOLOUR_HIGHPOINTS;
                            _dtmHighPoints.Add (&dtmCorner);
                        }
                    }
                else if (z1 == z2 && z1 == z3) {
                    _dtmHighPoints.Remove (&dtmCorner);
                    _dtmLowPoints.Remove (&dtmCorner);
                    dtmMidPoints.Remove (&dtmCorner);
                    dtmCorner.wColour = PENCOLOUR_FLATPOINTS;
                    _dtmFlatPoints.Add (&dtmCorner);
                }
                else if (z1 < z2 && z1 < z3) {
                    if (_dtmHighPoints.Match (&dtmCorner)) {
                        _dtmHighPoints.Remove (&dtmCorner);
                        dtmMidPoints.Add (&dtmCorner);
                    }
                    else if (!_dtmFlatPoints.Match (&dtmCorner) &&
                        !dtmMidPoints.Match (&dtmCorner)) {
                        dtmCorner.wColour = PENCOLOUR_LOWPOINTS;
                        _dtmLowPoints.Add (&dtmCorner);
                    }
                }
                else {
                    if (!_dtmFlatPoints.Match (&dtmCorner)) {
                        _dtmHighPoints.Remove (&dtmCorner);
                        _dtmLowPoints.Remove (&dtmCorner);
                        dtmMidPoints.Add (&dtmCorner);
                    }
                }
                wCorner1 ++;
                wCorner2 = AddOneRollOver (wCorner2, TRIA_COORDS);
                wCorner3 = AddOneRollOver (wCorner3, TRIA_COORDS);
            }
        _dtmTask.NextItem ();
        _dtmTask.IncBatchCounter ();
    }
    _dtmText.ProgressDot ();
    if (!_dtmTask.NoMoreItems (_dtmTrias.GetTotal ())) {
        return TASK_ONGOING;
    }
    _dtmHighPoints.ResetLimits ();
    _dtmFlatPoints.ResetLimits ();
    _dtmLowPoints.ResetLimits ();
    dtmMidPoints.Free ();
    _dtmText.Output (TEXT ("\r\nNumber of %s found: %lu\r\n"),
        _dtmHighPoints.GetDescription (), _dtmHighPoints.GetTotal () - dwHighAtStart);
    _dtmText.Output (TEXT ("Number of %s found: %lu\r\n"),
        _dtmFlatPoints.GetDescription (), _dtmFlatPoints.GetTotal () - dwFlatAtStart);
    _dtmText.Output (TEXT ("Number of %s found: %lu\r\n"),
        _dtmLowPoints.GetDescription (), _dtmLowPoints.GetTotal () - dwLowAtStart);
    return TASK_COMPLETED | TASK_REDRAW;
}
```

**Chapter09.cpp** has the same layout as source code files in earlier chapters in this book. It starts with the header files followed by child window IDs, task IDs, the task batch size constant FINDPOINTS_STEPSIZE which is used when finding high, flat and low points, and coloured pen numbers.

It then defines ten global variables, most of which are the same as in earlier chapters. The three points arrays *_dtmHighPoints*, *_dtmFlatPoints* and *_dtmLowPoints* contain high points, flat points and low points in the DTM found by the program.

Seven functions are then declared, followed by the C++ source code.

The functions *WinMain*, *WndProc*, *CarryOutTasks*, *DrawModel*, *InitShowDropdownMenu* and *InitMouseDropdownMenu* are similar to the equivalent functions in earlier chapters. After the message WM_CREATE in *WndProc*, the three points arrays are initialised to display points with different point styles: *_dtmHighPoints* as red plus signs, *_dtmFlatPoints* as light-blue circles, and *_dtmLowPoints* as dark-blue x-shaped crosses. The user can import triangles and find high, flat and low points based on the triangles in the DTM. *DrawModel* draws the triangles first, followed by the high points, the flat points and finally the low points.

The function *FindPointsStart* starts the task of finding high, flat and low points in the DTM. *hwnd* is the handle of the parent window and *uTaskID* is the task ID number. If there are no triangles in the triangles array *_dtmTrias*, the function displays an error message. If any of the three points arrays already contain some points, the function asks the user if they want to discard these points. If the user selects 'Yes', any existing points in the three points arrays are discarded. Finally, *FindPointsStart* displays a message in the text window and starts the task. The function returns TRUE if successful, or FALSE if the user cancels the task or if an error occurs.

The function *FindPointsCont* carries out the task of finding high, flat and low points in the DTM. *FindPointsCont* follows the standard task manager template as discussed in Chapter 1, looking at each triangle in the triangles array *_dtmTrias* in batches. If at the start of the task, as well as remembering initial totals in the three global points arrays, *FindPointsCont* also initialises a static fourth points array *dtmMidPoints*, which is only used by *FindPointsCont* and which will hold points at corners of triangles which are not high, flat or low points. As discussed in Chapter 1, it's important that *dtmMidPoints* is initialised before *FindPointsCont* checks if the task has been cancelled, as otherwise *dtmMidPoints* could be freed before it has been initialised, which could cause the program to stop working.

Within the while-loop in *FindPointsCont*, the z value of each corner of each triangle is compared to the z values of the other two corners of the same triangle in order to identify if each corner is a potential high point, flat point, low point or none of these (i.e. a mid-point). Depending on the result, the point is either added to or removed from the four points arrays: (i) Potential flat points are removed from the other points arrays and added to *_dtmFlatPoints*. (ii) Potential high and low points are only added to *_dtmHighPoints* and *_dtmLowPoints* if they are not already in any of the other points arrays. (iii) Points in *_dtmHighPoints* are removed from *_dtmHighPoints* and added to *dtmMidPoints* if the point is now a potential low or mid-point. (iv) Similarly, points in *_dtmLowPoints* are removed from *_dtmLowPoints* and added to *dtmMidPoints* if the point is now a potential high or mid-point.

These actions are summarised in the following table:

|  | _dtmHighPoints | _dtmFlatPoints | _dtmLowPoints | dtmMidPoints |
|---|---|---|---|---|
| High point ($z1 > z2$ and $z1 > z3$) | Add if no match found in _dtmFlatPoints and dtmMidPoints | Do nothing if match found | Remove if match found, and add to dtmMidPoints | Do nothing if match found |
| Flat point ($z1 = z2$ and $z1 = z3$) | Remove | Add | Remove | Remove |
| Low point ($z1 < z2$ and $z1 < z3$) | Remove if match found, and add to dtmMidPoints | Do nothing if match found | Add if no match found in _dtmFlatPoints and dtmMidPoints | Do nothing if match found |
| Mid-point (none of the above) | Remove if no match found in _dtmFlatPoints | Do nothing if match found | Remove if no match found in _dtmFlatPoints | Add if no match found in _dtmFlatPoints |

When points are added to the mid-points array, the coloured pen number does not matter because the mid-points array is never displayed in the graphics window. However, when added to the other three points arrays, the appropriate coloured pen number is set.

When the task is finished, *FindPointsCont* updates the minimum and maximum x,y,z values for each global points array, frees the contents of *dtmMidPoints* as it is no longer needed, and displays the numbers of points added to each of the three global points arrays. The function returns the TASK_ constants as discussed in Chapter 1.

# Running Chapter09

Before you can compile and run your program, you need to add the following nineteen source files to your Chapter09 project. Refer to Chapter 1 for how to do this:

| | | |
|---|---|---|
| **TextWnd.h** | **TextWnd.cpp** | |
| **FileInOut.h** | **FileInOut.cpp** | |
| **BigTask.h** | **BigTask.cpp** | |
| **Graphics.h** | **Graphics.cpp** | |
| **Colours.h** | **Colours.cpp** | |
| **Shapes.h** | **Shapes.cpp** | |
| **Points.cpp** | **Triangles.cpp** | |
| **Common.h** | **Common.cpp** | |
| **Chapter09.h** | **Chapter09.cpp** | **Chapter09.rc** |

You also need to add the Gdiplus.lib library file as an 'additional dependency' in your project's linker/input settings. Refer to Chapter 2 for how to do this. Finally, don't forget to set Chapter09 as your start-up project.

Otherwise, assuming you have compiled the code for Chapter09 successfully, and it is running, you can now test it out.

Start by importing your DTM of 3D triangles. Click on 'File' in the menu bar, then select 'Import' from the drop-down menu, and finally click on 'Triangles'. Next, select a file containing the triangles data. You can use the sample file Triangles.txt. Then click on 'Edit' in the menu bar, and select 'Find points' from the drop-down menu. If successful, the program's window should look something like this (the colours have been changed to make the points more prominent):

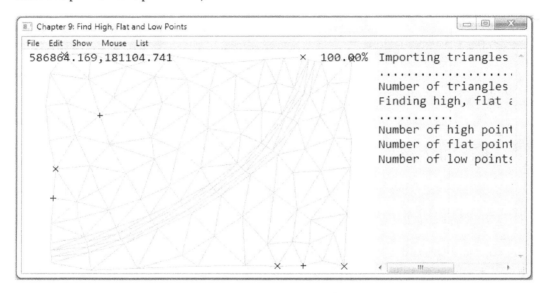

In the image above there are three high points (the +'s), six low points (the ×'s) and zero flat points (which would have been displayed as O's). Most of the high and low points are on the edge of the DTM. One high point is at the peak in the model near the top left-hand corner of the DTM. You can export any of the points arrays data (via 'File', 'Export') as CAD script files, as text files, or as JPEG files.

This type of information can be useful for identifying low points or flat points which could cause drainage problems in your DTM. For example, if you are designing a car park or a new road junction, rainwater could form unwanted puddles at the low points or flat points unless suitable drainage channels or gullies are provided.

As in previous chapters, to exit the program click on 'File' in the menu bar, select 'Exit' and then choose 'Yes' in the message box that appears.

# Chapter 10

## Create Flow Paths

Chapter 10 lists the source code for a program called **Chapter10** that creates flow paths when the user left-clicks the mouse over the DTM in the graphics window. The user can export the flow paths as CAD script files, as text files or as JPEG files.

The following files are discussed in this chapter:

**Chapter10.h**               **Chapter10.rc**               **Chapter10.cpp**

## Chapter10 Source Files

The first file is the header file:

**CHAPTER10.H**

```
#ifndef CHAPTER10_H
#define CHAPTER10_H

#define IDM_IMPORTTRIANGLES        101
#define IDM_EXPORTALLFLOWPATHS      102
#define IDM_EXPORTLASTFLOWPATH      103
#define IDM_EXPORTSCREEN            104
#define IDM_EXPORTMODEL             105
#define IDM_EXIT                    106

#define IDM_DELALLFLOWPATHS         201
#define IDM_DELLASTFLOWPATH         202

#define IDN_SHOWMENU                 2

#define IDM_SHOWFLOWPATHS           301
#define IDM_SHOWLASTFLOWPATH        302
#define IDM_SHOWTRIANGLES           303
#define IDM_COLOURBACKGROUND        304
#define IDM_COLOURCOORDSTEXT        305
#define IDM_COLOURFLOWPATHS         306
#define IDM_COLOURLASTFLOWPATH      307
#define IDM_COLOURTRIANGLES         308
#define IDM_ZOOMEXTENTS             309
#define IDM_REDRAW                  310

#define IDN_MOUSEMENU                3

#define IDM_MOUSEZOOM               401
#define IDM_MOUSEPAN                402
#define IDM_MOUSEFLOWPATH           403

#define IDM_LISTFLOWPATHSSTATS      501
#define IDM_LISTLASTFLOWPATHSTATS   502
#define IDM_LISTTRIANGLESSTATS      503
#define IDM_LISTFLOWPATHS           504
#define IDM_LISTLASTFLOWPATH        505
```

```
#define IDM_LISTTRIANGLES              506

#define IDM_ESCAPEKEY                  901

#endif // CHAPTER10_H
```

As in previous chapters, **Chapter10.h** contains ID numbers for menu bar options, drop-down menus and accelerator keys.

The second file is the resource script file:

## CHAPTER10.RC

```
#include <windows.h>
#include "Chapter10.h"

Chapter10 MENU {
    POPUP "&File" {
        POPUP "&Import" {
            MENUITEM "&Triangles",          IDM_IMPORTTRIANGLES
        }
        POPUP "&Export" {
            MENUITEM "&All flow paths",     IDM_EXPORTALLFLOWPATHS
            MENUITEM "&Last flow path",     IDM_EXPORTLASTFLOWPATH
            MENUITEM SEPARATOR
            MENUITEM "S&creen image",       IDM_EXPORTSCREEN
            MENUITEM "&Model image",        IDM_EXPORTMODEL
        }
        MENUITEM SEPARATOR
        MENUITEM "E&xit",                   IDM_EXIT
    }
    POPUP "&Edit" {
        MENUITEM "Delete &all flow paths",  IDM_DELALLFLOWPATHS
        MENUITEM "&Delete last flow path",  IDM_DELLASTFLOWPATH
    }
    POPUP "&Show" {
        MENUITEM "&Flow paths",             IDM_SHOWFLOWPATHS
        MENUITEM "&Last flow path",         IDM_SHOWLASTFLOWPATH
        MENUITEM "&Triangles",              IDM_SHOWTRIANGLES
        MENUITEM SEPARATOR
        POPUP "&Colour" {
            MENUITEM "Back&ground",         IDM_COLOURBACKGROUND
            MENUITEM "&Coords text",        IDM_COLOURCOORDSTEXT
            MENUITEM SEPARATOR
            MENUITEM "&Flow paths",         IDM_COLOURFLOWPATHS
            MENUITEM "&Last flow path",     IDM_COLOURLASTFLOWPATH
            MENUITEM "&Triangles",          IDM_COLOURTRIANGLES
        }
        MENUITEM SEPARATOR
        MENUITEM "&Zoom extents",           IDM_ZOOMEXTENTS
        MENUITEM "&Redraw",                 IDM_REDRAW
    }
    POPUP "&Mouse" {
        MENUITEM "&Zoom in/out",            IDM_MOUSEZOOM
        MENUITEM "&Pan",                    IDM_MOUSEPAN
        MENUITEM SEPARATOR
        MENUITEM "&Create flow path",       IDM_MOUSEFLOWPATH
    }
    POPUP "&List" {
        POPUP "&Statistics" {
```

```
                MENUITEM "&Flow paths",            IDM_LISTFLOWPATHSSTATS
                MENUITEM "&Last flow path",        IDM_LISTLASTFLOWPATHSTATS
                MENUITEM "&Triangles",             IDM_LISTTRIANGLESSTATS
            }
            MENUITEM SEPARATOR
            MENUITEM "&Flow paths",                IDM_LISTFLOWPATHS
            MENUITEM "&Last flow path",            IDM_LISTLASTFLOWPATH
            MENUITEM "&Triangles",                 IDM_LISTTRIANGLES
        }
}

Chapter10 ACCELERATORS {
    VK_ESCAPE,         IDM_ESCAPEKEY,          VIRTKEY, NOINVERT
    VK_DELETE,         IDM_DELLASTFLOWPATH,    VIRTKEY, NOINVERT
}
```

Like previous chapters, **Chapter10.rc** defines the contents of the program's menu bar and accelerator keys. There are two accelerator keys in Chapter10.rc, the second of which (the delete key) shares an IDM number with a menu bar option. There is no custom dialog box in this program.

The third file is the source code file, which includes function listings.

**CHAPTER10.CPP**

```cpp
#ifndef UNICODE
#define UNICODE
#endif

#include <windows.h>
#include <gdiplus.h>
using namespace Gdiplus;
#include <math.h>
#include "Chapter10.h"
#include "BigTask.h"
#include "FileInOut.h"
#include "TextWnd.h"
#include "Graphics.h"
#include "Colours.h"
#include "Shapes.h"
#include "Common.h"

#define ID_TEXTWND                      1
#define ID_DISPLAYWND                   2
#define ID_IMAGEEXPORT                  3

#define IDT_IMPORTTRIANGLES             11

#define IDT_EXPORTALLFLOWPATHS          21
#define IDT_EXPORTALLFLOWPATHSSCRIPT    22
#define IDT_EXPORTLASTFLOWPATH          23
#define IDT_EXPORTLASTFLOWPATHSCRIPT    24
#define IDT_EXPORTIMAGE                 25

#define IDT_GETFLOWPATH                 31

#define IDT_LISTFLOWPATHS               41
#define IDT_LISTLASTFLOWPATH            42
#define IDT_LISTTRIANGLES               43
```

```
#define CREATEFLOWPATH_STEPSIZE          20L

#define PENCOLOUR_FLOWPATHS              4
#define PENCOLOUR_LASTFLOWPATH           3
#define PENCOLOUR_TRIANGLES              11

struct DTMFLOWPATH {
    DTMCOORD cdStart, cdNow;
    DWORD dwTria;
};

DTMTEXTWINDOW _dtmText;
DTMFILEDATA _dtmFile;
DTMBIGTASK _dtmTask, _dtmTaskDisplay;
DTMDISPLAY _dtmDisplay;
DTMCOLOURS _dtmColours;
DTMLINES _dtmFlowPaths, _dtmLastFlowPath;
DTMTRIAS _dtmTrias;
DTMFLOWPATH _dtmFlowPath;

LRESULT CALLBACK WndProc (HWND, UINT, WPARAM, LPARAM);
BOOL CarryOutTasks (HWND);
WORD DrawModel (DTMFRAME *, DTMBIGTASK *);
void InitShowDropdownMenu (HMENU);
void InitMouseDropdownMenu (HMENU);
void DeleteFlowPaths (DTMLINES *);
BOOL CreateFlowPathStart (UINT);
WORD CreateFlowPathCont (void);
BOOL AddFlowPathLine (void);

int WINAPI WinMain (HINSTANCE hInst, HINSTANCE, PSTR, int nCmdShow) {
    return InitAndRunProgram (hInst, nCmdShow, TEXT ("Chapter10"),
        TEXT ("Chapter 10: Create flow paths"));
}

LRESULT CALLBACK WndProc (HWND hwnd, UINT message, WPARAM wParam, LPARAM lParam) {
    switch (message) {
        case WM_CREATE : {
            HINSTANCE hInst;

            hInst = ((LPCREATESTRUCT) lParam)->hInstance;
            _dtmText.Create (hwnd, ID_TEXTWND, hInst);
            _dtmFile.Init (hwnd);
            _dtmDisplay.Init (hwnd, 0, ID_DISPLAYWND, hInst,
                1.0, 4.0, 4.0, 4.0, 5.0, 1.0, 2.0, 0.5);
            _dtmDisplay.SetMouseAction (MOUSEACT_POINT);
            _dtmColours.Init ();
            _dtmFlowPaths.Init (TEXT ("flow paths"), PENCOLOUR_FLOWPATHS);
            _dtmLastFlowPath.Init (TEXT ("last flow paths"),
                PENCOLOUR_LASTFLOWPATH);
            _dtmTrias.Init (TEXT ("triangles"), PENCOLOUR_TRIANGLES, 0, FALSE);
            SetCoordToZero (&(_dtmFlowPath.cdStart));
            SetCoordToZero (&(_dtmFlowPath.cdNow));
            _dtmFlowPath.dwTria = 0L;
            return 0;
        }
        case WM_ENTERSIZEMOVE :
            _dtmDisplay.StartResizing ();
            return 0;
        case WM_SIZE :
            ResizeChildWindows (lParam);
```

```
            return 0;
    case WM_EXITSIZEMOVE :
        _dtmDisplay.StopResizing ();
        return 0;
    case WM_INITMENUPOPUP :
        if (HIWORD (lParam) == FALSE) {
            switch (LOWORD (lParam)) {
            case IDN_SHOWMENU :
                InitShowDropdownMenu ((HMENU) wParam);
                return 0;
            case IDN_MOUSEMENU :
                InitMouseDropdownMenu ((HMENU) wParam);
                return 0;
            default : break;
            }
        }
        break;
    case WM_COMMAND :
        if (HIWORD (wParam) == 0) {
            switch (LOWORD (wParam)) {
                case IDM_IMPORTTRIANGLES :
                    _dtmTrias.ImportStart (hwnd, IDT_IMPORTTRIANGLES);
                    return 0;
                case IDM_EXPORTALLFLOWPATHS :
                    if (_dtmLastFlowPath.GetTotal () != 0L) {
                        _dtmFlowPaths.TransferAll (&_dtmLastFlowPath,
                            PENCOLOUR_FLOWPATHS);
                        _dtmFlowPaths.ResetLimits ();
                        _dtmTaskDisplay.Start ();
                    }
                    _dtmFlowPaths.ExportStart (IDT_EXPORTALLFLOWPATHS,
                        IDT_EXPORTALLFLOWPATHSSCRIPT);
                    return 0;
                case IDM_EXPORTLASTFLOWPATH :
                    _dtmLastFlowPath.ExportStart (IDT_EXPORTLASTFLOWPATH,
                        IDT_EXPORTLASTFLOWPATHSCRIPT);
                    return 0;
                case IDM_EXPORTSCREEN :
                    ExportImage (FALSE, ID_IMAGEEXPORT);
                    return 0;
                case IDM_EXPORTMODEL :
                    ExportImage (TRUE, ID_IMAGEEXPORT);
                    return 0;
                case IDM_EXIT :
                    SendMessage (hwnd, WM_CLOSE, 0, 0);
                    return 0;
                case IDM_DELALLFLOWPATHS :
                    DeleteFlowPaths (&_dtmFlowPaths);
                    DeleteFlowPaths (&_dtmLastFlowPath);
                    return 0;
                case IDM_DELLASTFLOWPATH :
                    DeleteFlowPaths (&_dtmLastFlowPath);
                    return 0;
                case IDM_SHOWFLOWPATHS :
                    _dtmFlowPaths.FlipVisible ();
                    _dtmTaskDisplay.Start ();
                    return 0;
                case IDM_SHOWLASTFLOWPATH :
                    _dtmLastFlowPath.FlipVisible ();
                    _dtmTaskDisplay.Start ();
                    return 0;
```

```
            case IDM_SHOWTRIANGLES :
                _dtmTrias.FlipVisible ();
                _dtmTaskDisplay.Start ();
                return 0;
            case IDM_COLOURBACKGROUND :
                ChangeBackgroundColour (hwnd);
                return 0;
            case IDM_COLOURCOORDSTEXT :
                ChangeCoordsTextColour (hwnd);
                return 0;
            case IDM_COLOURFLOWPATHS :
                ChangePenColour (hwnd, PENCOLOUR_FLOWPATHS);
                return 0;
            case IDM_COLOURLASTFLOWPATH :
                ChangePenColour (hwnd, PENCOLOUR_LASTFLOWPATH);
                return 0;
            case IDM_COLOURTRIANGLES :
                ChangePenColour (hwnd, PENCOLOUR_TRIANGLES);
                return 0;
            case IDM_ZOOMEXTENTS :
                _dtmDisplay.ZoomExtents ();
                _dtmTaskDisplay.Start ();
                return 0;
            case IDM_REDRAW :
                _dtmTaskDisplay.Start ();
                return 0;
            case IDM_MOUSEZOOM :
                _dtmDisplay.SetMouseAction (MOUSEACT_ZOOM);
                return 0;
            case IDM_MOUSEPAN :
                _dtmDisplay.SetMouseAction (MOUSEACT_PAN);
                return 0;
            case IDM_MOUSEFLOWPATH :
                _dtmDisplay.SetMouseAction (MOUSEACT_POINT);
                return 0;
            case IDM_LISTFLOWPATHSSTATS :
                _dtmFlowPaths.ListStats ();
                return 0;
            case IDM_LISTLASTFLOWPATHSTATS :
                _dtmLastFlowPath.ListStats ();
                return 0;
            case IDM_LISTTRIANGLESSTATS :
                _dtmTrias.ListStats ();
                return 0;
            case IDM_LISTFLOWPATHS :
                _dtmFlowPaths.ListStart (IDT_LISTFLOWPATHS);
                return 0;
            case IDM_LISTLASTFLOWPATH :
                _dtmLastFlowPath.ListStart (IDT_LISTLASTFLOWPATH);
                return 0;
            case IDM_LISTTRIANGLES :
                _dtmTrias.ListStart (IDT_LISTTRIANGLES);
                return 0;
            default : break;
        }
    }
    else if (HIWORD (wParam) == 1) {
        if (LOWORD (wParam) == IDM_ESCAPEKEY) {
            _dtmTask.Quit (TRUE);
            _dtmTaskDisplay.Quit (TRUE);
            return 0;
```

```
                            }
                        else if (LOWORD (wParam) == IDM_DELLASTFLOWPATH) {
                            DeleteFlowPaths (&_dtmLastFlowPath);
                        }
                    }
                else if (LOWORD (wParam) == ID_DISPLAYWND) {
                    switch (HIWORD (wParam)) {
                        case DTM_REDRAW :
                            _dtmTaskDisplay.Start ();
                            return 0;
                        case DTM_DRAW_STOPPED :
                        case DTM_DRAW_COMPLETED :
                            _dtmDisplay.RepaintNow (REPAINT_ALL);
                            return 0;
                        case DTM_SELPOINT :
                            CreateFlowPathStart (IDT_GETFLOWPATH);
                            return 0;
                        default : return 0;
                    }
                }
                else if (LOWORD (wParam) == ID_IMAGEEXPORT) {
                    ProcessExportImageMessages (wParam, IDT_EXPORTIMAGE);
                    return 0;
                }
                break;
            case WM_CLOSE :
                AskCloseWindowMessage (hwnd);
                return 0;
            case WM_DESTROY:
                _dtmDisplay.Free ();
                _dtmColours.Free ();
                _dtmText.Destroy ();
                _dtmFile.FreeImportBuffer ();
                _dtmFlowPaths.Free ();
                _dtmLastFlowPath.Free ();
                _dtmTrias.Free ();
                PostQuitMessage (0);
                return 0;
            default : break;
        }
    return DefWindowProc (hwnd, message, wParam, lParam);
}

BOOL CarryOutTasks (HWND hwnd) {
    WORD wTaskStatus;

    if (!_dtmTask.IsBusy ()) {
        return FALSE;
    }
    if (_dtmTask.GetStage () == 0) {
        EnableMenuBar (hwnd, FALSE);
        _dtmDisplay.Enable (FALSE);
        _dtmTask.NextStage ();
    }
    switch (_dtmTask.GetID ()) {
        case IDT_IMPORTTRIANGLES :
            wTaskStatus = _dtmTrias.ImportCont (FALSE);
            break;
        case IDT_EXPORTALLFLOWPATHS :
            wTaskStatus = _dtmFlowPaths.ExportCont (FALSE);
            break;
```

```
            case IDT_EXPORTALLFLOWPATHSSCRIPT :
                wTaskStatus = _dtmFlowPaths.ExportCont (TRUE);
                break;
            case IDT_EXPORTLASTFLOWPATH :
                wTaskStatus = _dtmLastFlowPath.ExportCont (FALSE);
                break;
            case IDT_EXPORTLASTFLOWPATHSCRIPT :
                wTaskStatus = _dtmLastFlowPath.ExportCont (TRUE);
                break;
            case IDT_EXPORTIMAGE :
                wTaskStatus = DrawModel (_dtmDisplay.GetImageDtmPtr (), &_dtmTask);
                break;
            case IDT_GETFLOWPATH :
                wTaskStatus = CreateFlowPathCont ();
                break;
            case IDT_LISTFLOWPATHS :
                wTaskStatus = _dtmFlowPaths.ListCont ();
                break;
            case IDT_LISTLASTFLOWPATH :
                wTaskStatus = _dtmLastFlowPath.ListCont ();
                break;
            case IDT_LISTTRIANGLES :
                wTaskStatus = _dtmTrias.ListCont ();
                break;
            default :
                wTaskStatus = TASK_STOPPED;
                break;
        }
        if ((wTaskStatus & TASK_STOPPED) || (wTaskStatus & TASK_COMPLETED)) {
            EnableMenuBar (hwnd, TRUE);
            _dtmDisplay.Enable (TRUE);
            _dtmTask.Stop ();
        }
        if (wTaskStatus & TASK_COMPLETED) {
            switch (_dtmTask.GetID ()) {
                case IDT_IMPORTTRIANGLES :
                    AddShapeToDisplay (&_dtmTrias);
                    break;
                case IDT_GETFLOWPATH :
                    AddShapeToDisplay (&_dtmLastFlowPath);
                    break;
                default : break;
            }
        }
        if (wTaskStatus & TASK_REDRAW) {
            _dtmTaskDisplay.Start ();
        }
        return TRUE;
}

WORD DrawModel (DTMFRAME * pdtmFrame, DTMBIGTASK * pdtmTask) {
    if (pdtmFrame == NULL || !pdtmFrame->IsActive () ||
        !pdtmFrame->IsGdiOK () || pdtmTask == NULL) {
        return TASK_STOPPED;
    }
    if (pdtmTask->Quit ()) {
        pdtmFrame->NotifyParent (DTM_DRAW_STOPPED);
        return TASK_STOPPED;
    }
    switch (pdtmTask->GetStage ()) {
        case 1 :
```

```
                    pdtmFrame->ClearBackground ();
                    _dtmColours.SetPenWidths (pdtmFrame->GetPenWidth (),
                        pdtmFrame->GetVertExag ());
                    pdtmTask->NextStage ();
                    break;
            case 2 :
                    _dtmTrias.Draw (pdtmFrame, pdtmTask);
                    break;
            case 3 :
                    _dtmFlowPaths.Draw (pdtmFrame, pdtmTask);
                    break;
            case 4 :
                    _dtmLastFlowPath.Draw (pdtmFrame, pdtmTask);
                    break;
            default : break;
        }
        pdtmFrame->NotifyParent (DTM_DRAW_UPDATED);
        if (pdtmTask->GetStage () < 5) {
            return TASK_ONGOING;
        }
        pdtmFrame->NotifyParent (DTM_DRAW_COMPLETED);
        return TASK_COMPLETED;
}

void InitShowDropdownMenu (HMENU hMenu) {
    CheckMenuItem (hMenu, IDM_SHOWFLOWPATHS, MF_BYCOMMAND |
        (_dtmFlowPaths.IsVisible () ? MF_CHECKED : MF_UNCHECKED));
    CheckMenuItem (hMenu, IDM_SHOWLASTFLOWPATH, MF_BYCOMMAND |
        (_dtmLastFlowPath.IsVisible () ? MF_CHECKED : MF_UNCHECKED));
    CheckMenuItem (hMenu, IDM_SHOWTRIANGLES, MF_BYCOMMAND |
        (_dtmTrias.IsVisible () ? MF_CHECKED : MF_UNCHECKED));
}

void InitMouseDropdownMenu (HMENU hMenu) {
    DTMMOUSEACT mouseAction;

    mouseAction = _dtmDisplay.GetMouseAction ();
    CheckMenuItem (hMenu, IDM_MOUSEZOOM, MF_BYCOMMAND |
        (mouseAction == MOUSEACT_ZOOM ? MF_CHECKED : MF_UNCHECKED));
    CheckMenuItem (hMenu, IDM_MOUSEPAN, MF_BYCOMMAND |
        (mouseAction == MOUSEACT_PAN ? MF_CHECKED : MF_UNCHECKED));
    CheckMenuItem (hMenu, IDM_MOUSEFLOWPATH, MF_BYCOMMAND |
        (mouseAction == MOUSEACT_POINT ? MF_CHECKED : MF_UNCHECKED));
}

void DeleteFlowPaths (DTMLINES * pdtmFlowPaths) {
    if (!_dtmTask.IsBusy () && pdtmFlowPaths != NULL &&
        pdtmFlowPaths->GetTotal () != 0L) {
        pdtmFlowPaths->Free ();
        _dtmTaskDisplay.Start ();
    }
}

BOOL CreateFlowPathStart (UINT uTaskID) {
    if (_dtmLastFlowPath.GetTotal () != 0L) {
        _dtmFlowPaths.TransferAll (&_dtmLastFlowPath, PENCOLOUR_FLOWPATHS);
        _dtmFlowPaths.ResetLimits ();
        _dtmTaskDisplay.Start ();
    }
    _dtmFlowPath.cdStart.rX = _dtmDisplay.GetSelFromX ();
    _dtmFlowPath.cdStart.rY = _dtmDisplay.GetSelFromY ();
```

```
    _dtmFlowPath.dwTria = _dtmTrias.FromCoords (&(_dtmFlowPath.cdStart));
    if (_dtmFlowPath.dwTria >= _dtmTrias.GetTotal ()) {
        _dtmText.Output (TEXT ("No triangle found at %.3f, %.3f\r\n"),
            _dtmFlowPath.cdStart.rX, _dtmFlowPath.cdStart.rY);
        return FALSE;
    }
    if (!_dtmTrias.GetZ (_dtmFlowPath.dwTria, &(_dtmFlowPath.cdStart),
        &(_dtmFlowPath.cdStart.rZ))) {
        _dtmText.Output (TEXT ("No z value found at %.3f, %.3f\r\n"),
            _dtmFlowPath.cdStart.rX, _dtmFlowPath.cdStart.rY);
        return FALSE;
    }
    CopyCoords (&(_dtmFlowPath.cdNow), &(_dtmFlowPath.cdStart));
    _dtmTask.Start (uTaskID, CREATEFLOWPATH_STEPSIZE);
    return TRUE;
}

WORD CreateFlowPathCont (void) {
    if (_dtmTask.Quit ()) {
        _dtmText.Output (TEXT ("\r\nCreating flow path stopped\r\n"));
        return TASK_STOPPED | TASK_REDRAW;
    }
    _dtmTask.StartNewBatch ();
    while (_dtmFlowPath.dwTria <_dtmTrias.GetTotal () && !_dtmTask.AtEndOfBatch ()) {
        if (!AddFlowPathLine ()) {
            _dtmFlowPath.dwTria = _dtmTrias.GetTotal ();
            break;
        }
        _dtmTask.IncBatchCounter ();
    }
    _dtmText.ProgressDot ();
    if (_dtmFlowPath.dwTria <_dtmTrias.GetTotal ()) {
        return TASK_ONGOING;
    }
    if (_dtmLastFlowPath.GetTotal () == 0L) {
        _dtmText.Output (TEXT ("\r\nNo flow path created starting at %.3f, %.3f\r\n"),
            _dtmFlowPath.cdStart.rX, _dtmFlowPath.cdStart.rY);
    }
    else {
        _dtmText.Output (TEXT ("\r\nFlow path created from x, y: number of ") \
            TEXT ("lines, total length\r\n %.3f, %.3f: %lu, %.3f\r\n"),
            _dtmFlowPath.cdStart.rX, _dtmFlowPath.cdStart.rY,
            _dtmLastFlowPath.GetTotal (), _dtmLastFlowPath.GetLength ());
    }
    return TASK_COMPLETED | TASK_REDRAW;
}

BOOL AddFlowPathLine (void) {
    DOUBLE rSlope, rAngle, rX1, rY1, rZ1, rX2, rY2;
    DTMTRIA * pdtmTria;
    WORD wEdge;

    if (!_dtmTrias.GetSlope (_dtmFlowPath.dwTria, &rSlope, &rAngle)) {
        return FALSE;
    }
    if (rSlope == 0.0) {
        return FALSE;
    }
    rX1 = _dtmFlowPath.cdNow.rX;
    rY1 = _dtmFlowPath.cdNow.rY;
    rZ1 = _dtmFlowPath.cdNow.rZ;
```

```
    rAngle = rAngle * PI / 180.0;
    rX2 = rX1 + cos (rAngle);
    rY2 = rY1 + sin (rAngle);
    pdtmTria = _dtmTrias.GetPtr (_dtmFlowPath.dwTria);
    wEdge = 0;
    for (wEdge = 0; wEdge < TRIA_COORDS; wEdge ++) {
        DOUBLE rX3, rY3, rZ3, rX4, rY4, rZ4, rAlong1, rAlong2;

        _dtmTrias.GetEdge (pdtmTria, wEdge, &rX3, &rY3, &rZ3, &rX4, &rY4, &rZ4);
        if (DoLinesCross (rX1, rY1, rX2, rY2, rX3, rY3, rX4, rY4, &rAlong1, &rAlong2)) {
            if (rAlong1 >= FUZZFACTOR && rAlong2 > -FUZZFACTOR &&
                (rAlong2 - 1.0) < FUZZFACTOR) {
                DTMLINE dtmLine;
                DWORD dwNextTria;

                _dtmLastFlowPath.SetEnd (&dtmLine, 0, rX1, rY1, rZ1);
                _dtmLastFlowPath.SetEnd (&dtmLine, 1, rX3 + rAlong2 * (rX4 - rX3),
                    rY3 + rAlong2 * (rY4 - rY3), rZ3 + rAlong2 * (rZ4 - rZ3));
                if (!_dtmLastFlowPath.MatchingEnds (&dtmLine)) {
                    dtmLine.wColour = PENCOLOUR_LASTFLOWPATH;
                    _dtmLastFlowPath.AddNear (&dtmLine, FUZZFACTOR);
                    CopyCoords (&(_dtmFlowPath.cdNow), &(dtmLine.cdEnd [1]));
                }
                if (!_dtmTrias.NextClosest (_dtmFlowPath.cdNow.rX,
                    _dtmFlowPath.cdNow.rY, &dwNextTria, _dtmFlowPath.dwTria)) {
                    return FALSE;
                }
                _dtmFlowPath.dwTria = dwNextTria;
                return TRUE;
            }
        }
    }
    return FALSE;
}
```

**Chapter10.cpp** has the same layout as source code files in earlier chapters in this book. It starts with the header files, including <math.h> for the functions *cos* and *sin*, followed by child window IDs, task IDs, the task batch size constant CREATEFLOWPATH_STEPSIZE which is used when creating flow paths, and coloured pen numbers.

It then declares the structure DTMFLOWPATH which is used when creating flow paths. This structure contains three variables: *cdStart* is the x,y,z coordinates at the start of the flow path, *cdNow* is the x,y,z coordinates at the other end (or 'working end') of the flow path, and *dwTria* is the zero-based number of the triangle in *_dtmTrias* at *cdNow*. When lines are added to the flow path they join the flow path at *cdNow*. *cdNow* and *dwTria* are updated as the flow path grows.

Next, Chapter10.cpp defines ten global variables, most of which are the same as in earlier chapters. *_dtmFlowPaths* is a lines array of flow paths created by the program. *_dtmLastFlowPath* is a lines array of the last flow path created by the program. *_dtmFlowPath* is used when creating a flow path.

Nine functions are then declared, followed by the C++ source code.

The functions *WinMain*, *WndProc*, *CarryOutTasks*, *DrawModel*, *InitShowDropdownMenu* and *InitMouseDropdownMenu* are similar to the equivalent functions in earlier chapters. After the message WM_CREATE in *WndProc*, the graphics window's mouse action is set to MOUSEACT_POINT so that the user can start creating flow paths straight after importing the DTM. In other programs in this book and in Book One the mouse action defaults to MOUSEACT_ZOOM. Also after the message WM_CREATE, the variables in _dtmFlowPath_ are set to zero. When the user exports all the flow paths (IDM_EXPORTALLFLOWPATHS) any flow path lines in _dtmLastFlowPath_ are transferred to _dtmFlowPaths_, the maximum and minimum x,y,z values in _dtmFlowPaths_ are updated, and the graphics window updates its contents so that these changes are displayed even if the user cancels the export task. The user can import 3D triangles, create flow paths, and export flow paths. *DrawModel* draws the triangles first, followed by the non-last flow paths and then the last flow path.

---

In Chapters 4 and 6, when transferring selected triangles (Chapter 4) or points outside the DTM (Chapter 6) using the function *DTMSHAPES::TransferAll* (for example as part of an IDM 'export all' message), it was not necessary to call the function *DTMSHAPES:: ResetLimits* after the transfer because the triangles and points were all initially in the destination shapes array. Therefore the destination shapes array's minimum and maximum x,y,z values were still valid. However, in this chapter it is necessary to call *ResetLimits* after the IDM_EXPORTALLFLOWPATHS message because the flow path lines in _dtmLastFlowPath_ were not initially part of _dtmFlowPaths_.

---

The function *DeleteFlowPaths* deletes a lines array containing flow paths. *pdtmFlowPaths* points to the lines array. This function checks if the task manager is not busy, like the function *DeleteSelectedTriangles* in Chapter 4, before proceeding because it can be activated by the user pressing the delete key, which is one of the accelerator keys in Chapter10.rc, as well as via the menu bar. Accelerator keys cannot be disabled like menu-bar options when a task starts. Therefore *DeleteFlowPath* can still be called even when another task is active. After deleting the flow paths, the graphics window updates its contents to show that the flow paths have been removed.

The function *CreateFlowPathStart* starts the task that creates a flow path. *uTaskID* is the task ID number. The new flow path will be added to the lines array _dtmLastFlowPath_. If there is an existing flow path in _dtmLastFlowPath_, it is transferred to _dtmFlowPaths_, the minimum and maximum x,y,z values in _dtmFlowPaths_ are updated, and the graphics window updates its contents to show the changes. Next, *CreateFlowPathStart* copies the x,y coordinates of the mouse position into the start of the flow path in _dtmFlowPath_, as well as the zero-based number of the triangle in _dtmTrias_ at the x,y coordinates. If no triangle can be found, for example because the x,y coordinates are outside the DTM, an error message is displayed in the text window. Otherwise *CreateFlowPathStart* gets the z value at the start x,y coordinates, copies the x,y,z values into the other end of the flow path in _dtmFlowPath_, and starts the task. *CreateFlowPathStart* returns TRUE if successful, or FALSE if an error occurs.

The function *CreateFlowPathCont* carries out the task that creates a flow path. *CreateFlowPathCont* follows the standard task manager template as discussed in Chapter 1. However, instead of working its way through a shapes array, like other similar *...Cont* functions in earlier chapters, *CreateFlowPathCont* continues adding lines to the flow path, in batches, until the end of the flow path is reached. When no more lines can be added, *CreateFlowPathCont* sets the task's current item number to the end of *_dtmTrias* so that the task finishes. *CreateFlowPathCont* returns the TASK_ constants as discussed in Chapter 1.

The function *AddFlowPathLine* adds a line to the flow path in *_dtmLastFlowPath*. The start of the line to be added is at *cdNow*, the 'working end' of the flow path, in *_dtmFlowPath*. *AddFlowPathLine* starts by getting the slope and slope angle of the triangle *dwTria* in *_dtmFlowPath*, which is the triangle at the *cdNow* coordinates. If no slope can be found, or if the triangle is flat and therefore no further flow path if possible, the function exits. Otherwise it creates a short line, starting at *cdNow* and extending at the triangle's slope angle (converted from degrees to radians). The length of this line and the z value at the other end are not needed yet. *AddFlowPathLine* then checks if this potential flow path line intersects a far edge of the triangle, using the function *DoLinesCross*.

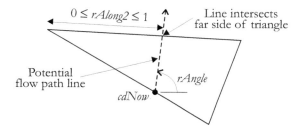

The line intersects a far edge when the following conditions are met:

```
rAlong1 > 0, rAlong2 >= 0 and rAlong2 <= 1
```

which, when using FUZZFACTOR, becomes:

```
rAlong1 >= FUZZFACTOR, rAlong2 > -FUZZFACTOR and (rAlong2 - 1) < FUZZFACTOR
```

*rAlong1* must be greater than zero otherwise *AddFlowPathLine* incorrectly interprets the start of the new line as being an intersection. This is because, except for the first line in the flow path, the start of the new line is always located on an edge of the triangle and therefore *rAlong1* equals zero at this location.

If the new line intersects a far edge, its coordinates at each end are set in *dtmLine*. If the ends of *dtmLine* do not match, the line is added to the flow path, and the 'working end' of the flow path is updated to the far end of the new line. Next, *AddFlowPathLine* finds the next triangle that shares the far edge of the current triangle. If no triangle can be found, the boundary of the DTM has been reached and the function exits. If a triangle can be found, its number is stored in *_dtmFlowPath* and the function exits ready for the next line to be added to the flow path.

If the new line does not intersect any far edge of the triangle, this is because the flow path has reached a triangle that slopes back towards the current triangle, thus creating a 'ditch' or a 'valley' in the DTM along the shared edge. *AddFlowPathLine* exits because it cannot add a new line in this situation.

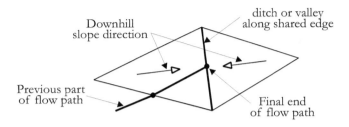

This program stops adding lines to the flow path when it reaches a ditch or a valley in the DTM created by two triangles both falling towards their shared edge. However, you could add code to your program to continue the flow path downhill along the shared edge or edges (for example go to the shared corner with the lower z value) until the end of the ditch or valley is reached, or until the flow path reaches the DTM boundary. The ditch or valley ends when it reaches a low point (see chapter 9), or when the flow is no longer restricted to a single direction, for example when a river reaches the sea.

Such code is not included in this program because it is possible for the user to determine the route of the ditch or valley by left-clicking the mouse close to the shared edge or edges to identify the route of the ditch or valley.

*AddFlowPathLine* returns TRUE if more lines can be added to the flow path, or FALSE if no more lines can be added to the flow path or if an error occurs.

## Running Chapter10

Before you can compile and run your program, you need to add the following nineteen source files to your Chapter10 project. Refer to Chapter 1 for how to do this:

| | | |
|---|---|---|
| **TextWnd.h** | **TextWnd.cpp** | |
| **FileInOut.h** | **FileInOut.cpp** | |
| **BigTask.h** | **BigTask.cpp** | |
| **Graphics.h** | **Graphics.cpp** | |
| **Colours.h** | **Colours.cpp** | |
| **Shapes.h** | **Shapes.cpp** | |
| **Lines.cpp** | **Triangles.cpp** | |
| **Common.h** | **Common.cpp** | |
| **Chapter10.h** | **Chapter10.cpp** | **Chapter10.rc** |

You also need to add the Gdiplus.lib library file as an 'additional dependency' in your project's linker/input settings. Refer to Chapter 2 for how to do this. Finally, don't forget to set Chapter10 as your start-up project.

Otherwise, assuming you have compiled the code for Chapter10 successfully, and it is running, you can now test it out.

Start by importing your DTM of 3D triangles. Click on 'File' in the menu bar, then select 'Import' from the drop-down menu, and finally click on 'Triangles'. Then select a file containing the triangles data. You can use the sample file Triangles.txt. Next, left-click the mouse in the graphics window over the DTM. As discussed in earlier chapters, there is a peak in the DTM in the top-left area of the model. If you left-click a few times around this peak, your program's window should look something like this (the colours have been changed to make the flow paths more prominent):

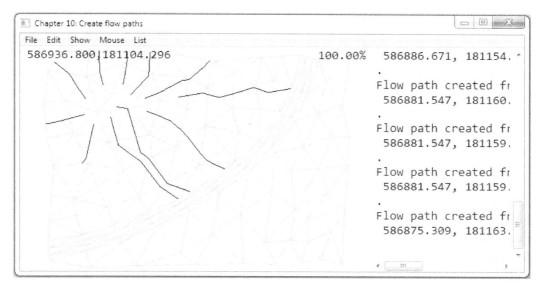

Note that when a flow path is added to the DTM, it is shown in a cyan or light-blue colour. When you add another flow path the light-blue flow path automatically changes to dark blue as it is transferred to the *_dtmFlowPaths* lines array. If you wish to delete the latest flow path (shown in light blue) you can do this by pressing the delete key or by clicking on 'Edit' in the menu bar and selecting 'Delete last flow path' from the drop-down menu. You might wish to have one finger over the delete key as you add flow paths to the model, enabling you to delete unwanted flow paths quickly, and keep just more interesting flow paths. You can also delete all flow paths (both dark blue and light blue) by clicking on 'Edit' in the menu bar and selecting 'Delete all flow paths'.

To export the flow paths, either as CAD script files or as text files, click on 'File' in the menu bar and select 'Export' from the drop-down menu. You can then export all the flow paths (the light-blue flow path combined with the dark-blue paths) or just the last flow path (shown in light blue). Flow paths can also be exported to JPEG files via 'File', 'Export' and then 'Screen image' or 'Model image'.

As discussed earlier, Chapter09 stops adding lines to a flow path when the flow path reaches a ditch or valley between two triangles, where both triangles fall downwards towards a shared edge. To determine the route of a ditch or valley in the DTM, continue creating flow paths to both sides of the shared edge, moving along the edge. The following image shows rows of flow paths identifying a ditch or valley in the lower-right area of the DTM. The image has been panned and zoomed (refer to Chapter 2):

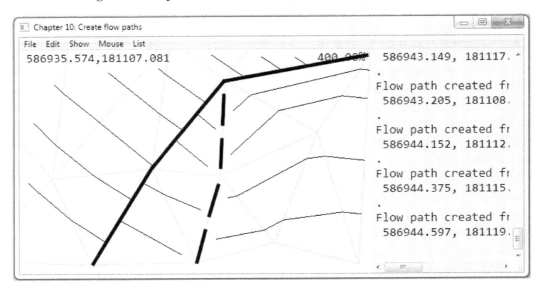

The thick black line (added to the image after the screen capture of the program) shows the route of a ditch or valley. Similarly, the thick black dashed line (also added to the image after the screen capture of the program) identifies a ridge or crest where adjacent triangles slope upwards to their shared edge, which can also be located using flow paths.

A further tool you could add to your version of Chapter10.cpp could be to calculate flow paths in reverse. The code in *AddFlowPathLine* could be adapted to add 180° to the slope angles depending on the value of a flag passed to the function which could be TRUE if downhill, or FALSE if uphill. Then flow paths would stop when they reach ridges or crests, instead of ditches or valleys. Uphill flow paths could be coloured red when added to the lines array *_dtmFlowPaths* to distinguish them from downhill flow paths (still coloured dark blue).

As in previous chapters, to exit the program click on 'File' in the menu bar, select 'Exit' and then choose 'Yes' in the message box that appears.

# Chapter 11

## Create DTM Boundary Lines

Chapter 11 lists the source code for a program called **Chapter11** that creates boundary lines around the DTM. These boundary lines can be separate boundaries, for example for DTMs that cover two separate areas, or one boundary can be inside another, for example for DTMs that contain lakes or other non-surveyed areas. The user can export the boundary lines as CAD script files, as text files or as JPEG files.

The following files are discussed in this chapter:

**Chapter11.h**　　　　　　**Chapter11.rc**　　　　　　**Chapter11.cpp**

## Chapter11 Source Files

The first file is the header file:

**CHAPTER11.H**

```
#ifndef CHAPTER11_H
#define CHAPTER11_H

#define IDM_IMPORTTRIANGLES         101
#define IDM_EXPORTBOUNDARIES        102
#define IDM_EXPORTSCREEN            103
#define IDM_EXPORTMODEL             104
#define IDM_EXIT                    105

#define IDM_GETBOUNDARIES           201

#define IDN_SHOWMENU                2

#define IDM_SHOWBOUNDARIES          301
#define IDM_SHOWTRIANGLES           302
#define IDM_COLOURBACKGROUND        303
#define IDM_COLOURCOORDSTEXT        304
#define IDM_COLOURBOUNDARIES        305
#define IDM_COLOURTRIANGLES         306
#define IDM_ZOOMEXTENTS             307
#define IDM_REDRAW                  308

#define IDN_MOUSEMENU               3

#define IDM_MOUSEZOOM               401
#define IDM_MOUSEPAN                402

#define IDM_LISTBOUNDARIESSTATS     501
#define IDM_LISTTRIANGLESSTATS      502
#define IDM_LISTBOUNDARIES          503
#define IDM_LISTTRIANGLES           504

#define IDM_ESCAPEKEY               901
```

```
#endif // CHAPTER11_H
```

As in previous chapters, **Chapter11.h** contains ID numbers for menu bar options, drop-down menus and accelerator keys.

The second file is the resource script file:

## CHAPTER11.RC

```
#include <windows.h>
#include "Chapter11.h"

Chapter11 MENU {
    POPUP "&File" {
        POPUP "&Import" {
            MENUITEM "&Triangles",          IDM_IMPORTTRIANGLES
        }
        POPUP "&Export" {
            MENUITEM "&Boundaries",         IDM_EXPORTBOUNDARIES
            MENUITEM SEPARATOR
            MENUITEM "S&creen image",       IDM_EXPORTSCREEN
            MENUITEM "&Model image",        IDM_EXPORTMODEL
        }
        MENUITEM SEPARATOR
        MENUITEM "E&xit",                   IDM_EXIT
    }
    POPUP "&Edit" {
        MENUITEM "Get boundaries",          IDM_GETBOUNDARIES
    }
    POPUP "&Show" {
        MENUITEM "&Boundaries",             IDM_SHOWBOUNDARIES
        MENUITEM "&Triangles",              IDM_SHOWTRIANGLES
        MENUITEM SEPARATOR
        POPUP "&Colour" {
            MENUITEM "Back&ground",         IDM_COLOURBACKGROUND
            MENUITEM "&Coords text",        IDM_COLOURCOORDSTEXT
            MENUITEM SEPARATOR
            MENUITEM "&Boundaries",         IDM_COLOURBOUNDARIES
            MENUITEM "&Triangles",          IDM_COLOURTRIANGLES
        }
        MENUITEM SEPARATOR
        MENUITEM "&Zoom extents",           IDM_ZOOMEXTENTS
        MENUITEM "&Redraw",                 IDM_REDRAW
    }
    POPUP "&Mouse" {
        MENUITEM "&Zoom in/out",            IDM_MOUSEZOOM
        MENUITEM "&Pan",                    IDM_MOUSEPAN
    }
    POPUP "&List" {
        POPUP "&Statistics" {
            MENUITEM "&Boundaries",         IDM_LISTBOUNDARIESSTATS
            MENUITEM "&Triangles",          IDM_LISTTRIANGLESSTATS
        }
        MENUITEM SEPARATOR
        MENUITEM "&Boundaries",             IDM_LISTBOUNDARIES
        MENUITEM "&Triangles",              IDM_LISTTRIANGLES
    }
}
```

```
Chapter11 ACCELERATORS {
    VK_ESCAPE,          IDM_ESCAPEKEY,            VIRTKEY, NOINVERT
}
```

Like previous chapters, **Chapter11.rc** defines the contents of the program's menu bar and accelerator keys. There is no custom dialog box in this program.

The third file is the source code file, which includes function listings.

## CHAPTER11.CPP

```cpp
#ifndef UNICODE
#define UNICODE
#endif

#include <windows.h>
#include <gdiplus.h>
using namespace Gdiplus;
#include "Chapter11.h"
#include "BigTask.h"
#include "FileInOut.h"
#include "TextWnd.h"
#include "Graphics.h"
#include "Colours.h"
#include "Shapes.h"
#include "Common.h"

#define ID_TEXTWND                      1
#define ID_DISPLAYWND                   2
#define ID_IMAGEEXPORT                  3

#define IDT_IMPORTTRIANGLES             11

#define IDT_EXPORTBOUNDARIES            21
#define IDT_EXPORTBOUNDARIESSCRIPT      22
#define IDT_EXPORTIMAGE                 23

#define IDT_GETBOUNDARIES               31

#define IDT_LISTBOUNDARIES              41
#define IDT_LISTTRIANGLES               42

#define GETBOUNDARIES_STEPSIZE          20L

#define PENCOLOUR_BOUNDARIES            3
#define PENCOLOUR_TRIANGLES             11

DTMTEXTWINDOW _dtmText;
DTMFILEDATA _dtmFile;
DTMBIGTASK _dtmTask, _dtmTaskDisplay;
DTMDISPLAY _dtmDisplay;
DTMCOLOURS _dtmColours;
DTMLINES _dtmBounds;
DTMTRIAS _dtmTrias;

LRESULT CALLBACK WndProc (HWND, UINT, WPARAM, LPARAM);
BOOL CarryOutTasks (HWND);
WORD DrawModel (DTMFRAME *, DTMBIGTASK *);
void InitShowDropdownMenu (HMENU);
void InitMouseDropdownMenu (HMENU);
```

```
BOOL GetBoundariesStart (HWND, UINT);
WORD GetBoundariesCont (void);

int WINAPI WinMain (HINSTANCE hInst, HINSTANCE, PSTR, int nCmdShow) {
    return InitAndRunProgram (hInst, nCmdShow, TEXT ("Chapter11"),
        TEXT ("Chapter 11: Create boundary lines"));
}

LRESULT CALLBACK WndProc (HWND hwnd, UINT message, WPARAM wParam, LPARAM lParam) {
    switch (message) {
        case WM_CREATE : {
            HINSTANCE hInst;

            hInst = ((LPCREATESTRUCT) lParam)->hInstance;
            _dtmText.Create (hwnd, ID_TEXTWND, hInst);
            _dtmFile.Init (hwnd);
            _dtmDisplay.Init (hwnd, 0, ID_DISPLAYWND, hInst,
                1.0, 4.0, 4.0, 4.0, 5.0, 1.0, 2.0, 0.5);
            _dtmColours.Init ();
            _dtmBounds.Init (TEXT ("boundary lines"), PENCOLOUR_BOUNDARIES);
            _dtmTrias.Init (TEXT ("triangles"), PENCOLOUR_TRIANGLES, 0, FALSE);
            return 0;
        }
        case WM_ENTERSIZEMOVE :
            _dtmDisplay.StartResizing ();
            return 0;
        case WM_SIZE :
            ResizeChildWindows (lParam);
            return 0;
        case WM_EXITSIZEMOVE :
            _dtmDisplay.StopResizing ();
            return 0;
        case WM_INITMENUPOPUP :
            if (HIWORD (lParam) == FALSE) {
                switch (LOWORD (lParam)) {
                case IDN_SHOWMENU :
                    InitShowDropdownMenu ((HMENU) wParam);
                    return 0;
                case IDN_MOUSEMENU :
                    InitMouseDropdownMenu ((HMENU) wParam);
                    return 0;
                default : break;
                }
            }
            break;
        case WM_COMMAND :
            if (HIWORD (wParam) == 0) {
                switch (LOWORD (wParam)) {
                    case IDM_IMPORTTRIANGLES :
                        _dtmTrias.ImportStart (hwnd, IDT_IMPORTTRIANGLES);
                        return 0;
                    case IDM_EXPORTBOUNDARIES :
                        _dtmBounds.ExportStart (IDT_EXPORTBOUNDARIES,
                            IDT_EXPORTBOUNDARIESSCRIPT);
                        return 0;
                    case IDM_EXPORTSCREEN :
                        ExportImage (FALSE, ID_IMAGEEXPORT);
                        return 0;
                    case IDM_EXPORTMODEL :
                        ExportImage (TRUE, ID_IMAGEEXPORT);
                        return 0;
```

```
                    case IDM_EXIT :
                        SendMessage (hwnd, WM_CLOSE, 0, 0);
                        return 0;
                    case IDM_GETBOUNDARIES :
                        GetBoundariesStart (hwnd, IDT_GETBOUNDARIES);
                        return 0;
                    case IDM_SHOWBOUNDARIES :
                        _dtmBounds.FlipVisible ();
                        _dtmTaskDisplay.Start ();
                        return 0;
                    case IDM_SHOWTRIANGLES :
                        _dtmTrias.FlipVisible ();
                        _dtmTaskDisplay.Start ();
                        return 0;
                    case IDM_COLOURBACKGROUND :
                        ChangeBackgroundColour (hwnd);
                        return 0;
                    case IDM_COLOURCOORDSTEXT :
                        ChangeCoordsTextColour (hwnd);
                        return 0;
                    case IDM_COLOURBOUNDARIES :
                        ChangePenColour (hwnd, PENCOLOUR_BOUNDARIES);
                        return 0;
                    case IDM_COLOURTRIANGLES :
                        ChangePenColour (hwnd, PENCOLOUR_TRIANGLES);
                        return 0;
                    case IDM_ZOOMEXTENTS :
                        _dtmDisplay.ZoomExtents ();
                        _dtmTaskDisplay.Start ();
                        return 0;
                    case IDM_REDRAW :
                        _dtmTaskDisplay.Start ();
                        return 0;
                    case IDM_MOUSEZOOM :
                        _dtmDisplay.SetMouseAction (MOUSEACT_ZOOM);
                        return 0;
                    case IDM_MOUSEPAN :
                        _dtmDisplay.SetMouseAction (MOUSEACT_PAN);
                        return 0;
                    case IDM_LISTBOUNDARIESSTATS :
                        _dtmBounds.ListStats ();
                        return 0;
                    case IDM_LISTTRIANGLESSTATS :
                        _dtmTrias.ListStats ();
                        return 0;
                    case IDM_LISTBOUNDARIES :
                        _dtmBounds.ListStart (IDT_LISTBOUNDARIES);
                        return 0;
                    case IDM_LISTTRIANGLES :
                        _dtmTrias.ListStart (IDT_LISTTRIANGLES);
                        return 0;
                    default : break;
                }
            }
            else if (HIWORD (wParam) == 1) {
                if (LOWORD (wParam) == IDM_ESCAPEKEY) {
                    _dtmTask.Quit (TRUE);
                    _dtmTaskDisplay.Quit (TRUE);
                    return 0;
                }
            }
        }
```

```
            else if (LOWORD (wParam) == ID_DISPLAYWND) {
                switch (HIWORD (wParam)) {
                    case DTM_REDRAW :
                        _dtmTaskDisplay.Start ();
                        return 0;
                    case DTM_DRAW_STOPPED :
                    case DTM_DRAW_COMPLETED :
                        _dtmDisplay.RepaintNow (REPAINT_ALL);
                        return 0;
                    default : return 0;
                }
            }
            else if (LOWORD (wParam) == ID_IMAGEEXPORT) {
                ProcessExportImageMessages (wParam, IDT_EXPORTIMAGE);
                return 0;
            }
            break;
        case WM_CLOSE :
            AskCloseWindowMessage (hwnd);
            return 0;
        case WM_DESTROY:
            _dtmDisplay.Free ();
            _dtmColours.Free ();
            _dtmText.Destroy ();
            _dtmFile.FreeImportBuffer ();
            _dtmBounds.Free ();
            _dtmTrias.Free ();
            PostQuitMessage (0);
            return 0;
        default : break;
    }
    return DefWindowProc (hwnd, message, wParam, lParam);
}

BOOL CarryOutTasks (HWND hwnd) {
    WORD wTaskStatus;

    if (!_dtmTask.IsBusy ()) {
        return FALSE;
    }
    if (_dtmTask.GetStage () == 0) {
        EnableMenuBar (hwnd, FALSE);
        _dtmDisplay.Enable (FALSE);
        _dtmTask.NextStage ();
    }
    switch (_dtmTask.GetID ()) {
        case IDT_IMPORTTRIANGLES :
            wTaskStatus = _dtmTrias.ImportCont (FALSE);
            break;
        case IDT_EXPORTBOUNDARIES :
            wTaskStatus = _dtmBounds.ExportCont (FALSE);
            break;
        case IDT_EXPORTBOUNDARIESSCRIPT :
            wTaskStatus = _dtmBounds.ExportCont (TRUE);
            break;
        case IDT_EXPORTIMAGE :
            wTaskStatus = DrawModel (_dtmDisplay.GetImageDtmPtr (), &_dtmTask);
            break;
        case IDT_GETBOUNDARIES :
            wTaskStatus = GetBoundariesCont ();
            break;
```

```
            case IDT_LISTBOUNDARIES :
                wTaskStatus = _dtmBounds.ListCont ();
                break;
            case IDT_LISTTRIANGLES :
                wTaskStatus = _dtmTrias.ListCont ();
                break;
            default :
                wTaskStatus = TASK_STOPPED;
                break;
    }
    if ((wTaskStatus & TASK_STOPPED) || (wTaskStatus & TASK_COMPLETED)) {
        EnableMenuBar (hwnd, TRUE);
        _dtmDisplay.Enable (TRUE);
        _dtmTask.Stop ();
    }
    if (wTaskStatus & TASK_COMPLETED) {
        switch (_dtmTask.GetID ()) {
            case IDT_IMPORTTRIANGLES :
                AddShapeToDisplay (&_dtmTrias);
                break;
            case IDT_GETBOUNDARIES :
                AddShapeToDisplay (&_dtmBounds);
                break;
            default : break;
        }
    }
    if (wTaskStatus & TASK_REDRAW) {
        _dtmTaskDisplay.Start ();
    }
    return TRUE;
}

WORD DrawModel (DTMFRAME * pdtmFrame, DTMBIGTASK * pdtmTask) {
    if (pdtmFrame == NULL || !pdtmFrame->IsActive () ||
        !pdtmFrame->IsGdiOK () || pdtmTask == NULL) {
        return TASK_STOPPED;
    }
    if (pdtmTask->Quit ()) {
        pdtmFrame->NotifyParent (DTM_DRAW_STOPPED);
        return TASK_STOPPED;
    }
    switch (pdtmTask->GetStage ()) {
        case 1 :
            pdtmFrame->ClearBackground ();
            _dtmColours.SetPenWidths (pdtmFrame->GetPenWidth (),
                pdtmFrame->GetVertExag ());
            pdtmTask->NextStage ();
            break;
        case 2 :
            _dtmTrias.Draw (pdtmFrame, pdtmTask);
            break;
        case 3 :
            _dtmBounds.Draw (pdtmFrame, pdtmTask);
            break;
        default : break;
    }
    pdtmFrame->NotifyParent (DTM_DRAW_UPDATED);
    if (pdtmTask->GetStage () < 4) {
        return TASK_ONGOING;
    }
    pdtmFrame->NotifyParent (DTM_DRAW_COMPLETED);
```

```
        return TASK_COMPLETED;
}

void InitShowDropdownMenu (HMENU hMenu) {
    CheckMenuItem (hMenu, IDM_SHOWBOUNDARIES, MF_BYCOMMAND |
        (_dtmBounds.IsVisible () ? MF_CHECKED : MF_UNCHECKED));
    CheckMenuItem (hMenu, IDM_SHOWTRIANGLES, MF_BYCOMMAND |
        (_dtmTrias.IsVisible () ? MF_CHECKED : MF_UNCHECKED));
}

void InitMouseDropdownMenu (HMENU hMenu) {
    DTMMOUSEACT mouseAction;

    mouseAction = _dtmDisplay.GetMouseAction ();
    CheckMenuItem (hMenu, IDM_MOUSEZOOM, MF_BYCOMMAND |
        (mouseAction == MOUSEACT_ZOOM ? MF_CHECKED : MF_UNCHECKED));
    CheckMenuItem (hMenu, IDM_MOUSEPAN, MF_BYCOMMAND |
        (mouseAction == MOUSEACT_PAN ? MF_CHECKED : MF_UNCHECKED));
}

BOOL GetBoundariesStart (HWND hwnd, UINT uTaskID) {
    if (_dtmTask.IsBusy ()) {
        _dtmText.Output (_szTaskBusyMessage);
        return FALSE;
    }
    if (_dtmTrias.GetTotal () == 0L) {
        _dtmText.Output (TEXT ("There are no %s available. Unable to ") \
            TEXT ("get boundaries\r\n"), _dtmTrias.GetDescription ());
        return FALSE;
    }
    if (_dtmBounds.GetTotal () != 0L) {
        int iMessage;

        iMessage = MessageBox (hwnd,
            TEXT ("Do you want to discard all boundary lines already created?"),
            TEXT ("Getting boundary lines "), MB_YESNOCANCEL | MB_ICONWARNING);
        if (iMessage == IDCANCEL) {
            return FALSE;
        }
        else if (iMessage == IDYES) {
            _dtmBounds.Free ();
        }
    }
    _dtmText.Output (TEXT ("Getting boundary lines\r\n"));
    _dtmTask.Start (uTaskID, GETBOUNDARIES_STEPSIZE);
    return TRUE;
}

WORD GetBoundariesCont (void) {
    static DTMLINES dtmNotBounds;
    static DWORD dwTotalAtStart;

    if (_dtmTask.AtStart ()) {
        dtmNotBounds.Init (NULL, 0);
        dwTotalAtStart = _dtmBounds.GetTotal ();
    }
    if (_dtmTask.Quit ()) {
        _dtmText.Output (TEXT ("\r\nGetting boundary lines stopped\r\n"));
        dtmNotBounds.Free ();
        return TASK_STOPPED | TASK_REDRAW;
    }
```

```
    _dtmTask.StartNewBatch ();
    while (!_dtmTask.NoMoreItems (_dtmTrias.GetTotal ()) && !_dtmTask.AtEndOfBatch ()) {
        DTMTRIA * pdtmTria;
        WORD wEdge;

        pdtmTria = _dtmTrias.GetPtr (_dtmTask.GetItemNumber ());
        for (wEdge = 0; wEdge < TRIA_COORDS; wEdge ++) {
            DTMLINE dtmBoundary;

            _dtmTrias.GetEdge (pdtmTria, wEdge,
                &(dtmBoundary.cdEnd [0]), &(dtmBoundary.cdEnd [1]));
            if (_dtmBounds.Match (&dtmBoundary)) {
                _dtmBounds.Remove (&dtmBoundary);
                dtmNotBounds.Add (&dtmBoundary);
            }
            else if (!dtmNotBounds.Match (&dtmBoundary)) {
                dtmBoundary.wColour = PENCOLOUR_BOUNDARIES;
                _dtmBounds.Add (&dtmBoundary);
            }
        }
        _dtmTask.NextItem ();
        _dtmTask.IncBatchCounter ();
    }
    _dtmText.ProgressDot ();
    if (!_dtmTask.NoMoreItems (_dtmTrias.GetTotal ())) {
        return TASK_ONGOING;
    }
    _dtmBounds.ResetLimits ();
    dtmNotBounds.Free ();
    _dtmText.Output (TEXT ("\r\nNumber of %s created: %lu\r\n"),
        _dtmBounds.GetDescription (), _dtmBounds.GetTotal () - dwTotalAtStart);
    return TASK_COMPLETED | TASK_REDRAW;
}
```

**Chapter11.cpp** has the same layout as source code files in earlier chapters in this book. It starts with the header files followed by child window IDs, task IDs, the task batch size constant GETBOUNDARIES_STEPSIZE which is used when creating the boundary or boundaries around the DTM, and coloured pen numbers.

It then defines eight global variables, most of which are the same as in earlier chapters. _dtmBounds_ contains the boundary lines created by the program.

Seven functions are then declared, followed by the C++ source code.

The functions _WinMain_, _WndProc_, _CarryOutTasks_, _DrawModel_, _InitShowDropdownMenu_ and _InitMouseDropdownMenu_ are similar to the equivalent functions in earlier chapters. The user can import triangles, create boundary lines and export boundary lines. _DrawModel_ draws the triangles first, followed by the boundary lines.

The function _GetBoundariesStart_ starts the task that creates boundary lines around the DTM triangles. _hwnd_ is the handle of the parent window and _uTaskID_ is the task ID number. If there are no triangles in the triangles array _dtmTrias_, the function displays an error message. If the lines array _dtmBounds_ already contains some boundary lines, the function asks the user if they want to discard these lines. If the user selects 'Yes', any existing boundary lines are discarded. Finally, _GetBoundariesStart_ displays a message in the text window and starts the task. The function returns TRUE if successful, or FALSE if the user cancels the task or an error occurs.

The function *GetBoundariesCont* carries out the task of creating boundary lines around the DTM triangles. *GetBoundariesCont* follows the standard task manager template as discussed in Chapter 1, looking at each triangle in the triangles array *_dtmTrias* in batches. If at the start of the task, as well as storing the number of lines already in *_dtmBounds*, the function initialises *dtmNotBounds* which is a lines array containing triangle edges which are not boundary lines. *dtmNotBounds* is only used within *GetBoundariesCont*. As discussed in Chapters 1 and 9, it's important that *dtmNotBounds* is initialised before *GetBoundariesCont* checks if the task has been cancelled, as otherwise *dtmNotBounds* could be freed before it has been initialised, which could cause the program to stop working. Within the while-loop, *GetBoundariesCont* looks at each edge of each triangle and stores it in *_dtmBounds* if no other triangle shares the edge, or in *dtmNotBounds* if the edge is shared with another triangle. This is achieved by the following two steps:

(i) If the edge is already in *_dtmBounds*, remove it from *_dtmBounds* and add it to *dtmNotBounds* because it is a shared edge.

(ii) If the edge is not in *_dtmBounds* and not in *dtmNotBounds*, add it to *_dtmBounds* because this edge is not shared with any other triangles, so far.

For example, all three edges of the first triangle in *_dtmTrias* will be added to *_dtmBounds*, and only transferred to *dtmNotBounds* if and when shared edges are identified while checking subsequent triangles in *_dtmTrias*. Triangle edges are only added to *dtmNotBounds* if they are initially in *_dtmBounds*. When the task is finished, *GetBoundariesCont* updates the minimum and maximum x,y,z values for *_dtmBounds*, frees the contents of *dtmNotBounds* as it is no longer needed, and displays the numbers of boundary lines added to *_dtmBounds*. The function returns the TASK_ constants as discussed in Chapter 1.

## Running Chapter11

Before you can compile and run your program, you need to add the following nineteen source files to your Chapter11 project. Refer to Chapter 1 for how to do this:

| | | |
|---|---|---|
| TextWnd.h | TextWnd.cpp | |
| FileInOut.h | FileInOut.cpp | |
| BigTask.h | BigTask.cpp | |
| Graphics.h | Graphics.cpp | |
| Colours.h | Colours.cpp | |
| Shapes.h | Shapes.cpp | |
| Lines.cpp | Triangles.cpp | |
| Common.h | Common.cpp | |
| Chapter11.h | Chapter11.cpp | Chapter11.rc |

You also need to add the Gdiplus.lib library file as an 'additional dependency' in your project's linker/input settings. Refer to Chapter 2 for how to do this. Finally, don't forget to set Chapter11 as your start-up project.

Otherwise, assuming you have compiled the code for Chapter11 successfully, and it is running, you can now test it out.

Start by importing your DTM of 3D triangles. Click on 'File' in the menu bar, then select 'Import' from the drop-down menu, and finally click on 'Triangles'. Next, select a file containing the triangles data. You can use the sample file Triangles.txt. Then click on 'Edit' in the menu bar, and select 'Get boundaries' from the drop-down menu. If successful, the program's window should look something like this (the colours have been changed to make the boundary lines more prominent):

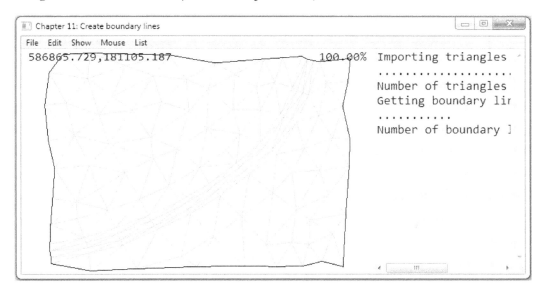

The boundary is the dark line around the outside of the model.

You can also try out the sample file Triangles_Ch11.txt which contains a DTM with two separate sets of triangles, one of which contains a hole. When you import this file, via 'File', 'Import', 'Triangles', click on 'Yes' to the message box asking if you wish to discard the existing triangles. Then create a new set of boundaries, via 'Edit', 'Get boundaries', again clicking on 'Yes' when a message box appears asking if you wish to discard existing boundary lines. If successful, the program's window should look like the image over the page.

You can also hide the triangles, via 'Show' in the menu and then 'Triangles' in the drop-down menu to remove the tick next to 'Triangles'. The triangles should no longer appear in the graphics window, making it easier to see all the boundaries and to identify any unwanted boundaries created by missing triangles. Chapter09 is better at identifying missing triangles in the DTM than Chapter04 in Chapter 4, which uses triangles filled with colour to identify holes and thus any missing triangles.

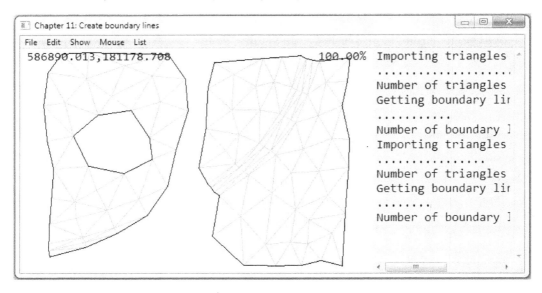

You can also export boundary lines as CAD script files, as text files or as JPEG files via 'File', 'Export'.

As in previous chapters, to exit the program click on 'File' in the menu bar, select 'Exit' and then choose 'Yes' in the message box that appears.

# Chapter 12

## Calculate Intersection Between Two DTMs

Chapter 12 lists the source code for a program called **Chapter12** that calculates the intersection between two DTMs, creating 3D lines along the intersection which can be exported as CAD script files, as text files or as JPEG files.

The following files are discussed in this chapter:

**Chapter12.h**                **Chapter12.rc**                **Chapter12.cpp**

## Chapter12 Source Files

The first file is the header file:

**CHAPTER12.H**

```
#ifndef CHAPTER12_H
#define CHAPTER12_H

#define IDM_IMPORTTRIANGLES1          101
#define IDM_IMPORTTRIANGLES2          102
#define IDM_EXPORTINTERSECTION        103
#define IDM_EXPORTSCREEN              104
#define IDM_EXPORTMODEL               105
#define IDM_EXIT                      106

#define IDM_GETINTERSECTION           201

#define IDN_SHOWMENU                  2

#define IDM_SHOWINTERSECTION          301
#define IDM_SHOWTRIANGLES1            302
#define IDM_SHOWTRIANGLES2            303
#define IDM_COLOURBACKGROUND          304
#define IDM_COLOURCOORDSTEXT          305
#define IDM_COLOURINTERSECTION        306
#define IDM_COLOURTRIANGLES1          307
#define IDM_COLOURTRIANGLES2          308
#define IDM_ZOOMEXTENTS               309
#define IDM_REDRAW                    310

#define IDN_MOUSEMENU                 3

#define IDM_MOUSEZOOM                 401
#define IDM_MOUSEPAN                  402

#define IDM_LISTINTERSECTIONSTATS     501
#define IDM_LISTTRIANGLES1STATS       502
#define IDM_LISTTRIANGLES2STATS       503
#define IDM_LISTINTERSECTION          504
#define IDM_LISTTRIANGLES1            505
#define IDM_LISTTRIANGLES2            506
```

```
#define IDM_ESCAPEKEY              901

#endif // CHAPTER12_H
```

As in previous chapters, **Chapter12.h** contains ID numbers for menu bar options, drop-down menus and accelerator keys.

The second file is the resource script file:

**CHAPTER12.RC**

```
#include <windows.h>
#include "Chapter12.h"

Chapter12 MENU {
    POPUP "&File" {
        POPUP "&Import" {
            MENUITEM "&Primary triangles",       IDM_IMPORTTRIANGLES1
            MENUITEM "&Secondary triangles",     IDM_IMPORTTRIANGLES2
        }
        POPUP "&Export" {
            MENUITEM "&Intersection",            IDM_EXPORTINTERSECTION
            MENUITEM SEPARATOR
            MENUITEM "S&creen image",            IDM_EXPORTSCREEN
            MENUITEM "&Model image",             IDM_EXPORTMODEL
        }
        MENUITEM SEPARATOR
        MENUITEM "E&xit",                        IDM_EXIT
    }
    POPUP "&Edit" {
        MENUITEM "Get &intersection",            IDM_GETINTERSECTION
    }
    POPUP "&Show" {
        MENUITEM "&Intersection",                IDM_SHOWINTERSECTION
        MENUITEM "&Primary triangles",           IDM_SHOWTRIANGLES1
        MENUITEM "&Secondary triangles",         IDM_SHOWTRIANGLES2
        MENUITEM SEPARATOR
        POPUP "&Colour" {
            MENUITEM "Back&ground",              IDM_COLOURBACKGROUND
            MENUITEM "&Coords text",             IDM_COLOURCOORDSTEXT
            MENUITEM SEPARATOR
            MENUITEM "&Intersection",            IDM_COLOURINTERSECTION
            MENUITEM "&Primary triangles",       IDM_COLOURTRIANGLES1
            MENUITEM "&Secondary triangles",     IDM_COLOURTRIANGLES2
        }
        MENUITEM SEPARATOR
        MENUITEM "&Zoom extents",                IDM_ZOOMEXTENTS
        MENUITEM "&Redraw",                      IDM_REDRAW
    }
    POPUP "&Mouse" {
        MENUITEM "&Zoom in/out",                 IDM_MOUSEZOOM
        MENUITEM "&Pan",                         IDM_MOUSEPAN
    }
    POPUP "&List" {
        POPUP "&Statistics" {
            MENUITEM "&Intersection",            IDM_LISTINTERSECTIONSTATS
            MENUITEM "&Primary triangles",       IDM_LISTTRIANGLES1STATS
            MENUITEM "&Secondary triangles",     IDM_LISTTRIANGLES2STATS
        }
        MENUITEM SEPARATOR
```

```
        MENUITEM "&Intersection",                    IDM_LISTINTERSECTION
        MENUITEM "&Primary triangles",               IDM_LISTTRIANGLES1
        MENUITEM "&Secondary triangles",             IDM_LISTTRIANGLES2
    }
}

Chapter12 ACCELERATORS {
    VK_ESCAPE,        IDM_ESCAPEKEY,               VIRTKEY, NOINVERT
}
```

Like previous chapters, **Chapter12.rc** defines the contents of the program's menu bar and accelerator keys. There is no custom dialog box in this program.

The third file is the source code file, which includes function listings.

## CHAPTER12.CPP

```
#ifndef UNICODE
#define UNICODE
#endif

#include <windows.h>
#include <gdiplus.h>
using namespace Gdiplus;
#include <math.h>
#include "Chapter12.h"
#include "BigTask.h"
#include "FileInOut.h"
#include "TextWnd.h"
#include "Graphics.h"
#include "Colours.h"
#include "Shapes.h"
#include "Common.h"

#define ID_TEXTWND                      1
#define ID_DISPLAYWND                   2
#define ID_IMAGEEXPORT                  3

#define IDT_IMPORTTRIANGLES1            11
#define IDT_IMPORTTRIANGLES2            12

#define IDT_EXPORTINTERSECTION          21
#define IDT_EXPORTINTERSECTIONSCRIPT    22
#define IDT_EXPORTIMAGE                 23

#define IDT_GETINTERSECTION             31

#define IDT_LISTINTERSECTION            41
#define IDT_LISTTRIANGLES1              42
#define IDT_LISTTRIANGLES2              43

#define GETINTERSECTION_STEPSIZE        20L

#define PENCOLOUR_INTERSECTION          0
#define PENCOLOUR_TRIANGLES1            11
#define PENCOLOUR_TRIANGLES2            4

DTMTEXTWINDOW _dtmText;
DTMFILEDATA _dtmFile;
DTMBIGTASK _dtmTask, _dtmTaskDisplay;
```

```
DTMDISPLAY _dtmDisplay;
DTMCOLOURS _dtmColours;
DTMLINES _dtmInter;
DTMTRIAS _dtmTrias1, _dtmTrias2;

LRESULT CALLBACK WndProc (HWND, UINT, WPARAM, LPARAM);
BOOL CarryOutTasks (HWND);
WORD DrawModel (DTMFRAME *, DTMBIGTASK *);
void InitShowDropdownMenu (HMENU);
void InitMouseDropdownMenu (HMENU);
BOOL GetIntersectionStart (HWND, UINT);
WORD GetIntersectionCont (void);
BOOL GetIntersectionLine (DTMTRIA *, DTMTRIA *, DTMLINE *);

int WINAPI WinMain (HINSTANCE hInst, HINSTANCE, PSTR, int nCmdShow) {
    return InitAndRunProgram (hInst, nCmdShow, TEXT ("Chapter12"),
        TEXT ("Chapter 12: Calculate intersection between DTMs"));
}

LRESULT CALLBACK WndProc (HWND hwnd, UINT message, WPARAM wParam, LPARAM lParam) {
    switch (message) {
        case WM_CREATE : {
            HINSTANCE hInst;

            hInst = ((LPCREATESTRUCT) lParam)->hInstance;
            _dtmText.Create (hwnd, ID_TEXTWND, hInst);
            _dtmFile.Init (hwnd);
            _dtmDisplay.Init (hwnd, 0, ID_DISPLAYWND, hInst,
                1.0, 4.0, 4.0, 4.0, 5.0, 1.0, 2.0, 0.5);
            _dtmColours.Init ();
            _dtmInter.Init (TEXT ("intersection lines"), PENCOLOUR_INTERSECTION);
            _dtmTrias1.Init (TEXT ("primary triangles"), PENCOLOUR_TRIANGLES1,
                0, FALSE);
            _dtmTrias2.Init (TEXT ("secondary triangles"), PENCOLOUR_TRIANGLES2,
                0, FALSE);
            return 0;
        }
        case WM_ENTERSIZEMOVE :
            _dtmDisplay.StartResizing ();
            return 0;
        case WM_SIZE :
            ResizeChildWindows (lParam);
            return 0;
        case WM_EXITSIZEMOVE :
            _dtmDisplay.StopResizing ();
            return 0;
        case WM_INITMENUPOPUP :
            if (HIWORD (lParam) == FALSE) {
                switch (LOWORD (lParam)) {
                case IDN_SHOWMENU :
                    InitShowDropdownMenu ((HMENU) wParam);
                    return 0;
                case IDN_MOUSEMENU :
                    InitMouseDropdownMenu ((HMENU) wParam);
                    return 0;
                default : break;
                }
            }
            break;
        case WM_COMMAND :
            if (HIWORD (wParam) == 0) {
```

```
switch (LOWORD (wParam)) {
    case IDM_IMPORTTRIANGLES1 :
        _dtmTrias1.ImportStart (hwnd, IDT_IMPORTTRIANGLES1);
        return 0;
    case IDM_IMPORTTRIANGLES2 :
        _dtmTrias2.ImportStart (hwnd, IDT_IMPORTTRIANGLES2);
        return 0;
    case IDM_EXPORTINTERSECTION :
        _dtmInter.ExportStart (IDT_EXPORTINTERSECTION,
            IDT_EXPORTINTERSECTIONSCRIPT);
        return 0;
    case IDM_EXPORTSCREEN :
        ExportImage (FALSE, ID_IMAGEEXPORT);
        return 0;
    case IDM_EXPORTMODEL :
        ExportImage (TRUE, ID_IMAGEEXPORT);
        return 0;
    case IDM_EXIT :
        SendMessage (hwnd, WM_CLOSE, 0, 0);
        return 0;
    case IDM_GETINTERSECTION :
        GetIntersectionStart (hwnd, IDT_GETINTERSECTION);
        return 0;
    case IDM_SHOWINTERSECTION :
        _dtmInter.FlipVisible ();
        _dtmTaskDisplay.Start ();
        return 0;
    case IDM_SHOWTRIANGLES1 :
        _dtmTrias1.FlipVisible ();
        _dtmTaskDisplay.Start ();
        return 0;
    case IDM_SHOWTRIANGLES2 :
        _dtmTrias2.FlipVisible ();
        _dtmTaskDisplay.Start ();
        return 0;
    case IDM_COLOURBACKGROUND :
        ChangeBackgroundColour (hwnd);
        return 0;
    case IDM_COLOURCOORDSTEXT :
        ChangeCoordsTextColour (hwnd);
        return 0;
    case IDM_COLOURINTERSECTION :
        ChangePenColour (hwnd, PENCOLOUR_INTERSECTION);
        return 0;
    case IDM_COLOURTRIANGLES1 :
        ChangePenColour (hwnd, PENCOLOUR_TRIANGLES1);
        return 0;
    case IDM_COLOURTRIANGLES2 :
        ChangePenColour (hwnd, PENCOLOUR_TRIANGLES2);
        return 0;
    case IDM_ZOOMEXTENTS :
        _dtmDisplay.ZoomExtents ();
        _dtmTaskDisplay.Start ();
        return 0;
    case IDM_REDRAW :
        _dtmTaskDisplay.Start ();
        return 0;
    case IDM_MOUSEZOOM :
        _dtmDisplay.SetMouseAction (MOUSEACT_ZOOM);
        return 0;
    case IDM_MOUSEPAN :
```

```
                    _dtmDisplay.SetMouseAction (MOUSEACT_PAN);
                    return 0;
                case IDM_LISTINTERSECTIONSTATS :
                    _dtmInter.ListStats ();
                    return 0;
                case IDM_LISTTRIANGLES1STATS :
                    _dtmTrias1.ListStats ();
                    return 0;
                case IDM_LISTTRIANGLES2STATS :
                    _dtmTrias2.ListStats ();
                    return 0;
                case IDM_LISTINTERSECTION :
                    _dtmInter.ListStart (IDT_LISTINTERSECTION);
                    return 0;
                case IDM_LISTTRIANGLES1 :
                    _dtmTrias1.ListStart (IDT_LISTTRIANGLES1);
                    return 0;
                case IDM_LISTTRIANGLES2 :
                    _dtmTrias2.ListStart (IDT_LISTTRIANGLES2);
                    return 0;
                default : break;
            }
        }
        else if (HIWORD (wParam) == 1) {
            if (LOWORD (wParam) == IDM_ESCAPEKEY) {
                _dtmTask.Quit (TRUE);
                _dtmTaskDisplay.Quit (TRUE);
                return 0;
            }
        }
        else if (LOWORD (wParam) == ID_DISPLAYWND) {
            switch (HIWORD (wParam)) {
                case DTM_REDRAW :
                    _dtmTaskDisplay.Start ();
                    return 0;
                case DTM_DRAW_STOPPED :
                case DTM_DRAW_COMPLETED :
                    _dtmDisplay.RepaintNow (REPAINT_ALL);
                    return 0;
                default : return 0;
            }
        }
        else if (LOWORD (wParam) == ID_IMAGEEXPORT) {
            ProcessExportImageMessages (wParam, IDT_EXPORTIMAGE);
            return 0;
        }
        break;
    case WM_CLOSE :
        AskCloseWindowMessage (hwnd);
        return 0;
    case WM_DESTROY:
        _dtmDisplay.Free ();
        _dtmColours.Free ();
        _dtmText.Destroy ();
        _dtmFile.FreeImportBuffer ();
        _dtmInter.Free ();
        _dtmTrias1.Free ();
        _dtmTrias2.Free ();
        PostQuitMessage (0);
        return 0;
    default : break;
```

```
    }
    return DefWindowProc (hwnd, message, wParam, lParam);
}

BOOL CarryOutTasks (HWND hwnd) {
    WORD wTaskStatus;

    if (!_dtmTask.IsBusy ()) {
        return FALSE;
    }
    if (_dtmTask.GetStage () == 0) {
        EnableMenuBar (hwnd, FALSE);
        _dtmDisplay.Enable (FALSE);
        _dtmTask.NextStage ();
    }
    switch (_dtmTask.GetID ()) {
        case IDT_IMPORTTRIANGLES1 :
            wTaskStatus = _dtmTrias1.ImportCont (FALSE);
            break;
        case IDT_IMPORTTRIANGLES2 :
            wTaskStatus = _dtmTrias2.ImportCont (FALSE);
            break;
        case IDT_EXPORTINTERSECTION :
            wTaskStatus = _dtmInter.ExportCont (FALSE);
            break;
        case IDT_EXPORTINTERSECTIONSCRIPT :
            wTaskStatus = _dtmInter.ExportCont (TRUE);
            break;
        case IDT_EXPORTIMAGE :
            wTaskStatus = DrawModel (_dtmDisplay.GetImageDtmPtr (), &_dtmTask);
            break;
        case IDT_GETINTERSECTION :
            wTaskStatus = GetIntersectionCont ();
            break;
        case IDT_LISTINTERSECTION :
            wTaskStatus = _dtmInter.ListCont ();
            break;
        case IDT_LISTTRIANGLES1 :
            wTaskStatus = _dtmTrias1.ListCont ();
            break;
        case IDT_LISTTRIANGLES2 :
            wTaskStatus = _dtmTrias2.ListCont ();
            break;
        default :
            wTaskStatus = TASK_STOPPED;
            break;
    }
    if ((wTaskStatus & TASK_STOPPED) || (wTaskStatus & TASK_COMPLETED)) {
        EnableMenuBar (hwnd, TRUE);
        _dtmDisplay.Enable (TRUE);
        _dtmTask.Stop ();
    }
    if (wTaskStatus & TASK_COMPLETED) {
        switch (_dtmTask.GetID ()) {
            case IDT_IMPORTTRIANGLES1 :
                AddShapeToDisplay (&_dtmTrias1);
                break;
            case IDT_IMPORTTRIANGLES2 :
                AddShapeToDisplay (&_dtmTrias2);
                break;
            case IDT_GETINTERSECTION :
```

```
                AddShapeToDisplay (&_dtmInter);
                break;
            default : break;
        }
    }
    if (wTaskStatus & TASK_REDRAW) {
        _dtmTaskDisplay.Start ();
    }
    return TRUE;
}

WORD DrawModel (DTMFRAME * pdtmFrame, DTMBIGTASK * pdtmTask) {
    if (pdtmFrame == NULL || !pdtmFrame->IsActive () ||
        !pdtmFrame->IsGdiOK () || pdtmTask == NULL) {
        return TASK_STOPPED;
    }
    if (pdtmTask->Quit ()) {
        pdtmFrame->NotifyParent (DTM_DRAW_STOPPED);
        return TASK_STOPPED;
    }
    switch (pdtmTask->GetStage ()) {
        case 1 :
            pdtmFrame->ClearBackground ();
            _dtmColours.SetPenWidths (pdtmFrame->GetPenWidth (),
                pdtmFrame->GetVertExag ());
            pdtmTask->NextStage ();
            break;
        case 2 :
            _dtmTrias1.Draw (pdtmFrame, pdtmTask);
            break;
        case 3 :
            _dtmTrias2.Draw (pdtmFrame, pdtmTask);
            break;
        case 4 :
            _dtmInter.Draw (pdtmFrame, pdtmTask);
            break;
        default : break;
    }
    pdtmFrame->NotifyParent (DTM_DRAW_UPDATED);
    if (pdtmTask->GetStage () < 5) {
        return TASK_ONGOING;
    }
    pdtmFrame->NotifyParent (DTM_DRAW_COMPLETED);
    return TASK_COMPLETED;
}

void InitShowDropdownMenu (HMENU hMenu) {
    CheckMenuItem (hMenu, IDM_SHOWINTERSECTION, MF_BYCOMMAND |
        (_dtmInter.IsVisible () ? MF_CHECKED : MF_UNCHECKED));
    CheckMenuItem (hMenu, IDM_SHOWTRIANGLES1, MF_BYCOMMAND |
        (_dtmTrias1.IsVisible () ? MF_CHECKED : MF_UNCHECKED));
    CheckMenuItem (hMenu, IDM_SHOWTRIANGLES2, MF_BYCOMMAND |
        (_dtmTrias2.IsVisible () ? MF_CHECKED : MF_UNCHECKED));
}

void InitMouseDropdownMenu (HMENU hMenu) {
    DTMMOUSEACT mouseAction;

    mouseAction = _dtmDisplay.GetMouseAction ();
    CheckMenuItem (hMenu, IDM_MOUSEZOOM, MF_BYCOMMAND |
        (mouseAction == MOUSEACT_ZOOM ? MF_CHECKED : MF_UNCHECKED));
```

```
        CheckMenuItem (hMenu, IDM_MOUSEPAN, MF_BYCOMMAND |
            (mouseAction == MOUSEACT_PAN ? MF_CHECKED : MF_UNCHECKED));
}

BOOL GetIntersectionStart (HWND hwnd, UINT uTaskID) {
    if (_dtmTask.IsBusy ()) {
        _dtmText.Output (_szTaskBusyMessage);
        return FALSE;
    }
    if (_dtmTrias1.GetTotal () == 0L) {
        _dtmText.Output (TEXT ("There are no %s available. ") \
            TEXT ("Unable to calculate %s\r\n"),
            _dtmTrias1.GetDescription (), _dtmInter.GetDescription ());
        return FALSE;
    }
    if (_dtmTrias2.GetTotal () == 0L) {
        _dtmText.Output (TEXT ("There are no %s available. ") \
            TEXT ("Unable to calculate %s\r\n"),
            _dtmTrias2.GetDescription (), _dtmInter.GetDescription ());
        return FALSE;
    }
    if (_dtmInter.GetTotal () != 0L) {
        int iMessage;

        iMessage = MessageBox (hwnd,
            TEXT ("Do you want to discard intersection lines already created?"),
            TEXT ("Intersection lines"), MB_YESNOCANCEL | MB_ICONWARNING);
        if (iMessage == IDCANCEL) {
            return FALSE;
        }
        else if (iMessage == IDYES) {
            _dtmInter.Free ();
        }
    }
    _dtmText.Output (TEXT ("Getting %s\r\n"), _dtmInter.GetDescription ());
    _dtmTask.Start (uTaskID, GETINTERSECTION_STEPSIZE);
    return TRUE;
}

WORD GetIntersectionCont (void) {
    static DWORD dwTotalAtStart;

    if (_dtmTask.AtStart ()) {
        dwTotalAtStart = _dtmInter.GetTotal ();
    }
    if (_dtmTask.Quit ()) {
        _dtmText.Output (TEXT ("\r\nGetting %s stopped\r\n"),
            _dtmInter.GetDescription ());
        return TASK_STOPPED | TASK_REDRAW;
    }
    _dtmTask.StartNewBatch ();
    while (!_dtmTask.NoMoreItems (_dtmTrias1.GetTotal ()) &&
        !_dtmTask.AtEndOfBatch ()) {
        DTMTRIA * pdtmTria1, * pdtmTria2;
        DWORD dwTria2;

        pdtmTria1 = _dtmTrias1.GetPtr (_dtmTask.GetItemNumber ());
        dwTria2 = 0L;
        pdtmTria2 = _dtmTrias2.GetPtr (dwTria2);
        while (dwTria2 < _dtmTrias2.GetTotal () &&
            pdtmTria2->cdMin.rX <= pdtmTria1->cdMax.rX) {
```

```
            DTMLINE dtmInter;

            if (GetIntersectionLine (pdtmTria1, pdtmTria2, &dtmInter)) {
                dtmInter.wColour = PENCOLOUR_INTERSECTION;
                _dtmInter.Add (&dtmInter);
            }
            dwTria2 ++;
            pdtmTria2 = _dtmTrias2.GetPtr (dwTria2);
        }
        _dtmTask.NextItem ();
        _dtmTask.IncBatchCounter ();
    }
    _dtmText.ProgressDot ();
    if (!_dtmTask.NoMoreItems (_dtmTrias1.GetTotal ())) {
        return TASK_ONGOING;
    }
    _dtmText.Output (TEXT ("\r\nNumber of %s created: %lu\r\n"),
        _dtmInter.GetDescription (), _dtmInter.GetTotal () - dwTotalAtStart);
    return TASK_COMPLETED | TASK_REDRAW;
}

BOOL GetIntersectionLine (DTMTRIA * pdtmTria1, DTMTRIA * pdtmTria2,
    DTMLINE * pdtmInter) {
    WORD wPlane;
    DOUBLE rX1, rY1, rZ1, rX2, rY2, rZ2;
    DOUBLE rFactorX [2], rFactorY [2], rFactorZ [2], rFx, rFy, rFz;
    DTMLINE dtmLine;
    DOUBLE rAlongTria1 [2], rAlongTria2 [2], rAlongFrom, rAlongTo;

    if (pdtmTria1 == NULL || pdtmTria2 == NULL || pdtmInter == NULL) {
        return FALSE;
    }
    if (pdtmTria1->cdMin.rX > pdtmTria2->cdMax.rX ||
        pdtmTria1->cdMin.rY > pdtmTria2->cdMax.rY ||
        pdtmTria1->cdMax.rY < pdtmTria2->cdMin.rY) {
        return FALSE;
    }
    for (wPlane = 0; wPlane < 2; wPlane ++) {
        DTMTRIA * pdtmTria;
        DOUBLE rX3, rY3, rZ3, rDenominator, rNumerator;

        pdtmTria = (wPlane == 0) ? pdtmTria1 : pdtmTria2;
        _dtmTrias1.GetCorner (pdtmTria, 0, &rX1, &rY1, &rZ1);
        _dtmTrias1.GetCorner (pdtmTria, 1, &rX2, &rY2, &rZ2);
        _dtmTrias1.GetCorner (pdtmTria, 2, &rX3, &rY3, &rZ3);
        rDenominator = (rX1 - rX2) * (rY1 - rY3) - (rX1 - rX3) * (rY1 - rY2);
        if (rDenominator == 0.0) {
            return FALSE;
        }
        rNumerator = (rY1 - rY3) * (rZ1 - rZ2) - (rY1 - rY2) * (rZ1 - rZ3);
        rFactorX [wPlane] = rNumerator / rDenominator;
        rNumerator = (rX1 - rX2) * (rZ1 - rZ3) - (rX1 - rX3) * (rZ1 - rZ2);
        rFactorY [wPlane] = rNumerator / rDenominator;
        rFactorZ [wPlane] = rZ1 - rFactorX [wPlane] * rX1 - rFactorY [wPlane] * rY1;
    }
    rFx = rFactorX [1] - rFactorX [0];
    rFy = rFactorY [1] - rFactorY [0];
    rFz = rFactorZ [1] - rFactorZ [0];
    if (fabs (rFx) < FUZZFACTOR && fabs (rFy) < FUZZFACTOR) {
        return FALSE;
    }
```

```
        if (fabs (rFx) > fabs (rFy)) {
            dtmLine.cdEnd [0].rY = min (pdtmTria1->cdMin.rY, pdtmTria2->cdMin.rY);
            dtmLine.cdEnd [0].rX = (rFz + rFy * dtmLine.cdEnd [0].rY) / -rFx;
            dtmLine.cdEnd [1].rY = max (pdtmTria1->cdMax.rY, pdtmTria2->cdMax.rY);
            dtmLine.cdEnd [1].rX = (rFz + rFy * dtmLine.cdEnd [1].rY) / -rFx;
        }
        else {
            dtmLine.cdEnd [0].rX = min (pdtmTria1->cdMin.rX, pdtmTria2->cdMin.rX);
            dtmLine.cdEnd [0].rY = (rFz + rFx * dtmLine.cdEnd [0].rX) / -rFy;
            dtmLine.cdEnd [1].rX = max (pdtmTria1->cdMax.rX, pdtmTria2->cdMax.rX);
            dtmLine.cdEnd [1].rY = (rFz + rFx * dtmLine.cdEnd [1].rX) / -rFy;
        }
        if (min (dtmLine.cdEnd [0].rX, dtmLine.cdEnd [1].rX) >
            max (pdtmTria1->cdMax.rX, pdtmTria2->cdMax.rX) ||
            min (dtmLine.cdEnd [0].rY, dtmLine.cdEnd [1].rY) >
            max (pdtmTria1->cdMax.rY, pdtmTria2->cdMax.rY) ||
            max (dtmLine.cdEnd [0].rX, dtmLine.cdEnd [1].rX) <
            min (pdtmTria1->cdMin.rX, pdtmTria2->cdMin.rX) ||
            max (dtmLine.cdEnd [0].rY, dtmLine.cdEnd [1].rY) <
            min (pdtmTria1->cdMin.rY, pdtmTria2->cdMin.rY)) {
            return FALSE;
        }
        for (wPlane = 0; wPlane < 2; wPlane ++) {
            DTMTRIA * pdtmTria;
            WORD wAlongCount, wEdge;

            pdtmTria = (wPlane == 0) ? pdtmTria1 : pdtmTria2;
            wAlongCount = 0;
            for (wEdge = 0; wEdge < TRIA_COORDS; wEdge ++) {
                DTMLINE dtmEdge;
                DOUBLE rAlong1, rAlong2;

                _dtmTrias1.GetEdge (pdtmTria, wEdge,
                    &(dtmEdge.cdEnd [0]), &(dtmEdge.cdEnd [1]));
                if (DoLinesCross (&dtmLine, &dtmEdge, & rAlong1, & rAlong2)) {
                    if (rAlong2 > -FUZZFACTOR && (rAlong2 - 1.0) < FUZZFACTOR &&
                        wAlongCount < 2) {
                        DOUBLE rDiff;

                        rDiff = 0.0;
                        if (wPlane == 0) {
                            rAlongTria1 [wAlongCount] = rAlong1;
                            if (wAlongCount == 1) {
                                rDiff = fabs (rAlongTria1 [1] - rAlongTria1 [0]);
                            }
                        }
                        else {
                            rAlongTria2 [wAlongCount] = rAlong1;
                            if (wAlongCount == 1) {
                                rDiff = fabs (rAlongTria2 [1] - rAlongTria2 [0]);
                            }
                        }
                        if (wAlongCount == 0 ||
                            (wAlongCount == 1 && rDiff >= FUZZFACTOR)) {
                            wAlongCount ++;
                        }
                    }
                }
            }
            if (wAlongCount != 2) {
                return FALSE;
```

```
        }
    }
    if (rAlongTria1 [1] < rAlongTria1 [0]) {
        DOUBLE rSwap;

        rSwap = rAlongTria1 [0];
        rAlongTria1 [0] = rAlongTria1 [1];
        rAlongTria1 [1] = rSwap;
    }
    if (rAlongTria2 [1] < rAlongTria2 [0]) {
        DOUBLE rSwap;

        rSwap = rAlongTria2 [0];
        rAlongTria2 [0] = rAlongTria2 [1];
        rAlongTria2 [1] = rSwap;
    }
    if (rAlongTria1 [0] > rAlongTria2 [1] || rAlongTria1 [1] < rAlongTria2 [0]) {
        return FALSE;
    }
    rAlongFrom = max (rAlongTria1 [0], rAlongTria2 [0]);
    rAlongTo = min (rAlongTria1 [1], rAlongTria2 [1]);
    _dtmInter.GetEnd (&dtmLine, 0, &rX1, &rY1);
    _dtmInter.GetEnd (&dtmLine, 1, &rX2, &rY2);
    pdtmInter->cdEnd [0].rX = rX1 + rAlongFrom * (rX2 - rX1);
    pdtmInter->cdEnd [0].rY = rY1 + rAlongFrom * (rY2 - rY1);
    pdtmInter->cdEnd [0].rZ = rFactorZ [0] + rFactorX [0] * pdtmInter->cdEnd [0].rX +
        rFactorY [0] * pdtmInter->cdEnd [0].rY;
    pdtmInter->cdEnd [1].rX = rX1 + rAlongTo * (rX2 - rX1);
    pdtmInter->cdEnd [1].rY = rY1 + rAlongTo * (rY2 - rY1);
    pdtmInter->cdEnd [1].rZ = rFactorZ [0] + rFactorX [0] * pdtmInter->cdEnd [1].rX +
        rFactorY [0] * pdtmInter->cdEnd [1].rY;
    return TRUE;
}
```

**Chapter12.cpp** has the same layout as source code files in earlier chapters in this book. It starts with the header files, including <math.h> for the function *fabs*, followed by child window IDs, task IDs, the task batch size constant GETINTERSECTION_ STEPSIZE which is used when creating the intersection lines, and coloured pen numbers.

It then defines nine global variables, most of which are the same as in earlier chapters. *_dtmInter* is a lines array containing the intersection line or lines. *_dtmTrias1* and *_dtmTrias2* are two triangles arrays containing the two DTMs.

Eight functions are then declared, followed by the C++ source code.

The functions *WinMain*, *WndProc*, *CarryOutTasks*, *DrawModel*, *InitShowDropdownMenu* and *InitMouseDropdownMenu* are similar to the equivalent functions in earlier chapters. The user can import two sets of triangles, and then create and export the intersection line or lines. *DrawModel* draws the two sets of triangles first, followed by the intersection line or lines.

The function *GetIntersectionStart* starts the task that creates the intersection lines. *hwnd* is the handle of the parent window and *uTaskID* is the task ID number. If there are no triangles in either of the two triangles arrays *_dtmTrias1* or *_dtmTrias2*, the function displays an error message. If the lines array *_dtmInter* already contains some intersection lines, the function asks the user if they want to discard these lines. If the user selects 'Yes', any existing intersection lines are discarded. Finally, *GetIntersectionStart* displays a message in the text window and starts the task. The function returns TRUE if successful, or FALSE if the user cancels the task or an error occurs.

The function *GetIntersectionCont* carries out the task that creates intersection lines. *GetIntersectionCont* follows the standard task manager template as discussed in Chapter 1, looking at each triangle in the first triangles array *_dtmTrias1* in batches. Within the main while-loop, the function enters a second while-loop that compares each triangle in *_dtmTrias1* with each triangle in the second triangles array *_dtmTrias2*. It exits this second while-loop either when it reaches the end of the second triangles array, or when it reaches a triangle in *_dtmTrias2* that is to the right of the triangle in *_dtmTrias1*. In this situation, as all the triangles in each triangles array are stored in ascending x value order, all subsequent triangles in *_dtmTrias2* cannot overlap the triangle in *_dtmTria1*. Otherwise, if *GetIntersectionCont* finds an intersection line, it is added to the lines array *_dtmInter*. When the task is finished, *GetIntersectionCont* displays the number of intersection lines added to *_dtmInter*. The function returns the TASK_ constants as discussed in Chapter 1.

The function *GetIntersectionLine* calculates the intersection line of two 3D planes which are based on the x,y,z values at the corners of two 3D triangles *pdtmTria1* and *pdtmTria2*. The extent of the line is limited to within the overlapping part of the triangles. *pdtmInter* points to a DTMLINE structure that will contain the intersection line when the function ends, if successful. *GetIntersectionLine* first checks if the two triangles overlap by comparing their minimum and maximum x,y values. The minimum x value of *pdtmTria2* is not compared to the maximum x value of *pdtmTria1* because that comparison is already carried out in *GetIntersectionCont*. If the triangles overlap, *GetIntersectionLine* calculates the three coefficients for the planes created by each triangle, using the following equations and the x,y,z values at each corner of each triangle (refer to "Defining a 3D Plane from Three 3D Points" in Appendix C):

$$b = \frac{(y_1 - y_3)(z_1 - z_2) - (y_1 - y_2)(z_1 - z_3)}{(x_1 - x_2)(y_1 - y_3) - (x_1 - x_3)(y_1 - y_2)}$$

$$c = \frac{(x_1 - x_2)(z_1 - z_3) - (x_1 - x_3)(z_1 - z_2)}{(x_1 - x_2)(y_1 - y_3) - (x_1 - x_3)(y_1 - y_2)}$$

$$a = z_1 - bx_1 - cy_1$$

where *rFactorX* is *b*, *rFactorY* is *c*, and *rFactorZ* is *a*. If the denominator in the first two equations above is zero, then there is no solution because the three points are collinear. Next, *GetIntersectionLine* calculates the difference in these coefficients for each plane, storing the differences in *rFx*, *rFy* and *rFz*. If *rFx* and *rFy* are both zero, then there is no intersection line because the two planes are coplanar. Then the function uses the following equations to obtain two 3D points on the line where the two planes intersect (refer to "Intersection of Two 3D Planes" in Appendix C). The equations it uses depend on which of *rFx* or *rFy* is greater:

If $|b_1 - b_2| > |c_1 - c_2|$ then:                    If $|c_1 - c_2| \geq |b_1 - b_2|$ then:

$$y_1 = y_{min}$$                                        $$x_1 = x_{min}$$

$$x_1 = \frac{(a_2 - a_1) + (c_2 - c_1)y_1}{(b_1 - b_2)}$$          $$y_1 = \frac{(a_2 - a_1) + (b_2 - b_1)x_1}{(c_1 - c_2)}$$

$$y_2 = y_{max}$$                                        $$x_2 = x_{max}$$

$$x_2 = \frac{(a_2 - a_1) + (c_2 - c_1)y_2}{(b_1 - b_2)}$$          $$y_2 = \frac{(a_2 - a_1) + (b_2 - b_1)x_2}{(c_1 - c_2)}$$

where $x_{min}$ $y_{min}$ and $x_{max}$ $y_{max}$ are the minimum and maximum x,y values of the rectangle that surrounds both triangles. The x,y values are stored in each end of the DTMLINE structure *dtmLine*. z values are not needed at this stage. Next, *GetIntersectionLine* checks that the line overlaps both triangles, exiting if it does not. The function then compares the intersection line with each side of each triangle, storing the fraction of the distance along the line to the intersection point in two arrays *rAlongTria1* and *rAlongTria2* when the line and an edge cross. The line and edge cross when:

```
rAlong2 >= 0 and rAlong2 <= 1
```

which, when using FUZZFACTOR, becomes:

```
rAlong2 > -FUZZFACTOR and (rAlong2 - 1.0) < FUZZFACTOR
```

Because the intersection line can cross all three edges of a triangle if it crosses a corner, *GetIntersectionLine* checks that the two values stored in each array *rAlongTria1* and *rAlongTria2* are not the same as that would create an intersection line with zero length. If either array does not contain two values, *GetIntersectionLine* exits.

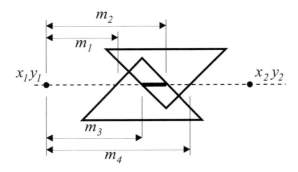

*rAlongTria1* is the equivalent of $m_1$ and $m_2$ in the diagram above, and *rAlongTria2* is the equivalent of $m_3$ and $m_4$. Next, *GetIntersectionLine* swaps the values in each array if they are not in ascending order, and exits if the two arrays do not overlap, for example if $m_2 < m_3$ or $m_1 > m_4$. Finally, *rAlongFrom* and *rAlongTo* contain the maximum and minimum values of the arrays *rAlongTria1* and *rAlongTria2* (the equivalent of the maximum

of $m_1$ and $m_3$ and the minimum of $m_2$ and $m_4$) and the following equations are used for calculating the x,y,z values at each end of the intersection line that is within the overlapping section of both triangles:

$$x = x_1 + m(x_2 - x_1)$$

$$y = y_1 + m(y_2 - y_1)$$

$$z = a_1 + b_1 x + c_1 y$$

where $m$ is *rAlongFrom* for the start of the line and *rAlongTo* for the end of the line, and $a_1 b_1 c_1$ are the plane coefficients *rFactorX*, *rFactorY* and *rFactorZ* for the first plane.

*GetIntersectionLine* returns TRUE if successful, or FALSE if there is no intersection line for the two triangles within the triangles' overlapping area or if an error occurs.

## Running Chapter12

Before you can compile and run your program, you need to add the following nineteen source files to your Chapter12 project. Refer to Chapter 1 for how to do this:

| | | |
|---|---|---|
| TextWnd.h | TextWnd.cpp | |
| FileInOut.h | FileInOut.cpp | |
| BigTask.h | BigTask.cpp | |
| Graphics.h | Graphics.cpp | |
| Colours.h | Colours.cpp | |
| Shapes.h | Shapes.cpp | |
| Lines.cpp | Triangles.cpp | |
| Common.h | Common.cpp | |
| Chapter12.h | Chapter12.cpp | Chapter12.rc |

You also need to add the Gdiplus.lib library file as an 'additional dependency' in your project's linker/input settings. Refer to Chapter 2 for how to do this. Finally, don't forget to set Chapter12 as your start-up project.

Otherwise, assuming you have compiled the code for Chapter12 successfully, and it is running, you can now test it out.

Start by importing your two DTMs of 3D triangles, one after the other. Click on 'File' in the menu bar, then select 'Import' from the drop-down menu, and finally click on 'Primary triangles' for the first DTM or 'Secondary triangles' for the second DTM. Next, select a file containing the triangles data. You can use the sample files Triangles.txt for the first DTM and TrianglesA_Ch12.txt for the second DTM. If both DTMs are imported successfully, the primary DTM should appear as green triangles and the secondary DTM as blue triangles, as shown in the following image (the colours have been changed to make it easier to differentiate between the two sets of triangles):

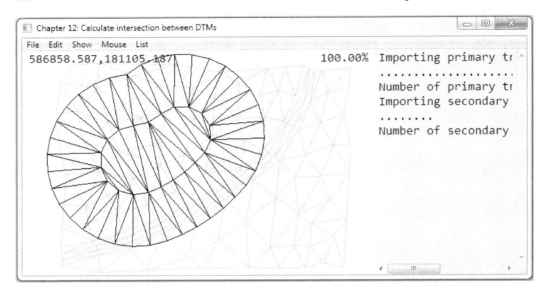

The secondary DTM is a flat-bottomed hole with sloping sides, for example a proposed balancing pond. Currently, the extent of the side slopes is upwards to the same z value as the highest z value in the primary DTM.

To calculate where these sloping sides intersect the primary DTM, click on 'Edit' in the menu bar and then select 'Get intersection' from the drop-down menu. A red loop of intersection lines should appear as in the following image (again, the colours have been changed to make it easier to identify the intersection lines):

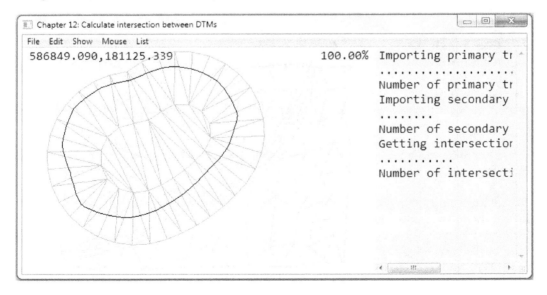

You can export the intersection lines as CAD script files or as text files by clicking on 'File' in the menu bar, selecting 'Export' from the drop-down menu, and then 'Intersection' from the next menu. The exported CAD script files can be used in your

CAD program to create a new boundary in your secondary model, for example trimming the extents of the sloping sides in our balancing pond example.

If the secondary DTM contains parts that are above the primary DTM and other parts that are below the primary DTM, for example areas of cut and other areas of fill, the intersection lines will be around the edge of the model where it intersects the primary DTM, as in the previous example, but also along any boundary or boundaries between the cut areas and the fill areas.

To see an example of this, import the sample file TrianglesB_Ch12.txt via 'File', 'Import', 'Secondary triangles' again (answering 'Yes' when the program asks if you want to discard any existing triangles in the secondary DTM). Your program's window should look something like this (the intersection lines from the previous example have been hidden via 'Show', 'Intersection' in the menu bar):

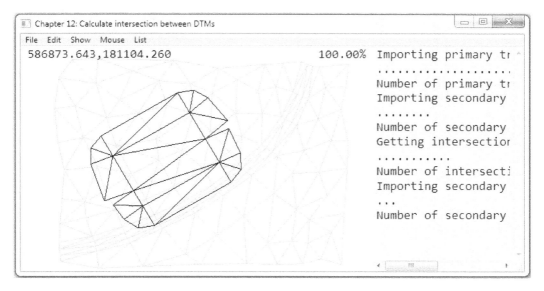

This secondary DTM contains a central gently-sloping rectangular area. Around this rectangle is a combination of upward slopes where the rectangle cuts into the primary DTM (the cut area), and downward slopes where the rectangle extends above the primary DTM (the fill area). To determine where the upward slopes switch to downward slopes, I initially created a simple DTM containing four 3D points that define the corners of the central rectangular area. Using the program in this chapter, I identified the boundary between cut and fill across the rectangular area. The upward slopes switch to downward slopes where this boundary intersects the edge of the central rectangle. If you import TrianglesB_Ch12.txt into the program in Chapter 5 and create contour groups, the extents of the slopes should be clearer.

Next, create new intersection lines via 'Edit', 'Get Intersection' (again answering 'Yes' to discard existing intersection lines). The program's window should look like the image over the page (you may need to 'unhide' intersection lines via 'Show' in the menu bar).

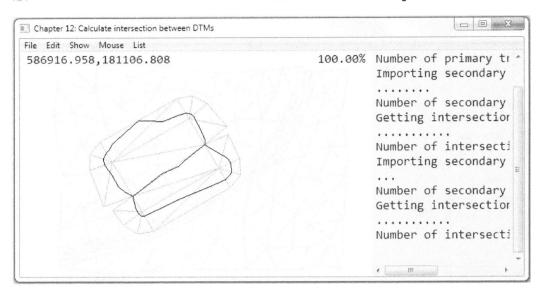

Note how the intersection lines form an approximate figure of 8, with the upper loop surrounding the area of cut and the lower loop encircling the area of fill. This secondary DTM, with its central gently-sloping rectangular area, could for example be a model for the slab foundations of a building, where the back half is dug into the existing slope and the front half extends outwards on top of piled-up excavated material.

Again, the intersection lines can be exported as a CAD script file to use in your CAD program to adjust the edges of the slopes to tie-in with the primary DTM.

To adjust the edges of your DTM to the intersection line or lines created by the program in this chapter, follow these steps in your CAD program:

(i) Import the CAD script file that contains the intersection lines into your CAD drawing of your secondary DTM.
(ii) Delete (or freeze) points that are outside the boundary (or boundaries) created by the intersection lines.
(iii) Use the lisp routine POINTSONLINES (see Appendix A) to add 3D points at each end of the intersection lines to your CAD drawing.
(iv) Use the lisp routine EXTRACTPOINTS (refer to Appendix A again) to export these new 3D points, along with any existing 3D points within the boundary formed by the intersection lines, to a new 'points data' text file.
(v) Finally, import this points file into the program in Chapter 4 to create a new DTM of your secondary model with the extents of the model trimmed to the intersection lines.

As in previous chapters, to exit the program click on 'File' in the menu bar, select 'Exit' and then choose 'Yes' in the message box that appears.

# Chapter 13

## Calculate Difference in Z Values Between DTMs

Chapter 13 lists the source code for a program called **Chapter13** that calculates the difference in z values between two DTMs, creating a set of 3D points with z values equal to the differences across the DTMs. The 3D points can be exported as CAD script files, as text files or as JPEG files. The user can also obtain difference in z values at individual locations by left-clicking the mouse in the graphics window.

The following files are discussed in this chapter:

**Chapter13.h**          **Chapter13.rc**          **Chapter13.cpp**

## Chapter13 Source Files

The first file is the header file:

**CHAPTER13.H**

```
#ifndef CHAPTER13_H
#define CHAPTER13_H

#define IDM_IMPORTTRIANGLES1       101
#define IDM_IMPORTTRIANGLES2       102
#define IDM_EXPORTDIFFERENCE       103
#define IDM_EXPORTSCREEN           104
#define IDM_EXPORTMODEL            105
#define IDM_EXIT                   106

#define IDM_GETDIFFERENCE          201

#define IDN_SHOWMENU               2

#define IDM_SHOWDIFFERENCE         301
#define IDM_SHOWTRIANGLES1         302
#define IDM_SHOWTRIANGLES2         303
#define IDM_COLOURBACKGROUND       304
#define IDM_COLOURCOORDSTEXT       305
#define IDM_COLOURDIFFERENCE       306
#define IDM_COLOURTRIANGLES1       307
#define IDM_COLOURTRIANGLES2       308
#define IDM_ZOOMEXTENTS            309
#define IDM_REDRAW                 310

#define IDN_MOUSEMENU              3

#define IDM_MOUSEZOOM              401
#define IDM_MOUSEPAN              402
#define IDM_MOUSEDIFFERENCE        403

#define IDM_LISTDIFFERENCESTATS    501
#define IDM_LISTTRIANGLES1STATS    502
#define IDM_LISTTRIANGLES2STATS    503
```

```
#define IDM_LISTDIFFERENCE          504
#define IDM_LISTTRIANGLES1          505
#define IDM_LISTTRIANGLES2          506

#define IDM_ESCAPEKEY               901

#endif // CHAPTER13_H
```

As in previous chapters, **Chapter13.h** contains ID numbers for menu bar options, drop-down menus and accelerator keys.

The second file is the resource script file:

**CHAPTER13.RC**

```
#include <windows.h>
#include "Chapter13.h"

Chapter13 MENU {
    POPUP "&File" {
        POPUP "&Import" {
            MENUITEM "&Primary triangles",      IDM_IMPORTTRIANGLES1
            MENUITEM "&Secondary triangles",    IDM_IMPORTTRIANGLES2
        }
        POPUP "&Export" {
            MENUITEM "&Difference points",      IDM_EXPORTDIFFERENCE
            MENUITEM SEPARATOR
            MENUITEM "S&creen image",           IDM_EXPORTSCREEN
            MENUITEM "&Model image",            IDM_EXPORTMODEL
        }
        MENUITEM SEPARATOR
        MENUITEM "E&xit",                       IDM_EXIT
    }
    POPUP "&Edit" {
        MENUITEM "Calculate difference",        IDM_GETDIFFERENCE
    }
    POPUP "&Show" {
        MENUITEM "&Difference points",          IDM_SHOWDIFFERENCE
        MENUITEM "&Primary triangles",          IDM_SHOWTRIANGLES1
        MENUITEM "&Secondary triangles",        IDM_SHOWTRIANGLES2
        MENUITEM SEPARATOR
        POPUP "&Colour" {
            MENUITEM "Back&ground",             IDM_COLOURBACKGROUND
            MENUITEM "&Coords text",            IDM_COLOURCOORDSTEXT
            MENUITEM SEPARATOR
            MENUITEM "&Difference points",      IDM_COLOURDIFFERENCE
            MENUITEM "&Primary triangles",      IDM_COLOURTRIANGLES1
            MENUITEM "&Secondary triangles",    IDM_COLOURTRIANGLES2
        }
        MENUITEM SEPARATOR
        MENUITEM "&Zoom extents",               IDM_ZOOMEXTENTS
        MENUITEM "&Redraw",                     IDM_REDRAW
    }
    POPUP "&Mouse" {
        MENUITEM "&Zoom in/out",                IDM_MOUSEZOOM
        MENUITEM "&Pan",                        IDM_MOUSEPAN
        MENUITEM SEPARATOR
        MENUITEM "&Difference",                 IDM_MOUSEDIFFERENCE
    }
    POPUP "&List" {
```

```
        POPUP "&Statistics" {
            MENUITEM "&Difference points",        IDM_LISTDIFFERENCESTATS
            MENUITEM "&Primary triangles",        IDM_LISTTRIANGLES1STATS
            MENUITEM "&Secondary triangles",      IDM_LISTTRIANGLES2STATS
        }
        MENUITEM SEPARATOR
        MENUITEM "&Difference points",            IDM_LISTDIFFERENCE
        MENUITEM "&Primary triangles",            IDM_LISTTRIANGLES1
        MENUITEM "&Secondary triangles",          IDM_LISTTRIANGLES2
    }
}

Chapter13 ACCELERATORS {
    VK_ESCAPE,        IDM_ESCAPEKEY,               VIRTKEY, NOINVERT
}
```

Like previous chapters, **Chapter13.rc** defines the contents of the program's menu bar and accelerator keys. There is no custom dialog box in this program.

The third file is the source code file, which includes function listings.

## CHAPTER13.CPP

```
#ifndef UNICODE
#define UNICODE
#endif

#include <windows.h>
#include <gdiplus.h>
using namespace Gdiplus;
#include "Chapter13.h"
#include "BigTask.h"
#include "FileInOut.h"
#include "TextWnd.h"
#include "Graphics.h"
#include "Colours.h"
#include "Shapes.h"
#include "Common.h"

#define ID_TEXTWND                    1
#define ID_DISPLAYWND                 2
#define ID_IMAGEEXPORT                3

#define IDT_IMPORTTRIANGLES1          11
#define IDT_IMPORTTRIANGLES2          12

#define IDT_EXPORTDIFFERENCE          21
#define IDT_EXPORTDIFFERENCESCRIPT    22
#define IDT_EXPORTIMAGE               23

#define IDT_GETDIFFERENCE             31

#define IDT_LISTDIFFERENCE            41
#define IDT_LISTTRIANGLES1            42
#define IDT_LISTTRIANGLES2            43

#define GETDIFFERENCE_STEPSIZE        20L

#define PENCOLOUR_DIFFERENCE          0
#define PENCOLOUR_TRIANGLES1          11
```

```
#define PENCOLOUR_TRIANGLES2          4

#define DIFF_PROXIMITY                0.001

DTMTEXTWINDOW _dtmText;
DTMFILEDATA _dtmFile;
DTMBIGTASK _dtmTask, _dtmTaskDisplay;
DTMDISPLAY _dtmDisplay;
DTMCOLOURS _dtmColours;
DTMPOINTS _dtmDiffs;
DTMTRIAS _dtmTrias1, _dtmTrias2;

LRESULT CALLBACK WndProc (HWND, UINT, WPARAM, LPARAM);
BOOL CarryOutTasks (HWND);
WORD DrawModel (DTMFRAME *, DTMBIGTASK *);
void InitShowDropdownMenu (HMENU);
void InitMouseDropdownMenu (HMENU);
BOOL GetDifferenceStart (HWND, UINT);
WORD GetDifferenceCont (void);
BOOL GetDifferenceAtCorners (DTMTRIAS *, DTMTRIAS *, DOUBLE);
BOOL GetDifferenceAtCrossingEdges (void);
void GetDifferenceAtMouse (void);

int WINAPI WinMain (HINSTANCE hInst, HINSTANCE, PSTR, int nCmdShow) {
    return InitAndRunProgram (hInst, nCmdShow, TEXT ("Chapter13"),
        TEXT ("Chapter 13: Calculate difference in Z values between DTMs"));
}

LRESULT CALLBACK WndProc (HWND hwnd, UINT message, WPARAM wParam, LPARAM lParam) {
    switch (message) {
        case WM_CREATE : {
            HINSTANCE hInst;

            hInst = ((LPCREATESTRUCT) lParam)->hInstance;
            _dtmText.Create (hwnd, ID_TEXTWND, hInst);
            _dtmFile.Init (hwnd);
            _dtmDisplay.Init (hwnd, 0, ID_DISPLAYWND, hInst,
                1.0, 4.0, 4.0, 4.0, 5.0, 1.0, 2.0, 0.5);
            _dtmColours.Init ();
            _dtmDiffs.Init (TEXT ("difference points"), PENCOLOUR_DIFFERENCE,
                POINTSTYLE_CROSS);
            _dtmTrias1.Init (TEXT ("primary triangles"), PENCOLOUR_TRIANGLES1,
                0, FALSE);
            _dtmTrias2.Init (TEXT ("secondary triangles"), PENCOLOUR_TRIANGLES2,
                0, FALSE);
            return 0;
        }
        case WM_ENTERSIZEMOVE :
            _dtmDisplay.StartResizing ();
            return 0;
        case WM_SIZE :
            ResizeChildWindows (lParam);
            return 0;
        case WM_EXITSIZEMOVE :
            _dtmDisplay.StopResizing ();
            return 0;
        case WM_INITMENUPOPUP :
            if (HIWORD (lParam) == FALSE) {
                switch (LOWORD (lParam)) {
                case IDN_SHOWMENU :
                    InitShowDropdownMenu ((HMENU) wParam);
```

```
                    return 0;
            case IDN_MOUSEMENU :
                InitMouseDropdownMenu ((HMENU) wParam);
                return 0;
            default : break;
            }
        }
    break;
case WM_COMMAND :
    if (HIWORD (wParam) == 0) {
        switch (LOWORD (wParam)) {
            case IDM_IMPORTTRIANGLES1 :
                _dtmTrias1.ImportStart (hwnd, IDT_IMPORTTRIANGLES1);
                return 0;
            case IDM_IMPORTTRIANGLES2 :
                _dtmTrias2.ImportStart (hwnd, IDT_IMPORTTRIANGLES2);
                return 0;
            case IDM_EXPORTDIFFERENCE :
                _dtmDiffs.ExportStart (IDT_EXPORTDIFFERENCE,
                    IDT_EXPORTDIFFERENCESCRIPT);
                return 0;
            case IDM_EXPORTSCREEN :
                ExportImage (FALSE, ID_IMAGEEXPORT);
                return 0;
            case IDM_EXPORTMODEL :
                ExportImage (TRUE, ID_IMAGEEXPORT);
                return 0;
            case IDM_EXIT :
                SendMessage (hwnd, WM_CLOSE, 0, 0);
                return 0;
            case IDM_GETDIFFERENCE :
                GetDifferenceStart (hwnd, IDT_GETDIFFERENCE);
                return 0;
            case IDM_SHOWDIFFERENCE :
                _dtmDiffs.FlipVisible ();
                _dtmTaskDisplay.Start ();
                return 0;
            case IDM_SHOWTRIANGLES1 :
                _dtmTrias1.FlipVisible ();
                _dtmTaskDisplay.Start ();
                return 0;
            case IDM_SHOWTRIANGLES2 :
                _dtmTrias2.FlipVisible ();
                _dtmTaskDisplay.Start ();
                return 0;
            case IDM_COLOURBACKGROUND :
                ChangeBackgroundColour (hwnd);
                return 0;
            case IDM_COLOURCOORDSTEXT :
                ChangeCoordsTextColour (hwnd);
                return 0;
            case IDM_COLOURDIFFERENCE :
                ChangePenColour (hwnd, PENCOLOUR_DIFFERENCE);
                return 0;
            case IDM_COLOURTRIANGLES1 :
                ChangePenColour (hwnd, PENCOLOUR_TRIANGLES1);
                return 0;
            case IDM_COLOURTRIANGLES2 :
                ChangePenColour (hwnd, PENCOLOUR_TRIANGLES2);
                return 0;
            case IDM_ZOOMEXTENTS :
```

```
                    _dtmDisplay.ZoomExtents ();
                    _dtmTaskDisplay.Start ();
                    return 0;
                case IDM_REDRAW :
                    _dtmTaskDisplay.Start ();
                    return 0;
                case IDM_MOUSEZOOM :
                    _dtmDisplay.SetMouseAction (MOUSEACT_ZOOM);
                    return 0;
                case IDM_MOUSEPAN :
                    _dtmDisplay.SetMouseAction (MOUSEACT_PAN);
                    return 0;
                case IDM_MOUSEDIFFERENCE :
                    _dtmDisplay.SetMouseAction (MOUSEACT_POINT);
                    return 0;
                case IDM_LISTDIFFERENCESTATS :
                    _dtmDiffs.ListStats ();
                    return 0;
                case IDM_LISTTRIANGLES1STATS :
                    _dtmTrias1.ListStats ();
                    return 0;
                case IDM_LISTTRIANGLES2STATS :
                    _dtmTrias2.ListStats ();
                    return 0;
                case IDM_LISTDIFFERENCE :
                    _dtmDiffs.ListStart (IDT_LISTDIFFERENCE);
                    return 0;
                case IDM_LISTTRIANGLES1 :
                    _dtmTrias1.ListStart (IDT_LISTTRIANGLES1);
                    return 0;
                case IDM_LISTTRIANGLES2 :
                    _dtmTrias2.ListStart (IDT_LISTTRIANGLES2);
                    return 0;
                default : break;
            }
        }
        else if (HIWORD (wParam) == 1) {
            if (LOWORD (wParam) == IDM_ESCAPEKEY) {
                _dtmTask.Quit (TRUE);
                _dtmTaskDisplay.Quit (TRUE);
                return 0;
            }
        }
        else if (LOWORD (wParam) == ID_DISPLAYWND) {
            switch (HIWORD (wParam)) {
                case DTM_REDRAW :
                    _dtmTaskDisplay.Start ();
                    return 0;
                case DTM_DRAW_STOPPED :
                case DTM_DRAW_COMPLETED :
                    _dtmDisplay.RepaintNow (REPAINT_ALL);
                    return 0;
                case DTM_SELPOINT :
                    GetDifferenceAtMouse ();
                    return 0;
                default : return 0;
            }
        }
        else if (LOWORD (wParam) == ID_IMAGEEXPORT) {
            ProcessExportImageMessages (wParam, IDT_EXPORTIMAGE);
            return 0;
```

```
                    }
                    break;
            case WM_CLOSE :
                AskCloseWindowMessage (hwnd);
                return 0;
            case WM_DESTROY:
                _dtmDisplay.Free ();
                _dtmColours.Free ();
                _dtmText.Destroy ();
                _dtmFile.FreeImportBuffer ();
                _dtmDiffs.Free ();
                _dtmTrias1.Free ();
                _dtmTrias2.Free ();
                PostQuitMessage (0);
                return 0;
            default : break;
    }
    return DefWindowProc (hwnd, message, wParam, lParam);
}

BOOL CarryOutTasks (HWND hwnd) {
    WORD wTaskStatus;

    if (!_dtmTask.IsBusy ()) {
        return FALSE;
    }
    if (_dtmTask.GetStage () == 0) {
        EnableMenuBar (hwnd, FALSE);
        _dtmDisplay.Enable (FALSE);
        _dtmTask.NextStage ();
    }
    switch (_dtmTask.GetID ()) {
        case IDT_IMPORTTRIANGLES1 :
            wTaskStatus = _dtmTrias1.ImportCont (FALSE);
            break;
        case IDT_IMPORTTRIANGLES2 :
            wTaskStatus = _dtmTrias2.ImportCont (FALSE);
            break;
        case IDT_EXPORTDIFFERENCE :
            wTaskStatus = _dtmDiffs.ExportCont (FALSE);
            break;
        case IDT_EXPORTDIFFERENCESCRIPT :
            wTaskStatus = _dtmDiffs.ExportCont (TRUE);
            break;
        case IDT_EXPORTIMAGE :
            wTaskStatus = DrawModel (_dtmDisplay.GetImageDtmPtr (), &_dtmTask);
            break;
        case IDT_GETDIFFERENCE :
            wTaskStatus = GetDifferenceCont ();
            break;
        case IDT_LISTDIFFERENCE :
            wTaskStatus = _dtmDiffs.ListCont ();
            break;
        case IDT_LISTTRIANGLES1 :
            wTaskStatus = _dtmTrias1.ListCont ();
            break;
        case IDT_LISTTRIANGLES2 :
            wTaskStatus = _dtmTrias2.ListCont ();
            break;
        default :
            wTaskStatus = TASK_STOPPED;
```

```
                break;
        }
        if ((wTaskStatus & TASK_STOPPED) || (wTaskStatus & TASK_COMPLETED)) {
            EnableMenuBar (hwnd, TRUE);
            _dtmDisplay.Enable (TRUE);
            _dtmTask.Stop ();
        }
        if (wTaskStatus & TASK_COMPLETED) {
            switch (_dtmTask.GetID ()) {
                case IDT_IMPORTTRIANGLES1 :
                    AddShapeToDisplay (&_dtmTrias1);
                    break;
                case IDT_IMPORTTRIANGLES2 :
                    AddShapeToDisplay (&_dtmTrias2);
                    break;
                case IDT_GETDIFFERENCE :
                    AddShapeToDisplay (&_dtmDiffs);
                    break;
                default : break;
            }
        }
        if (wTaskStatus & TASK_REDRAW) {
            _dtmTaskDisplay.Start ();
        }
        return TRUE;
}

WORD DrawModel (DTMFRAME * pdtmFrame, DTMBIGTASK * pdtmTask) {
    if (pdtmFrame == NULL || !pdtmFrame->IsActive () ||
        !pdtmFrame->IsGdiOK () || pdtmTask == NULL) {
        return TASK_STOPPED;
    }
    if (pdtmTask->Quit ()) {
        pdtmFrame->NotifyParent (DTM_DRAW_STOPPED);
        return TASK_STOPPED;
    }
    switch (pdtmTask->GetStage ()) {
        case 1 :
            pdtmFrame->ClearBackground ();
            _dtmColours.SetPenWidths (pdtmFrame->GetPenWidth (),
                pdtmFrame->GetVertExag ());
            pdtmTask->NextStage ();
            break;
        case 2 :
            _dtmTrias1.Draw (pdtmFrame, pdtmTask);
            break;
        case 3 :
            _dtmTrias2.Draw (pdtmFrame, pdtmTask);
            break;
        case 4 :
            _dtmDiffs.Draw (pdtmFrame, pdtmTask);
            break;
        default : break;
    }
    pdtmFrame->NotifyParent (DTM_DRAW_UPDATED);
    if (pdtmTask->GetStage () < 5) {
        return TASK_ONGOING;
    }
    pdtmFrame->NotifyParent (DTM_DRAW_COMPLETED);
    return TASK_COMPLETED;
}
```

```
void InitShowDropdownMenu (HMENU hMenu) {
    CheckMenuItem (hMenu, IDM_SHOWDIFFERENCE, MF_BYCOMMAND |
        (_dtmDiffs.IsVisible () ? MF_CHECKED : MF_UNCHECKED));
    CheckMenuItem (hMenu, IDM_SHOWTRIANGLES1, MF_BYCOMMAND |
        (_dtmTrias1.IsVisible () ? MF_CHECKED : MF_UNCHECKED));
    CheckMenuItem (hMenu, IDM_SHOWTRIANGLES2, MF_BYCOMMAND |
        (_dtmTrias2.IsVisible () ? MF_CHECKED : MF_UNCHECKED));
}

void InitMouseDropdownMenu (HMENU hMenu) {
    DTMMOUSEACT mouseAction;

    mouseAction = _dtmDisplay.GetMouseAction ();
    CheckMenuItem (hMenu, IDM_MOUSEZOOM, MF_BYCOMMAND |
        (mouseAction == MOUSEACT_ZOOM ? MF_CHECKED : MF_UNCHECKED));
    CheckMenuItem (hMenu, IDM_MOUSEPAN, MF_BYCOMMAND |
        (mouseAction == MOUSEACT_PAN ? MF_CHECKED : MF_UNCHECKED));
    CheckMenuItem (hMenu, IDM_MOUSEDIFFERENCE, MF_BYCOMMAND |
        (mouseAction == MOUSEACT_POINT ? MF_CHECKED : MF_UNCHECKED));
}

BOOL GetDifferenceStart (HWND hwnd, UINT uTaskID) {
    if (_dtmTask.IsBusy ()) {
        _dtmText.Output (_szTaskBusyMessage);
        return FALSE;
    }
    if (_dtmTrias1.GetTotal () == 0L) {
        _dtmText.Output (TEXT ("There are no %s available. ") \
            TEXT ("Unable to calculate %s\r\n"),
            _dtmTrias1.GetDescription (), _dtmDiffs.GetDescription ());
        return FALSE;
    }
    if (_dtmTrias2.GetTotal () == 0L) {
        _dtmText.Output (TEXT ("There are no %s available. ") \
            TEXT ("Unable to calculate %s\r\n"),
            _dtmTrias2.GetDescription (), _dtmDiffs.GetDescription ());
        return FALSE;
    }
    if (_dtmDiffs.GetTotal () != 0L) {
        int iMessage;

        iMessage = MessageBox (hwnd,
            TEXT ("Do you want to discard difference points already created?"),
            TEXT ("Difference points"), MB_YESNOCANCEL | MB_ICONWARNING);
        if (iMessage == IDCANCEL) {
            return FALSE;
        }
        else if (iMessage == IDYES) {
            _dtmDiffs.Free ();
        }
    }
    _dtmText.Output (TEXT ("Getting %s\r\n"), _dtmDiffs.GetDescription ());
    _dtmTask.Start (uTaskID, GETDIFFERENCE_STEPSIZE);
    return TRUE;
}

WORD GetDifferenceCont (void) {
    static DWORD dwTotalAtStart;
```

```
    if (_dtmTask.Quit ()) {
        _dtmText.Output (TEXT ("\r\nGetting %s stopped\r\n"),
            _dtmDiffs.GetDescription ());
        return TASK_STOPPED | TASK_REDRAW;
    }
    switch (_dtmTask.GetStage ()) {
        case 1 :
            if (_dtmTask.AtStart ()) {
                dwTotalAtStart = _dtmDiffs.GetTotal ();
                _dtmText.Output (TEXT ("Stage 1:\r\n"));
            }
            if (!GetDifferenceAtCorners (&_dtmTrias1, &_dtmTrias2, 1.0)) {
                _dtmTask.NextStage ();
            }
            return TASK_ONGOING;
        case 2 :
            if (_dtmTask.AtStart ()) {
                _dtmText.Output (TEXT ("\r\nStage 2:\r\n"));
            }
            if (!GetDifferenceAtCorners (&_dtmTrias2, &_dtmTrias1, -1.0)) {
                _dtmTask.NextStage ();
            }
            return TASK_ONGOING;
        case 3 :
            if (_dtmTask.AtStart ()) {
                _dtmText.Output (TEXT ("\r\nStage 3:\r\n"));
            }
            if (GetDifferenceAtCrossingEdges ()) {
                return TASK_ONGOING;
            }
            break;
        default : break;
    }
    _dtmText.Output (TEXT ("\r\nNumber of %s created: %lu\r\n"),
        _dtmDiffs.GetDescription (), _dtmDiffs.GetTotal () - dwTotalAtStart);
    return TASK_COMPLETED | TASK_REDRAW;
}

BOOL GetDifferenceAtCorners (DTMTRIAS * pdtmTrias1, DTMTRIAS * pdtmTrias2,
    DOUBLE rSign) {

    if (pdtmTrias1 == NULL || pdtmTrias2 == NULL) {
        return FALSE;
    }
    _dtmTask.StartNewBatch ();
    while (!_dtmTask.NoMoreItems (pdtmTrias1->GetTotal ()) &&
        !_dtmTask.AtEndOfBatch ()) {
        DTMTRIA * pdtmTria1;
        WORD wCorner;

        pdtmTria1 = pdtmTrias1->GetPtr (_dtmTask.GetItemNumber ());
        if (pdtmTria1->cdMin.rX > pdtmTrias2->GetMaxX ()) {
            _dtmTask.SetItemNumber (pdtmTrias1->GetTotal ());
            break;
        }
        for (wCorner = 0; wCorner < TRIA_COORDS; wCorner ++) {
            DTMPOINT dtmDiff;
            DOUBLE rZ;

            CopyCoords (&(dtmDiff.cdPoint), &(pdtmTria1->cdCorner [wCorner]));
            if (pdtmTrias2->GetZ (&(dtmDiff.cdPoint), &rZ)) {
```

```
                dtmDiff.cdPoint.rZ = (rZ - dtmDiff.cdPoint.rZ) * rSign;
                dtmDiff.wColour = PENCOLOUR_DIFFERENCE;
                _dtmDiffs.AddNear (&dtmDiff, DIFF_PROXIMITY);
            }
        }
        _dtmTask.NextItem ();
        _dtmTask.IncBatchCounter ();
    }
    _dtmText.ProgressDot ();
    return !_dtmTask.NoMoreItems (pdtmTrias1->GetTotal ());
}

BOOL GetDifferenceAtCrossingEdges (void) {
    _dtmTask.StartNewBatch ();
    while (!_dtmTask.NoMoreItems (_dtmTrias1.GetTotal ()) &&
        !_dtmTask.AtEndOfBatch ()) {
        DTMTRIA * pdtmTria1, * pdtmTria2;
        DWORD dwTria2;

        pdtmTria1 = _dtmTrias1.GetPtr (_dtmTask.GetItemNumber ());
        dwTria2 = 0L;
        pdtmTria2 = _dtmTrias2.GetPtr (dwTria2);
        while (dwTria2 < _dtmTrias2.GetTotal () &&
            pdtmTria2->cdMin.rX <= pdtmTria1->cdMax.rX) {
            WORD wEdge1;

            if (pdtmTria1->cdMax.rY < pdtmTria2->cdMin.rY ||
                pdtmTria1->cdMin.rX > pdtmTria2->cdMax.rX ||
                pdtmTria1->cdMin.rY > pdtmTria2->cdMax.rY) {
                dwTria2 ++;
                pdtmTria2 = _dtmTrias2.GetPtr (dwTria2);
                continue;
            }
            for (wEdge1 = 0; wEdge1 < TRIA_COORDS; wEdge1 ++) {
                DOUBLE rX1, rY1, rZ1, rX2, rY2, rZ2;
                WORD wEdge2;

                _dtmTrias1.GetEdge (pdtmTria1, wEdge1, &rX1, &rY1, &rZ1,
                    &rX2, &rY2, &rZ2);
                for (wEdge2 = 0; wEdge2 < TRIA_COORDS; wEdge2 ++) {
                    DOUBLE rX3, rY3, rZ3, rX4, rY4, rZ4, rAlong1, rAlong2;

                    _dtmTrias2.GetEdge (pdtmTria2, wEdge2, &rX3, &rY3, &rZ3,
                        &rX4, &rY4, &rZ4);
                    if (DoLinesCross (rX1, rY1, rX2, rY2, rX3, rY3, rX4, rY4,
                        &rAlong1, &rAlong2)) {
                        if (rAlong1 >= FUZZFACTOR && (1.0 - rAlong1) >= FUZZFACTOR &&
                            rAlong2 >= FUZZFACTOR && (1.0 - rAlong2) >= FUZZFACTOR) {
                            DTMPOINT dtmDiff;

                            dtmDiff.cdPoint.rX = rX1 + rAlong1 * (rX2 - rX1);
                            dtmDiff.cdPoint.rY = rY1 + rAlong1 * (rY2 - rY1);
                            dtmDiff.cdPoint.rZ = (rZ3 + rAlong2 * (rZ4 - rZ3)) -
                                (rZ1 + rAlong1 * (rZ2 - rZ1));
                            dtmDiff.wColour = PENCOLOUR_DIFFERENCE;
                            _dtmDiffs.AddNear (&dtmDiff, DIFF_PROXIMITY);
                        }
                    }
                }
            }
            dwTria2 ++;
```

```
            pdtmTria2 = _dtmTrias2.GetPtr (dwTria2);
        }
        _dtmTask.NextItem ();
        _dtmTask.IncBatchCounter ();
    }
    _dtmText.ProgressDot ();
    return !_dtmTask.NoMoreItems (_dtmTrias1.GetTotal ());
}

void GetDifferenceAtMouse (void) {
    DTMCOORD dtmMouse;
    DOUBLE rLevel1, rLevel2;

    dtmMouse.rX = _dtmDisplay.GetSelFromX ();
    dtmMouse.rY = _dtmDisplay.GetSelFromY ();
    if (_dtmTrias1.GetZ (&dtmMouse, &rLevel1) &&
        _dtmTrias2.GetZ (&dtmMouse, &rLevel2)) {
        _dtmText.Output (TEXT ("z values at %.3f, %.3f:\r\n"),
            dtmMouse.rX, dtmMouse.rY);
        _dtmText.Output (TEXT (" primary triangles: %.3f\r\n"), rLevel1);
        _dtmText.Output (TEXT (" secondary triangles: %.3f\r\n"), rLevel2);
        _dtmText.Output (TEXT (" difference: %.3f\r\n"), rLevel2 - rLevel1);
    }
    else {
        _dtmText.Output (TEXT ("Unable to find difference at %.3f, %.3f\r\n"),
            dtmMouse.rX, dtmMouse.rY);
    }
}
```

**Chapter13.cpp** has the same layout as source code files in earlier chapters in this book. It starts with the header files, followed by child window IDs, task IDs, the task batch size constant GETDIFFERENCE_STEPSIZE which is used when calculating the difference in z values, and coloured pen numbers. There is an additional constant DIFF_ PROXIMITY which sets the proximity, or how close, points can be for them to be treated as if they're the same. It is similar to COORD_PROXIMITY in Chapter 3.

Chapter13.cpp then defines nine global variables, most of which are the same as in earlier chapters. _dtmDiffs is a points array that contains the points with z values equal to the difference in z values between the two DTMS. _dtmTrias1 and _dtmTrias2 are two triangles arrays that contain the two DTMs.

Ten functions are then declared, followed by the C++ source code.

The functions *WinMain*, *WndProc*, *CarryOutTasks*, *DrawModel*, *InitShowDropdownMenu* and *InitMouseDropdownMenu* are similar to the equivalent functions in earlier chapters. The user can import two sets of triangles, calculate the differences in z values between the two sets of triangles storing the data as points, and then export the points. *DrawModel* draws the two sets of triangles first, followed by the points.

The function *GetDifferenceStart* starts the task that calculates the difference in z values. *hwnd* is the handle of the parent window and *uTaskID* is the task ID number. If there are no triangles in either of the two triangles arrays _dtmTrias1 or _dtmTrias2, the function displays an error message. If the points array _dtmDiffs already contains some points, the function asks the user if they want to discard this data. If the user selects 'Yes', any existing points are discarded. Finally, *GetDifferenceStart* displays a message in the text window and starts the task. The function returns TRUE if successful, or FALSE if the user cancels the task or an error occurs.

The function *GetDifferenceCont* carries out the task that calculates the difference in z values. *GetDifferenceCont* follows the standard task manager template as discussed in Chapter 1. It divides the task into three stages: (i) get differences at the corners of the triangles in *_dtmTrias1*, (ii) get differences at the corners of the triangles in *_dtmTrias2*, and (iii) get differences where the edges of the triangles in *_dtmTrias1* cross the edges of the triangles in *_dtmTrias2*. Stages 1 and 2 both call the function *GetDifferenceAtCorners*, with the sign of the last value passed to the function reversed in Stage 2 so that difference in z values remain as *_dtmTrias1* subtracted from *_dtmTrias2*. Stage 3 falls through the end of the switch-statement when the task is finished, and the number of points added to *_dtmDiffs* is displayed in the text window. The function returns the TASK_ constants as discussed in Chapter 1.

The function *GetDifferenceAtCorners* calculates the difference in z values between the two triangles arrays *pdtmTrias1* and *pdtmTrias2* at the x,y positions of each corner of each triangle in *pdtmTrias1*. *rSign* is either 1.0 if *pdtmTrias1* is subtracted from *pdtmTrias2*, or -1.0 if *pdtmTrias2* is subtracted from *pdtmTrias1*. *GetDifferenceAtCorners* looks through the triangles in *pdtmTrias1* in batches. It uses a break-statement to exit its while-loop early if the current triangle in *pdtmTrias1* is to the right of the overall maximum x value of *pdtmTrias2*. This is because, as the triangles are stored in ascending x value order, all subsequent triangles in *pdtmTrias1* will also be to the right of *pdtmTrias2*. Therefore no further difference in z values can be calculated as no more triangles will overlap. It also sets the task item number to the end of *pdtmTrias1* to indicate that this stage of the task is complete. Otherwise if still within the limits of *pdtmTrias2*, *GetDifferenceAtCorners* gets the coordinates at each corner of the current triangle in *pdtmTrias1* and obtains the z value at the same x,y coordinates in *pdtmTrias2*. If successful, the difference in z values is stored as the z value of a new point at the current corner's x,y coordinates, and the new point is added to the *_dtmDiffs* points array. The function returns TRUE if it has not yet reached the end of *pdtmTrias1*, or FALSE if it has reached the end or if an error occurs. It does not return TASK_ constants despite using task manager functions.

The function *GetDifferenceAtCrossingEdges* calculates the difference in z values between the two triangles arrays at the x,y positions where the edges of triangles in *_dtmTrias1* cross the edges of triangles in *_dtmTrias2*. *GetDifferenceAtCrossingEdges* looks through the triangles in *_dtmTrias1* in batches comparing each triangle, in an inner while-loop, with each triangle in *_dtmTrias2*. It exits the inner while-loop when it reaches the end of the *_dtmTrias2*, or when the triangles in *_dtmTrias2* are to the right of the triangle in *_dtmTrias1*. Within the inner while-loop, *GetDifferenceAtCrossingEdges* first checks if the two triangles overlap, and uses the continue-statement if they do not overlap to return to the beginning of the while-loop. Otherwise it compares each edge of the triangle in *_dtmTrias1* with each edge of the triangle in *_dtmTrias2*, adding a new point to *_dtmDiffs* if the edges cross between their ends. The z value of the new point is the difference in z values between the two edges where they cross. The edges cross between their ends when:

```
rAlong1 > 0, rAlong1 < 1, rAlong2 > 0 and rAlong2 < 1
```

which when using FUZZFACTOR becomes:

```
rAlong1 >= FUZZFACTOR, (1 - rAlong1) >= FUZZFACTOR,
rAlong2 >= FUZZFACTOR and (1 - rAlong2) >= FUZZFACTOR,
```

*GetDifferenceAtCrossingEdges* returns TRUE if it has not yet reached the end of *_dtmTrias1*, or FALSE if it has reached the end or if an error occurs. It does not return TASK_ constants despite using task manager functions.

The function *GetDifferenceAtMouse* displays the z values and the difference in z values between *_dtmTrias1* and *_dtmTrias2* at the x,y location where the user has left-clicked the mouse in the graphics window. The function displays the values in the text window, or an error message if the difference in z value cannot be calculated because the mouse's position is outside one or both of the DTMs.

## Running Chapter13

Before you can compile and run your program, you need to add the following nineteen source files to your Chapter13 project. Refer to Chapter 1 for how to do this:

| | | |
|---|---|---|
| **TextWnd.h** | **TextWnd.cpp** | |
| **FileInOut.h** | **FileInOut.cpp** | |
| **BigTask.h** | **BigTask.cpp** | |
| **Graphics.h** | **Graphics.cpp** | |
| **Colours.h** | **Colours.cpp** | |
| **Shapes.h** | **Shapes.cpp** | |
| **Points.cpp** | **Triangles.cpp** | |
| **Common.h** | **Common.cpp** | |
| **Chapter13.h** | **Chapter13.cpp** | **Chapter13.rc** |

You also need to add the Gdiplus.lib library file as an 'additional dependency' in your project's linker/input settings. Refer to Chapter 2 for how to do this. Finally, don't forget to set Chapter13 as your start-up project.

Otherwise, assuming you have compiled the code for Chapter13 successfully, and it is running, you can now test it out.

Start by importing your two DTMs of 3D triangles, one after the other. Click on 'File' in the menu bar, then select 'Import' from the drop-down menu, and finally click on 'Primary triangles' for the first DTM or 'Secondary triangles' for the second DTM. Next, select a file containing the triangles data. You can use the sample files Triangles.txt for the first DTM and TrianglesA_Ch13.txt for the second DTM.

TrianglesA_Ch13.txt is based on the sample file TrianglesA_Ch12.txt used in Chapter 12, except that the extents of the model have been trimmed (using a CAD program) to the intersection line created in Chapter 12 (refer to Chapter 12 for how to do this).

If both DTMs are imported successfully, the primary DTM should appear as green triangles and the secondary DTM as blue triangles, as shown in the following image (the colours have been changed to make it easier to differentiate between the two sets of triangles):

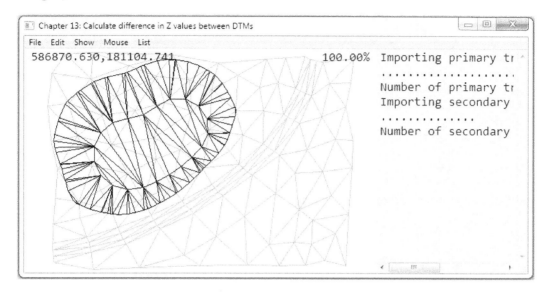

To calculate the difference in z values between the two DTMs, click on 'Edit' in the menu bar and select 'Calculate difference' from the drop-down menu. If successful, the program's window should look something like this (again, the colours have been changed to make the point crosses more prominent):

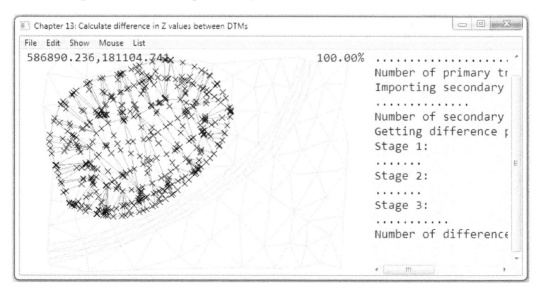

In our example, 495 points have been created.

You can then export this data by clicking on 'File' in the menu bar, selecting 'Export' in the drop-down menu and then 'Difference points'.

If you click on 'List' in the menu bar, select 'Statistics' from the drop-down menu and then 'Difference points', the minimum and maximum x,y,z values of the points are displayed. In our example the minimum z value is -3.499 and the maximum z value is 0.001. The z values are actually the difference in z values between the two DTMs. Therefore the maximum depth of cut between the two models is 3.499 units. The maximum height of fill is 0.001 units. This second value is a rounding error, as it should be zero because the secondary DTM is all cut, representing a balancing pond cut out of the primary DTM, and its extents have been trimmed to tie into the primary DTM.

If you import the second Chapter 13 sample file TrianglesB_Ch13.txt via 'File', 'Import', 'Secondary triangles' (and answer 'Yes' when the program asks if you want to discard any existing secondary triangles), and then create a new set of points via 'Edit', 'Calculate difference' (again, answering 'Yes' to discard any existing difference points), the program's window should look something like this:

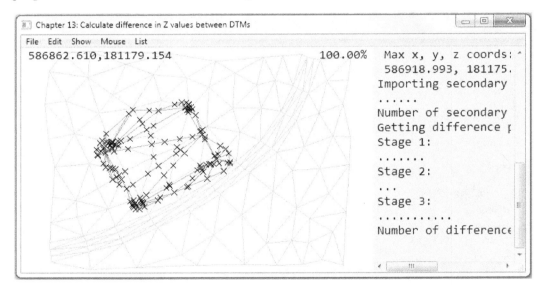

This model is smaller. If you click on 'List', 'Statistics', 'Difference points' again, it shows that this model creates 148 difference points, the maximum depth of cut is 0.628 units and the maximum height of fill is 1.000 units.

If you click on 'Mouse' in the menu bar and select 'Difference' from the drop-down menu, then when you left-click your mouse in the graphics window the values of each DTM and the difference in z values are displayed in the text window. If z values cannot be calculated for both DTMs because you left-clicked outside the extents of either or both DTMs, an error message is displayed. Negative difference z values indicate locations where the secondary DTM is below the primary DTM. Positive difference z values indicate locations where the secondary DTM is above the primary DTM.

As in previous chapters, to exit the program click on 'File' in the menu bar, select 'Exit' and then choose 'Yes' in the message box that appears.

The points data created by the program in Chapter 13 can be used for many purposes such as calculating the minimum and maximum differences in z values (i.e. the maximum depth of cut and the maximum height of fill) as already mentioned. The data can also be used for calculating cut and fill volumes by following these steps:

(i) Import the points data into the program in Chapter 4 ('File', 'Import', 'Points'). You can also import breaklines and boundaries if necessary.

(ii) Click on 'Edit' then 'Create triangles' in the Chapter 4 program to create a new DTM where the z values are based on the differences in z values between the original primary and secondary DTMs. On my computer, the model based on TrianglesA_Ch13.txt containing 495 points took about seven minutes to complete. Once the model is created, it might be necessary to swap some triangle edges if some of the triangles still cross breaklines, and to delete flat triangles around the edge of the DTM if a boundary was not imported.

(iii) Click on 'File', 'Export', 'All triangles' to export the new DTM as a text file.

(iv) Import that text file into the program in Chapter 8 ('File', 'Import', 'Triangles').

(v) Click on 'Edit' then 'Total area and volume' in the Chapter 8 program to display in the text window the total area and volume for the new DTM.

For the differences DTM created from TrianglesA_Ch13.txt the total volume on my computer is -4013.485 cubic units. This value is negative because TrianglesA_Ch13.txt represents a hole, or pond, dug out of the original Triangles.txt sample file. Negative volumes represent cut. Positive volumes represent fill. The volume calculated on your computer will be slightly different if you swapped different triangles to me in (ii) above.

For the differences DTM created from TrianglesB_Ch13.txt the total volume on my computer is -23.024 cubic units. This value is much smaller because it is a combination of fill and cut. Ideally the volume should be zero to indicate that all excavated 'cut' material is used up as fill material, therefore not requiring additional material to be imported to site, or surplus material to be removed. In reality some of the cut material will be 'lost' due to compaction and other site processes. So the total volume would ideally be a factor (for example ten percent) of the cut volume to avoid the need to import extra fill material.

To separate out the cut and fill volumes for this last DTM, the DTM would need to be split in two. This can be done by exporting the DTM in the program in Chapter 4 as a CAD script file, then importing that file into your CAD program, where you can separate or split the data before using the lisp routine EXTRACTTRIAS (see Appendix A) to export the DTM triangles into separate text files, one for cut, the other for fill, to be re-imported separately into the program in Chapter 8.

The following images show the DTMs created in the program in Chapter 4, imported into the program in Chapter 8, for the two sets of differences in z values created by the program in this chapter.

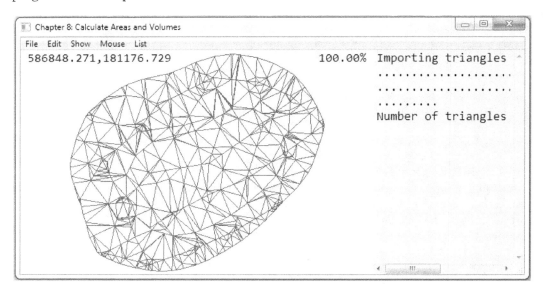

The DTM above is based on the differences in z values between the sample files Triangles.txt and TrianglesA_Ch13.txt. It contains 888 triangles.

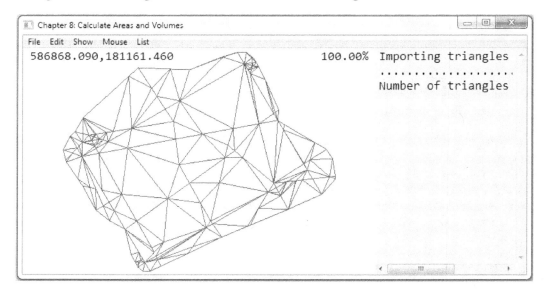

The DTM above is based on the differences in z values between the sample files Triangles.txt and TrianglesB_Ch13.txt. It contains 248 triangles.

# Chapter 14

## Create a Section Through a DTM

Chapter 14 lists the source code for a program called **Chapter14** that creates a section through a DTM along a path that includes lines and/or arcs. The section's chainage and x,y,z values, and section high and low points can be exported as CAD script files, as text files or as JPEG files. The user can switch views between the DTM's plan model and the section model. The user can also obtain x,y,z values, chainages and offsets from the path at individual locations by left-clicking the mouse in the graphics window.

The following files are discussed in this chapter:

**Chapter14.h**          **Chapter14.rc**          **Chapter14.cpp**

## Chapter14 Source Files

The first file is the header file:

**CHAPTER14.H**

```
#ifndef CHAPTER14_H
#define CHAPTER14_H

#define IDM_IMPORTTRIANGLES       101
#define IDM_IMPORTPATHS           102
#define IDM_EXPORTSECTIONS        103
#define IDM_EXPORTPLANPOINTS      104
#define IDM_EXPORTHILOPOINTS      105
#define IDM_EXPORTSCREEN          106
#define IDM_EXPORTMODEL           107
#define IDM_EXIT                  108

#define IDM_GETSECTIONS           201

#define IDN_SHOWMENU              2

#define IDM_SHOWTRIANGLES         301
#define IDM_SHOWPATHS             302
#define IDM_SHOWSECTIONS          303
#define IDM_SHOWPLANPOINTS        304
#define IDM_SHOWHILOPOINTS        305
#define IDM_COLOURBACKGROUND      306
#define IDM_COLOURCOORDSTEXT      307
#define IDM_COLOURTRIANGLES       308
#define IDM_COLOURPATHS           309
#define IDM_COLOURSECTIONS        310
#define IDM_COLOURPLANPOINTS      311
#define IDM_COLOURVERTLINES       312
#define IDM_COLOURHILOPOINTS      313
#define IDM_ZOOMEXTENTS           314
#define IDM_REDRAW                315
```

```
#define IDN_MOUSEMENU              3

#define IDM_MOUSEZOOM              401
#define IDM_MOUSEPAN               402
#define IDM_MOUSECOORDS            403

#define IDM_LISTTRIANGLESSTATS     501
#define IDM_LISTPATHSSTATS         502
#define IDM_LISTSECTIONSSTATS      503
#define IDM_LISTPLANPOINTSSTATS    504
#define IDM_LISTHILOPOINTSSTATS    505
#define IDM_LISTTRIANGLES          506
#define IDM_LISTPATHS              507
#define IDM_LISTSECTIONS           508
#define IDM_LISTPLANPOINTS         509
#define IDM_LISTHILOPOINTS         510

#define IDN_VIEWMENU               5

#define IDM_VIEWPLAN               601
#define IDM_VIEWSECTIONS           602

#define IDM_ESCAPEKEY              901

#endif // CHAPTER14_H
```

As in previous chapters, **Chapter14.h** contains ID numbers for menu bar options, drop-down menus (one more than in previous chapters) and accelerator keys.

The second file is the resource script file:

## CHAPTER14.RC

```
#include <windows.h>
#include "Chapter14.h"

Chapter14 MENU {
    POPUP "&File" {
        POPUP "&Import" {
            MENUITEM "&Triangles",          IDM_IMPORTTRIANGLES
            MENUITEM "P&aths",              IDM_IMPORTPATHS
        }
        POPUP "&Export" {
            MENUITEM "&Sections",           IDM_EXPORTSECTIONS
            MENUITEM "&Plan points",        IDM_EXPORTPLANPOINTS
            MENUITEM "&High/low points",    IDM_EXPORTHILOPOINTS
            MENUITEM SEPARATOR
            MENUITEM "S&creen image",       IDM_EXPORTSCREEN
            MENUITEM "&Model image",        IDM_EXPORTMODEL
        }
        MENUITEM SEPARATOR
        MENUITEM "E&xit",                   IDM_EXIT
    }
    POPUP "&Edit" {
        MENUITEM "Calculate section",       IDM_GETSECTIONS
    }
    POPUP "&Show" {
        MENUITEM "&Triangles",              IDM_SHOWTRIANGLES
        MENUITEM "P&aths",                  IDM_SHOWPATHS
        MENUITEM "&Sections",               IDM_SHOWSECTIONS
```

```
            MENUITEM "&Plan points",              IDM_SHOWPLANPOINTS
            MENUITEM "&High/low points",          IDM_SHOWHILOPOINTS
            MENUITEM SEPARATOR
            POPUP "&Colour" {
                MENUITEM "Back&ground",           IDM_COLOURBACKGROUND
                MENUITEM "&Coords text",          IDM_COLOURCOORDSTEXT
                MENUITEM SEPARATOR
                MENUITEM "&Triangles",            IDM_COLOURTRIANGLES
                MENUITEM "P&aths",                IDM_COLOURPATHS
                MENUITEM "&Sections",             IDM_COLOURSECTIONS
                MENUITEM "&Plan points",          IDM_COLOURPLANPOINTS
                MENUITEM "&Vertical lines",       IDM_COLOURVERTLINES
                MENUITEM "&High/low points",      IDM_COLOURHILOPOINTS
            }
            MENUITEM SEPARATOR
            MENUITEM "&Zoom extents",             IDM_ZOOMEXTENTS
            MENUITEM "&Redraw",                   IDM_REDRAW
        }
        POPUP "&Mouse" {
            MENUITEM "&Zoom in/out",              IDM_MOUSEZOOM
            MENUITEM "&Pan",                      IDM_MOUSEPAN
            MENUITEM SEPARATOR
            MENUITEM "&Coordinates",              IDM_MOUSECOORDS
        }
        POPUP "&List" {
            POPUP "&Statistics" {
                MENUITEM "&Triangles",            IDM_LISTTRIANGLESSTATS
                MENUITEM "P&aths",                IDM_LISTPATHSSTATS
                MENUITEM "&Sections",             IDM_LISTSECTIONSSTATS
                MENUITEM "&Plan points",          IDM_LISTPLANPOINTSSTATS
                MENUITEM "&High/low points",      IDM_LISTHILOPOINTSSTATS
            }
            MENUITEM SEPARATOR
            MENUITEM "&Triangles",                IDM_LISTTRIANGLES
            MENUITEM "P&aths",                    IDM_LISTPATHS
            MENUITEM "&Sections",                 IDM_LISTSECTIONS
            MENUITEM "&Plan points",              IDM_LISTPLANPOINTS
            MENUITEM "&High/low points",          IDM_LISTHILOPOINTS
        }
        POPUP "&View" {
            MENUITEM "&Plan",                     IDM_VIEWPLAN
            MENUITEM "&Section",                  IDM_VIEWSECTIONS
        }
}

Chapter14 ACCELERATORS {
    VK_ESCAPE,        IDM_ESCAPEKEY,              VIRTKEY, NOINVERT
}
```

Like previous chapters, **Chapter14.rc** defines the contents of the program's menu bar and accelerator keys. There is an additional option 'View' in the menu bar to enable the user to switch views between the DTM's plan model and the section model. There is no custom dialog box in this program.

The third file is the source code file, which includes function listings.

**CHAPTER14.CPP**

```
#ifndef UNICODE
#define UNICODE
```

```
#endif

#include <windows.h>
#include <gdiplus.h>
using namespace Gdiplus;
#include <math.h>
#include "Chapter14.h"
#include "BigTask.h"
#include "FileInOut.h"
#include "TextWnd.h"
#include "Graphics.h"
#include "Colours.h"
#include "Shapes.h"
#include "Common.h"

#define ID_TEXTWND                      1
#define ID_DISPLAYWND                   2
#define ID_IMAGEEXPORT                  3

#define IDT_IMPORTTRIANGLES             11
#define IDT_IMPORTPATHS                 12

#define IDT_EXPORTPLANPOINTS            21
#define IDT_EXPORTPLANPOINTSSCRIPT      22
#define IDT_EXPORTSECTIONS              23
#define IDT_EXPORTSECTIONSSCRIPT        24
#define IDT_EXPORTHILOPOINTS            25
#define IDT_EXPORTHILOPOINTSSCRIPT      26
#define IDT_EXPORTIMAGE                 27

#define IDT_GETSECTIONS                 31
#define IDT_GETSECTIONSCURVEPOINTS      32

#define IDT_LISTTRIANGLES               41
#define IDT_LISTPATHS                   42
#define IDT_LISTSECTIONS                43
#define IDT_LISTPLANPOINTS              44
#define IDT_LISTHILOPOINTS              45

#define MODEL_PLAN                      1
#define MODEL_SECTIONS                  2

#define GETSECTIONS_STEPSIZE            20L

#define PENCOLOUR_PLANPOINTS            4
#define PENCOLOUR_TRIANGLES             11
#define PENCOLOUR_PATHS                 9
#define PENCOLOUR_SECTIONS              9
#define PENCOLOUR_HILOPOINTS            0
#define PENCOLOUR_SECTVERTLINES         8

#define VERTICAL_EXAG                   10.0

#define NODE_MAX_COUNT                  10

#define NODE_EMPTY                      0
#define NODE_STARTOREND                 1
#define NODE_HILOPOINT                  2
#define NODE_ATEDGE                     4
```

```
#define SECTZVAL_SECTLINE          0.0
#define SECTZVAL_ABOVE             1.0
#define SECTZVAL_BELOW             -1.0
#define SECTZVAL_HILOPOINT         0.0

#define SECTVLINE_INITLEN          0.1
#define SECTVLINE_BEYONDMINMAX     0.5

#define MAX_ARC_STEPINC            1.0

struct DTMNODE {
    DTMCOORD cdPoint;
    DOUBLE rAlong;
    DOUBLE rChainage;
    WORD wType;
};

DTMTEXTWINDOW _dtmText;
DTMFILEDATA _dtmFile;
DTMBIGTASK _dtmTask, _dtmTaskDisplay;
DTMDISPLAY _dtmDisplay;
DTMMODEL _dtmModel;
DTMCOLOURS _dtmColours;
DTMTRIAS _dtmTrias;
DTMPATHS _dtmPaths;
DTMLINES _dtmSects;
DTMPOINTS _dtmPlanPoints, _dtmHiLoPoints;

LRESULT CALLBACK WndProc (HWND, UINT, WPARAM, LPARAM);
BOOL CarryOutTasks (HWND);
WORD DrawModel (DTMFRAME *, DTMBIGTASK *);
void InitShowDropdownMenu (HMENU);
void InitMouseDropdownMenu (HMENU);
void InitViewDropdownMenu (HMENU);
BOOL GetSectionsStart (HWND, UINT, UINT);
WORD GetSectionsCont (BOOL);
BOOL GetNodesAlongArc (DTMPATH *, DTMTRIA *, DTMNODE *);
BOOL IsAngleBetween (DOUBLE *, DOUBLE, DOUBLE);
BOOL AddNode (DTMNODE *, DOUBLE, DOUBLE, DOUBLE, DOUBLE, DOUBLE, WORD);
BOOL DoLineAndCircleCross (DOUBLE, DOUBLE, DOUBLE, DOUBLE,
    DOUBLE, DOUBLE, DOUBLE, DOUBLE *, DOUBLE *);
BOOL GetNodesAlongLine (DTMPATH *, DTMTRIA *, DTMNODE *);
BOOL CreateSectionsFromNodes (DTMPATH *, DTMTRIA *, DTMNODE *, BOOL);
void GetCoordsAtMouse (void);

int WINAPI WinMain (HINSTANCE hInst, HINSTANCE, PSTR, int nCmdShow) {
    return InitAndRunProgram (hInst, nCmdShow, TEXT ("Chapter14"),
        TEXT ("Chapter 14: Create section through DTM"));
}

LRESULT CALLBACK WndProc (HWND hwnd, UINT message, WPARAM wParam, LPARAM lParam) {
    switch (message) {
        case WM_CREATE : {
            HINSTANCE hInst;

            hInst = ((LPCREATESTRUCT) lParam)->hInstance;
            _dtmText.Create (hwnd, ID_TEXTWND, hInst);
            _dtmFile.Init (hwnd);
            _dtmDisplay.Init (hwnd, MODEL_PLAN, ID_DISPLAYWND, hInst,
                1.0, 4.0, 4.0, 10.0, 11.0, 1.0, 2.0, 0.5);
            _dtmModel.Init (MODEL_SECTIONS, VERTICAL_EXAG);
```

```
        _dtmColours.Init ();
        _dtmTrias.Init (TEXT ("triangles"), PENCOLOUR_TRIANGLES, 0, FALSE);
        _dtmPaths.Init (TEXT ("path elements"), PENCOLOUR_PATHS);
        _dtmSects.Init (TEXT ("section lines"), PENCOLOUR_SECTIONS);
        _dtmPlanPoints.Init (TEXT ("section points"), PENCOLOUR_PLANPOINTS,
            POINTSTYLE_PLUS);
        _dtmHiLoPoints.Init (TEXT ("high and low points"), PENCOLOUR_HILOPOINTS,
            POINTSTYLE_CROSS);
        return 0;
    }
case WM_ENTERSIZEMOVE :
    _dtmDisplay.StartResizing ();
    return 0;
case WM_SIZE :
    ResizeChildWindows (lParam);
    return 0;
case WM_EXITSIZEMOVE :
    _dtmDisplay.StopResizing ();
    return 0;
case WM_INITMENUPOPUP :
    if (HIWORD (lParam) == FALSE) {
        switch (LOWORD (lParam)) {
            case IDN_SHOWMENU :
                InitShowDropdownMenu ((HMENU) wParam);
                return 0;
            case IDN_MOUSEMENU :
                InitMouseDropdownMenu ((HMENU) wParam);
                return 0;
            case IDN_VIEWMENU :
                InitViewDropdownMenu ((HMENU) wParam);
                return 0;
            default : break;
        }
    }
    break;
case WM_COMMAND :
    if (HIWORD (wParam) == 0) {
        switch (LOWORD (wParam)) {
            case IDM_IMPORTTRIANGLES :
                _dtmTrias.ImportStart (hwnd, IDT_IMPORTTRIANGLES);
                return 0;
            case IDM_IMPORTPATHS :
                _dtmPaths.ImportStart (hwnd, IDT_IMPORTPATHS);
                return 0;
            case IDM_EXPORTSECTIONS :
                _dtmSects.ExportStart (IDT_EXPORTSECTIONS,
                    IDT_EXPORTSECTIONSSCRIPT);
                return 0;
            case IDM_EXPORTPLANPOINTS :
                _dtmPlanPoints.ExportStart (IDT_EXPORTPLANPOINTS,
                    IDT_EXPORTPLANPOINTSSCRIPT);
                return 0;
            case IDM_EXPORTHILOPOINTS :
                _dtmHiLoPoints.ExportStart (IDT_EXPORTHILOPOINTS,
                    IDT_EXPORTHILOPOINTSSCRIPT);
                return 0;
            case IDM_EXPORTSCREEN :
                ExportImage (FALSE, ID_IMAGEEXPORT);
                return 0;
            case IDM_EXPORTMODEL :
                ExportImage (TRUE, ID_IMAGEEXPORT);
```

```
            return 0;
        case IDM_EXIT :
            SendMessage (hwnd, WM_CLOSE, 0, 0);
            return 0;
        case IDM_GETSECTIONS :
            GetSectionsStart (hwnd, IDT_GETSECTIONS,
                IDT_GETSECTIONSCURVEPOINTS);
            return 0;
        case IDM_SHOWTRIANGLES :
            _dtmTrias.FlipVisible ();
            _dtmTaskDisplay.Start ();
            return 0;
        case IDM_SHOWPATHS :
            _dtmPaths.FlipVisible ();
            _dtmTaskDisplay.Start ();
            return 0;
        case IDM_SHOWSECTIONS :
            _dtmSects.FlipVisible ();
            _dtmTaskDisplay.Start ();
            return 0;
        case IDM_SHOWPLANPOINTS :
            _dtmPlanPoints.FlipVisible ();
            _dtmTaskDisplay.Start ();
            return 0;
        case IDM_SHOWHILOPOINTS :
            _dtmHiLoPoints.FlipVisible ();
            _dtmTaskDisplay.Start ();
            return 0;
        case IDM_COLOURBACKGROUND :
            ChangeBackgroundColour (hwnd);
            return 0;
        case IDM_COLOURCOORDSTEXT :
            ChangeCoordsTextColour (hwnd);
            return 0;
        case IDM_COLOURTRIANGLES :
            ChangePenColour (hwnd, PENCOLOUR_TRIANGLES);
            return 0;
        case IDM_COLOURPATHS :
            ChangePenColour (hwnd, PENCOLOUR_PATHS);
            return 0;
        case IDM_COLOURSECTIONS :
            ChangePenColour (hwnd, PENCOLOUR_SECTIONS);
            return 0;
        case IDM_COLOURPLANPOINTS :
            ChangePenColour (hwnd, PENCOLOUR_PLANPOINTS);
            return 0;
        case IDM_COLOURVERTLINES :
            ChangePenColour (hwnd, PENCOLOUR_SECTVERTLINES);
            return 0;
        case IDM_COLOURHILOPOINTS :
            ChangePenColour (hwnd, PENCOLOUR_HILOPOINTS);
            return 0;
        case IDM_ZOOMEXTENTS :
            _dtmDisplay.ZoomExtents ();
            _dtmTaskDisplay.Start ();
            return 0;
        case IDM_REDRAW :
            _dtmTaskDisplay.Start ();
            return 0;
        case IDM_MOUSEZOOM :
            _dtmDisplay.SetMouseAction (MOUSEACT_ZOOM);
```

```
                            return 0;
                    case IDM_MOUSEPAN :
                        _dtmDisplay.SetMouseAction (MOUSEACT_PAN);
                        return 0;
                    case IDM_MOUSECOORDS :
                        _dtmDisplay.SetMouseAction (MOUSEACT_POINT);
                        return 0;
                    case IDM_LISTTRIANGLESSTATS :
                        _dtmTrias.ListStats ();
                        return 0;
                    case IDM_LISTPATHSSTATS :
                        _dtmPaths.ListStats ();
                        return 0;
                    case IDM_LISTSECTIONSSTATS :
                        _dtmSects.ListStats ();
                        return 0;
                    case IDM_LISTPLANPOINTSSTATS :
                        _dtmPlanPoints.ListStats ();
                        return 0;
                    case IDM_LISTHILOPOINTSSTATS :
                        _dtmHiLoPoints.ListStats ();
                        return 0;
                    case IDM_LISTTRIANGLES :
                        _dtmTrias.ListStart (IDT_LISTTRIANGLES);
                        return 0;
                    case IDM_LISTPATHS :
                        _dtmPaths.ListStart (IDT_LISTPATHS);
                        return 0;
                    case IDM_LISTSECTIONS :
                        _dtmSects.ListStart (IDT_LISTSECTIONS);
                        return 0;
                    case IDM_LISTPLANPOINTS :
                        _dtmPlanPoints.ListStart (IDT_LISTPLANPOINTS);
                        return 0;
                    case IDM_LISTHILOPOINTS :
                        _dtmHiLoPoints.ListStart (IDT_LISTHILOPOINTS);
                        return 0;
                    case IDM_VIEWPLAN :
                        _dtmDisplay.SetView (MODEL_PLAN, &_dtmModel);
                        _dtmTaskDisplay.Start ();
                        return 0;
                    case IDM_VIEWSECTIONS :
                        _dtmDisplay.SetView (MODEL_SECTIONS, &_dtmModel);
                        _dtmTaskDisplay.Start ();
                        return 0;
                    default : break;
            }
        }
        else if (HIWORD (wParam) == 1) {
            if (LOWORD (wParam) == IDM_ESCAPEKEY) {
                _dtmTask.Quit (TRUE);
                _dtmTaskDisplay.Quit (TRUE);
                return 0;
            }
        }
        else if (LOWORD (wParam) == ID_DISPLAYWND) {
            switch (HIWORD (wParam)) {
                case DTM_REDRAW :
                    _dtmTaskDisplay.Start ();
                    return 0;
                case DTM_DRAW_STOPPED :
```

```
                            case DTM_DRAW_COMPLETED :
                                _dtmDisplay.RepaintNow (REPAINT_ALL);
                                return 0;
                            case DTM_SELPOINT :
                                GetCoordsAtMouse ();
                                return 0;
                            default : return 0;
                    }
                }
                else if (LOWORD (wParam) == ID_IMAGEEXPORT) {
                    ProcessExportImageMessages (wParam, IDT_EXPORTIMAGE);
                    return 0;
                }
                break;
            case WM_CLOSE :
                AskCloseWindowMessage (hwnd);
                return 0;
            case WM_DESTROY:
                _dtmDisplay.Free ();
                _dtmColours.Free ();
                _dtmText.Destroy ();
                _dtmFile.FreeImportBuffer ();
                _dtmTrias.Free ();
                _dtmPaths.Free ();
                _dtmSects.Free ();
                _dtmPlanPoints.Free ();
                _dtmHiLoPoints.Free ();
                PostQuitMessage (0);
                return 0;
            default : break;
        }
        return DefWindowProc (hwnd, message, wParam, lParam);
}

BOOL CarryOutTasks (HWND hwnd) {
    WORD wTaskStatus;

    if (!_dtmTask.IsBusy ()) {
        return FALSE;
    }
    if (_dtmTask.GetStage () == 0) {
        EnableMenuBar (hwnd, FALSE);
        _dtmDisplay.Enable (FALSE);
        _dtmTask.NextStage ();
    }
    switch (_dtmTask.GetID ()) {
        case IDT_IMPORTTRIANGLES :
            wTaskStatus = _dtmTrias.ImportCont (FALSE);
            break;
        case IDT_IMPORTPATHS :
            wTaskStatus = _dtmPaths.ImportCont (FALSE);
            break;
        case IDT_EXPORTSECTIONS :
            wTaskStatus = _dtmSects.ExportCont (FALSE);
            break;
        case IDT_EXPORTSECTIONSSCRIPT :
            wTaskStatus = _dtmSects.ExportCont (TRUE, VERTICAL_EXAG);
            break;
        case IDT_EXPORTPLANPOINTS :
            wTaskStatus = _dtmPlanPoints.ExportCont (FALSE);
            break;
```

```
        case IDT_EXPORTPLANPOINTSSCRIPT :
            wTaskStatus = _dtmPlanPoints.ExportCont (TRUE);
            break;
        case IDT_EXPORTHILOPOINTS :
            wTaskStatus = _dtmHiLoPoints.ExportCont (FALSE);
            break;
        case IDT_EXPORTHILOPOINTSSCRIPT :
            wTaskStatus = _dtmHiLoPoints.ExportCont (TRUE, VERTICAL_EXAG);
            break;
        case IDT_EXPORTIMAGE :
            wTaskStatus = DrawModel (_dtmDisplay.GetImageDtmPtr (), &_dtmTask);
            break;
        case IDT_GETSECTIONS :
            wTaskStatus = GetSectionsCont (FALSE);
            break;
        case IDT_GETSECTIONSCURVEPOINTS :
            wTaskStatus = GetSectionsCont (TRUE);
            break;
        case IDT_LISTTRIANGLES :
            wTaskStatus = _dtmTrias.ListCont ();
            break;
        case IDT_LISTPATHS :
            wTaskStatus = _dtmPaths.ListCont ();
            break;
        case IDT_LISTSECTIONS :
            wTaskStatus = _dtmSects.ListCont ();
            break;
        case IDT_LISTPLANPOINTS :
            wTaskStatus = _dtmPlanPoints.ListCont ();
            break;
        case IDT_LISTHILOPOINTS :
            wTaskStatus = _dtmHiLoPoints.ListCont ();
            break;
        default :
            wTaskStatus = TASK_STOPPED;
            break;
    }
    if ((wTaskStatus & TASK_STOPPED) || (wTaskStatus & TASK_COMPLETED)) {
        EnableMenuBar (hwnd, TRUE);
        _dtmDisplay.Enable (TRUE);
        _dtmTask.Stop ();
    }
    if (wTaskStatus & TASK_COMPLETED) {
        switch (_dtmTask.GetID ()) {
            case IDT_IMPORTTRIANGLES :
                _dtmDisplay.SetView (MODEL_PLAN, &_dtmModel);
                AddShapeToDisplay (&_dtmTrias);
                break;
            case IDT_IMPORTPATHS :
                _dtmDisplay.SetView (MODEL_PLAN, &_dtmModel);
                AddShapeToDisplay (&_dtmPaths);
                break;
            case IDT_GETSECTIONS :
            case IDT_GETSECTIONSCURVEPOINTS :
                _dtmDisplay.SetView (MODEL_PLAN, &_dtmModel);
                AddShapeToDisplay (&_dtmPlanPoints);
                _dtmDisplay.SetView (MODEL_SECTIONS, &_dtmModel);
                AddShapeToDisplay (&_dtmSects);
                AddShapeToDisplay (&_dtmHiLoPoints);
                break;
            default : break;
```

```
            }
        }
        if (wTaskStatus & TASK_REDRAW) {
            _dtmTaskDisplay.Start ();
        }
        return TRUE;
}

WORD DrawModel (DTMFRAME * pdtmFrame, DTMBIGTASK * pdtmTask) {
    if (pdtmFrame == NULL || !pdtmFrame->IsActive () ||
        !pdtmFrame->IsGdiOK () || pdtmTask == NULL) {
        return TASK_STOPPED;
    }
    if (pdtmTask->Quit ()) {
        pdtmFrame->NotifyParent (DTM_DRAW_STOPPED);
        return TASK_STOPPED;
    }
    switch (pdtmTask->GetStage ()) {
        case 1 :
            pdtmFrame->ClearBackground ();
            _dtmColours.SetPenWidths (pdtmFrame->GetPenWidth (),
                pdtmFrame->GetVertExag ());
            pdtmTask->NextStage ();
            break;
        case 2 :
            if (pdtmFrame->GetModelID () == MODEL_PLAN) {
                _dtmTrias.Draw (pdtmFrame, pdtmTask);
            }
            else {
                _dtmSects.Draw (pdtmFrame, pdtmTask);
            }
            break;
        case 3 :
            if (pdtmFrame->GetModelID () == MODEL_PLAN) {
                _dtmPaths.Draw (pdtmFrame, pdtmTask);
            }
            else {
                _dtmHiLoPoints.Draw (pdtmFrame, pdtmTask);
            }
            break;
        case 4 :
            if (pdtmFrame->GetModelID () == MODEL_PLAN) {
                _dtmPlanPoints.Draw (pdtmFrame, pdtmTask);
            }
            else {
                pdtmTask->NextStage ();
            }
            break;
        default : break;
    }
    pdtmFrame->NotifyParent (DTM_DRAW_UPDATED);
    if (pdtmTask->GetStage () < 5) {
        return TASK_ONGOING;
    }
    pdtmFrame->NotifyParent (DTM_DRAW_COMPLETED);
    return TASK_COMPLETED;
}

void InitShowDropdownMenu (HMENU hMenu) {
    CheckMenuItem (hMenu, IDM_SHOWTRIANGLES, MF_BYCOMMAND |
        (_dtmTrias.IsVisible () ? MF_CHECKED : MF_UNCHECKED));
```

```
        CheckMenuItem (hMenu, IDM_SHOWPATHS, MF_BYCOMMAND |
            (_dtmPaths.IsVisible () ? MF_CHECKED : MF_UNCHECKED));
        CheckMenuItem (hMenu, IDM_SHOWSECTIONS, MF_BYCOMMAND |
            (_dtmSects.IsVisible () ? MF_CHECKED : MF_UNCHECKED));
        CheckMenuItem (hMenu, IDM_SHOWPLANPOINTS, MF_BYCOMMAND |
            (_dtmPlanPoints.IsVisible () ? MF_CHECKED : MF_UNCHECKED));
        CheckMenuItem (hMenu, IDM_SHOWHILOPOINTS, MF_BYCOMMAND |
            (_dtmHiLoPoints.IsVisible () ? MF_CHECKED : MF_UNCHECKED));
}

void InitMouseDropdownMenu (HMENU hMenu) {
    DTMMOUSEACT mouseAction;

    mouseAction = _dtmDisplay.GetMouseAction ();
    CheckMenuItem (hMenu, IDM_MOUSEZOOM, MF_BYCOMMAND |
        (mouseAction == MOUSEACT_ZOOM ? MF_CHECKED : MF_UNCHECKED));
    CheckMenuItem (hMenu, IDM_MOUSEPAN, MF_BYCOMMAND |
        (mouseAction == MOUSEACT_PAN ? MF_CHECKED : MF_UNCHECKED));
    CheckMenuItem (hMenu, IDM_MOUSECOORDS, MF_BYCOMMAND |
        (mouseAction == MOUSEACT_POINT ? MF_CHECKED : MF_UNCHECKED));
}

void InitViewDropdownMenu (HMENU hMenu) {
    UINT uModelID;

    uModelID = _dtmDisplay.GetModelID ();
    CheckMenuItem (hMenu, IDM_VIEWPLAN, MF_BYCOMMAND |
        (uModelID == MODEL_PLAN ? MF_CHECKED : MF_UNCHECKED));
    CheckMenuItem (hMenu, IDM_VIEWSECTIONS, MF_BYCOMMAND |
        (uModelID == MODEL_SECTIONS ? MF_CHECKED : MF_UNCHECKED));
}

BOOL GetSectionsStart (HWND hwnd, UINT uTaskID, UINT uTaskIDwithCurvePoints) {
    int iMessage;

    if (_dtmTask.IsBusy ()) {
        _dtmText.Output (_szTaskBusyMessage);
        return FALSE;
    }
    if (_dtmTrias.GetTotal () == 0L) {
        _dtmText.Output (TEXT ("There are no %s available. ") \
            TEXT ("Unable to calculate %s\r\n"),
            _dtmTrias.GetDescription (), _dtmSects.GetDescription ());
        return FALSE;
    }
    if (_dtmPaths.GetTotal () == 0L) {
        _dtmText.Output (TEXT ("There are no %s available. ") \
            TEXT ("Unable to calculate %s\r\n"),
            _dtmPaths.GetDescription (), _dtmSects.GetDescription ());
        return FALSE;
    }
    if (_dtmSects.GetTotal () != 0L || _dtmPlanPoints.GetTotal () != 0L ||
        _dtmHiLoPoints.GetTotal () != 0L) {
        iMessage = MessageBox (hwnd,
            TEXT ("Do you want to discard sections and points already created?"),
            TEXT ("Create sections"), MB_YESNOCANCEL | MB_ICONWARNING);
        if (iMessage == IDCANCEL) {
            return FALSE;
        }
        else if (iMessage == IDYES) {
            _dtmSects.Free ();
```

```
                _dtmPlanPoints.Free ();
                _dtmHiLoPoints.Free ();
        }
    }
    iMessage = MessageBox (hwnd,
        TEXT ("Include intermediate plan points along curves?"),
        TEXT ("Create sections"), MB_YESNOCANCEL);
    if (iMessage == IDCANCEL) {
        return FALSE;
    }
    _dtmText.Output (TEXT ("Getting %s\r\n"), _dtmSects.GetDescription ());
    if (iMessage == IDNO) {
        _dtmTask.Start (uTaskID, GETSECTIONS_STEPSIZE);
    }
    else {
        _dtmTask.Start (uTaskIDwithCurvePoints, GETSECTIONS_STEPSIZE);
    }
    return TRUE;
}

WORD GetSectionsCont (BOOL fWithCurvePoints) {
    static DWORD dwTotalAtStart;
    DWORD dwSect;
    DOUBLE rMinY, rMaxY;

    if (_dtmTask.AtStart ()) {
        dwTotalAtStart = _dtmSects.GetTotal ();
    }
    if (_dtmTask.Quit ()) {
        _dtmText.Output (TEXT ("\r\nGetting %s stopped\r\n"),
            _dtmSects.GetDescription ());
        return TASK_STOPPED | TASK_REDRAW;
    }
    _dtmTask.StartNewBatch ();
    while (!_dtmTask.NoMoreItems (_dtmPaths.GetTotal ()) && !_dtmTask.AtEndOfBatch ()) {
        DTMPATH * pdtmPath;
        DWORD dwTria;

        pdtmPath = _dtmPaths.GetPtr (_dtmTask.GetItemNumber ());
        dwTria = 0L;
        while (dwTria < _dtmTrias.GetTotal ()) {
            DTMTRIA * pdtmTria;

            pdtmTria = _dtmTrias.GetPtr (dwTria);
            if (pdtmTria->cdMin.rX > pdtmPath->cdMax.rX) {
                dwTria = _dtmTrias.GetTotal ();
                break;
            }
            if (!(pdtmTria->cdMin.rY > pdtmPath->cdMax.rY ||
                pdtmTria->cdMax.rX < pdtmPath->cdMin.rX ||
                pdtmTria->cdMax.rY < pdtmPath->cdMin.rY)) {
                WORD wNode;
                DTMNODE dtmNodes [NODE_MAX_COUNT];

                for (wNode = 0; wNode < NODE_MAX_COUNT; wNode ++) {
                    dtmNodes [wNode].wType = NODE_EMPTY;
                }
                if (pdtmPath->fCurved) {
                    GetNodesAlongArc (pdtmPath, pdtmTria, dtmNodes);
                }
                else {
```

```
                    GetNodesAlongLine (pdtmPath, pdtmTria, dtmNodes);
                }
                CreateSectionsFromNodes (pdtmPath, pdtmTria, dtmNodes,
                    fWithCurvePoints);
            }
            dwTria ++;
        }
        _dtmTask.NextItem ();
        _dtmTask.IncBatchCounter ();
    }
    _dtmText.ProgressDot ();
    if (!_dtmTask.NoMoreItems (_dtmPaths.GetTotal ())) {
        return TASK_ONGOING;
    }
    rMinY = _dtmSects.GetMinY () - SECTVLINE_BEYONDMINMAX;
    rMaxY = _dtmSects.GetMaxY () + SECTVLINE_BEYONDMINMAX;
    dwSect = 0L;
    while (dwSect < _dtmSects.GetTotal ()) {
        DTMLINE * pdtmSect;

        pdtmSect = _dtmSects.GetPtr (dwSect);
        if (pdtmSect->cdEnd [1].rZ == SECTZVAL_ABOVE) {
            pdtmSect->cdEnd [1].rY = rMaxY;
            _dtmSects.SetShapeLimits (pdtmSect);
        }
        else if (pdtmSect->cdEnd [0].rZ == SECTZVAL_BELOW) {
            pdtmSect->cdEnd [0].rY = rMinY;
            _dtmSects.SetShapeLimits (pdtmSect);
        }
        dwSect ++;
    }
    _dtmSects.ReorderAll ();
    _dtmSects.ResetLimits ();
    _dtmText.Output (TEXT ("\r\nNumber of %s created: %lu\r\n"),
        _dtmSects.GetDescription (), _dtmSects.GetTotal () - dwTotalAtStart);
    return TASK_COMPLETED | TASK_REDRAW;
}


BOOL GetNodesAlongArc (DTMPATH * pdtmPath, DTMTRIA * pdtmTria, DTMNODE * pdtmNodes) {
    WORD wEdge;
    DOUBLE rAngleFrom, rAngleTo, rChainageFrom, rChainageTo, rX1, rY1, rZ1,
        rX2, rY2, rZ2, rAngle, rSlope;

    if (pdtmPath == NULL || pdtmTria == NULL || pdtmNodes == NULL) {
        return FALSE;
    }
    if (pdtmPath->rAngleSweep < 0.0) {
        rAngleFrom = pdtmPath->rAngleFrom + pdtmPath->rAngleSweep;
        rAngleTo = pdtmPath->rAngleFrom;
        if (rAngleFrom < 0.0) {
            rAngleFrom += 360.0;
            rAngleTo += 360.0;
        }
        rChainageFrom = pdtmPath->rChainage + pdtmPath->rLength * pdtmPath->rDirection;
        rChainageTo = pdtmPath->rChainage;
        _dtmPaths.GetEnd (pdtmPath, 1, &rX1, &rY1);
        _dtmPaths.GetEnd (pdtmPath, 0, &rX2, &rY2);
    }
    else {
        rAngleFrom = pdtmPath->rAngleFrom;
        rAngleTo = pdtmPath->rAngleFrom + pdtmPath->rAngleSweep;
```

```
            rChainageFrom = pdtmPath->rChainage;
            rChainageTo = pdtmPath->rChainage + pdtmPath->rLength * pdtmPath->rDirection;
            _dtmPaths.GetEnd (pdtmPath, 0, &rX1, &rY1);
            _dtmPaths.GetEnd (pdtmPath, 1, &rX2, &rY2);
        }
        if (_dtmTrias.IsInside (pdtmTria, rX1, rY1, TRUE)) {
            if (_dtmTrias.GetZ (pdtmTria, rX1, rY1, &rZ1)) {
                AddNode (pdtmNodes, rAngleFrom, rChainageFrom, rX1, rY1, rZ1,
                    NODE_STARTOREND);
            }
        }
        if (_dtmTrias.IsInside (pdtmTria, rX2, rY2, TRUE)) {
            if (_dtmTrias.GetZ (pdtmTria, rX2, rY2, &rZ2)) {
                AddNode (pdtmNodes, rAngleTo, rChainageTo, rX2, rY2, rZ2, NODE_STARTOREND);
            }
        }
    }
    _dtmTrias.GetSlope (pdtmTria, &rSlope, &rAngle);
    if (rSlope != 0.0) {
        DOUBLE rAngleRads;
        WORD wLowThenHigh;

        rAngleRads = rAngle * (PI / 180.0);
        for (wLowThenHigh = 0; wLowThenHigh < 2; wLowThenHigh ++) {
            rX1 = pdtmPath->cdCentre.rX + pdtmPath->rRadius * cos (rAngleRads);
            rY1 = pdtmPath->cdCentre.rY + pdtmPath->rRadius * sin (rAngleRads);
            if (_dtmTrias.IsInside (pdtmTria, rX1, rY1, TRUE) &&
                IsAngleBetween (&rAngle, rAngleFrom, rAngleTo)) {
                if (_dtmTrias.GetZ (pdtmTria, rX1, rY1, &rZ1)) {
                    DOUBLE rChainage;

                    rChainage = rChainageFrom + (rChainageTo - rChainageFrom) *
                        (rAngle - rAngleFrom) / (rAngleTo - rAngleFrom);
                    AddNode (pdtmNodes, rAngle, rChainage, rX1, rY1, rZ1,
                        NODE_HILOPOINT);
                }
            }
            rAngleRads += PI;
            rAngle += 180.0;
            while (rAngle >= 360.0) {
                rAngle -= 360.0;
            }
        }
    }
    for (wEdge = 0; wEdge < TRIA_COORDS; wEdge ++) {
        DOUBLE rAlong1, rAlong2, rX3, rY3, rZ3;

        _dtmTrias.GetEdge (pdtmTria, wEdge, &rX1, &rY1, &rZ1, &rX2, &rY2, &rZ2);
        if (DoLineAndCircleCross (rX1, rY1, rX2, rY2, pdtmPath->cdCentre.rX,
            pdtmPath->cdCentre.rY, pdtmPath->rRadius, &rAlong1, &rAlong2)) {
            WORD wWhichAlong;

            for (wWhichAlong = 0; wWhichAlong < 2; wWhichAlong ++) {
                DOUBLE rAlong;

                rAlong = (wWhichAlong == 0) ? rAlong1 : rAlong2;
                if (rAlong > -FUZZFACTOR && (rAlong - 1.0) < FUZZFACTOR) {
                    rX3 = rX1 + rAlong * (rX2 - rX1);
                    rY3 = rY1 + rAlong * (rY2 - rY1);
                    rZ3 = rZ1 + rAlong * (rZ2 - rZ1);
                    rAngle = GetAngle (rY3 - pdtmPath->cdCentre.rY,
                        rX3 - pdtmPath->cdCentre.rX);
```

```
                    if (IsAngleBetween (&rAngle, rAngleFrom, rAngleTo)) {
                        DOUBLE rChainage;

                        rChainage = rChainageFrom + (rChainageTo - rChainageFrom)
                            * (rAngle - rAngleFrom) / (rAngleTo - rAngleFrom);
                        AddNode (pdtmNodes, rAngle, rChainage, rX3, rY3, rZ3,
                            NODE_ATEDGE);
                    }
                }
                if (rAlong2 == rAlong1) {
                    break;
                }
            }
        }
    }
    return TRUE;
}

BOOL IsAngleBetween (DOUBLE * prAngle, DOUBLE rAngleFrom, DOUBLE rAngleTo) {
    if (prAngle == NULL) {
        return FALSE;
    }
    if (*prAngle >= rAngleFrom && *prAngle <= rAngleTo) {
        return TRUE;
    }
    if (*prAngle + 360.0 >= rAngleFrom && *prAngle + 360.0 <= rAngleTo) {
                // update provided angle so it's between range values
        *prAngle += 360.0;
        return TRUE;
    }
    return FALSE;
}

BOOL AddNode (DTMNODE * pdtmNodes, DOUBLE rAlong, DOUBLE rChainage,
    DOUBLE rX, DOUBLE rY, DOUBLE rZ, WORD wNodeType) {
    DTMNODE * pdtmCurNode;
    WORD wNode;

    if (pdtmNodes == NULL) {
        return FALSE;
    }
    pdtmCurNode = pdtmNodes;
    wNode = 0;
    while (wNode < NODE_MAX_COUNT) {
        if (pdtmCurNode->wType == NODE_EMPTY) {
            SetCoord (&(pdtmCurNode->cdPoint), rX, rY, rZ);
            pdtmCurNode->rAlong = rAlong;
            pdtmCurNode->rChainage = rChainage;
            pdtmCurNode->wType = wNodeType;
            return TRUE;
        }
        else if (fabs (pdtmCurNode->rAlong - rAlong) < FUZZFACTOR) {
            pdtmCurNode->wType |= wNodeType;
            return TRUE;
        }
        else if (rAlong < pdtmCurNode->rAlong) {
            WORD wEmptyNode;
            DTMNODE * pdtmMoveTo;
            DWORD dwBytesMoved;
```

```
                wEmptyNode = wNode + 1;
                while (wEmptyNode < NODE_MAX_COUNT &&
                    (pdtmNodes + wEmptyNode)->wType != NODE_EMPTY) {
                    wEmptyNode ++;
                }
                if (wEmptyNode == NODE_MAX_COUNT) {
                    return FALSE;
                }
                pdtmMoveTo = pdtmCurNode + 1;
                dwBytesMoved = (wEmptyNode - wNode) * sizeof (DTMNODE);
                MoveMemory (pdtmMoveTo, pdtmCurNode, dwBytesMoved);
                SetCoord (&(pdtmCurNode->cdPoint), rX, rY, rZ);
                pdtmCurNode->rAlong = rAlong;
                pdtmCurNode->rChainage = rChainage;
                pdtmCurNode->wType = wNodeType;
                return TRUE;
        }
        wNode ++;
        pdtmCurNode ++;
    }
    return FALSE;
}

BOOL DoLineAndCircleCross (DOUBLE rX1, DOUBLE rY1, DOUBLE rX2, DOUBLE rY2,
    DOUBLE rXc, DOUBLE rYc, DOUBLE rRadius, DOUBLE * prAlong1, DOUBLE * prAlong2) {
    DOUBLE rX21, rY21, rX1c, rY1c, rQuadA, rQuadB, rQuadC, rB24AC;

    if (prAlong1 == NULL || prAlong2 == NULL) {
        return FALSE;
    }
    rX21 = rX2 - rX1;
    rY21 = rY2 - rY1;
    rX1c = rX1 - rXc;
    rY1c = rY1 - rYc;
    rQuadA = pow (rX21, 2.0) + pow (rY21, 2.0);
    if (rQuadA == 0.0) {
        return FALSE;
    }
    rQuadB = 2.0 * rX1c * rX21 + 2.0 * rY1c * rY21;
    rQuadC = pow (rX1c, 2.0) + pow (rY1c, 2.0) - pow (rRadius, 2.0);
    rB24AC = pow (rQuadB, 2.0) - 4.0 * rQuadA * rQuadC;
    if (rB24AC < 0.0) {
        return FALSE;
    }
    if (rB24AC == 0.0) {
        *prAlong1 = -rQuadB / (2.0 * rQuadA);
        *prAlong2 = *prAlong1;
    }
    else {
        *prAlong1 = (-rQuadB + sqrt (rB24AC)) / (2.0 * rQuadA);
        *prAlong2 = (-rQuadB - sqrt (rB24AC)) / (2.0 * rQuadA);
    }
    return TRUE;
}

BOOL GetNodesAlongLine (DTMPATH * pdtmPath, DTMTRIA * pdtmTria, DTMNODE * pdtmNodes) {
    WORD wEdge;
    DOUBLE rChainageFrom, rChainageTo, rX1, rY1, rZ, rX2, rY2;

    if (pdtmPath == NULL || pdtmTria == NULL || pdtmNodes == NULL) {
        return FALSE;
```

```
    }
    rChainageFrom = pdtmPath->rChainage;
    rChainageTo = pdtmPath->rChainage + pdtmPath->rLength * pdtmPath->rDirection;
    _dtmPaths.GetEnd (pdtmPath, 0, &rX1, &rY1);
    if (_dtmTrias.IsInside (pdtmTria, rX1, rY1, TRUE)) {
        if (_dtmTrias.GetZ (pdtmTria, rX1, rY1, &rZ)) {
            AddNode (pdtmNodes, 0.0, rChainageFrom, rX1, rY1, rZ, NODE_STARTOREND);
        }
    }
    _dtmPaths.GetEnd (pdtmPath, 1, &rX2, &rY2);
    if (_dtmTrias.IsInside (pdtmTria, rX2, rY2, TRUE)) {
        if (_dtmTrias.GetZ (pdtmTria, rX2, rY2, &rZ)) {
            AddNode (pdtmNodes, 1.0, rChainageTo, rX2, rY2, rZ, NODE_STARTOREND);
        }
    }
    for (wEdge = 0; wEdge < TRIA_COORDS; wEdge ++) {
        DOUBLE rX3, rY3, rZ3, rX4, rY4, rZ4, rAlong1, rAlong2, rX, rY, rChainage;

        _dtmTrias.GetEdge (pdtmTria, wEdge, &rX3, &rY3, &rZ3, &rX4, &rY4, &rZ4);
        if (DoLinesCross (rX1, rY1, rX2, rY2, rX3, rY3, rX4, rY4, &rAlong1, &rAlong2)) {
            if (rAlong1 > -FUZZFACTOR && (rAlong1 - 1.0) < FUZZFACTOR &&
                rAlong2 > -FUZZFACTOR && (rAlong2 - 1.0) < FUZZFACTOR) {
                rX = rX3 + rAlong2 * (rX4 - rX3);
                rY = rY3 + rAlong2 * (rY4 - rY3);
                rZ = rZ3 + rAlong2 * (rZ4 - rZ3);
                rChainage = rChainageFrom + rAlong1 * (rChainageTo - rChainageFrom);
                AddNode (pdtmNodes, rAlong1, rChainage, rX, rY, rZ, NODE_ATEDGE);
            }
        }
    }
    return TRUE;
}

BOOL CreateSectionsFromNodes (DTMPATH * pdtmPath, DTMTRIA * pdtmTria,
    DTMNODE * pdtmNodes, BOOL fWithCurvePoints) {
    DTMLINE dtmSect;
    WORD wNode;

    if (pdtmPath == NULL || pdtmTria == NULL || pdtmNodes == NULL) {
        return FALSE;
    }
    if (pdtmNodes->wType == NODE_EMPTY || (pdtmNodes + 1)->wType == NODE_EMPTY) {
        return FALSE;
    }
    dtmSect.wColour = PENCOLOUR_SECTIONS;
    wNode = 0;
    while (wNode + 1 < NODE_MAX_COUNT && (pdtmNodes + wNode)->wType != NODE_EMPTY &&
        (pdtmNodes + wNode + 1)->wType != NODE_EMPTY) {
        WORD wFromTo;
        DOUBLE rAngle [2], rChainage [2], rZ [2];

        rAngle [0] = (pdtmNodes + wNode)->rAlong;
        rAngle [1] = (pdtmNodes + wNode + 1)->rAlong;
        if (pdtmPath->fCurved) {
            DOUBLE rMidAngle, rX, rY;

            rMidAngle = (PI / 180.0) * (rAngle [0] + rAngle [1]) / 2.0;
            rX = pdtmPath->cdCentre.rX + pdtmPath->rRadius * cos (rMidAngle);
            rY = pdtmPath->cdCentre.rY + pdtmPath->rRadius * sin (rMidAngle);
            if (!_dtmTrias.IsInside (pdtmTria, rX, rY, TRUE)) {
                wNode ++;
```

```
                    continue;
                }
            }
            for (wFromTo = 0; wFromTo < 2; wFromTo ++) {
                DTMNODE * pdtmNode;
                DTMPOINT dtmPoint;
                DTMLINE dtmVert;

                pdtmNode = pdtmNodes + wNode + wFromTo;
                rChainage [wFromTo] = pdtmNode->rChainage;
                rZ [wFromTo] = pdtmNode->cdPoint.rZ;
                CopyCoords (&(dtmPoint.cdPoint), &(pdtmNode->cdPoint));
                dtmPoint.wColour = (pdtmNode->wType & NODE_HILOPOINT) ?
                    PENCOLOUR_HILOPOINTS : PENCOLOUR_PLANPOINTS;
                _dtmPlanPoints.AddNear (&dtmPoint, FUZZFACTOR);
                dtmVert.wColour = PENCOLOUR_SECTVERTLINES;
                if (pdtmNode->wType & NODE_STARTOREND) {
                    _dtmSects.SetEnd (&dtmVert, 0, rChainage [wFromTo], rZ [wFromTo],
                        SECTZVAL_ABOVE);
                    _dtmSects.SetEnd (&dtmVert, 1, rChainage [wFromTo],
                        rZ [wFromTo] + SECTVLINE_INITLEN, SECTZVAL_ABOVE);
                    _dtmSects.AddNear (&dtmVert, FUZZFACTOR);
                }
                if (pdtmNode->wType & NODE_ATEDGE) {
                    _dtmSects.SetEnd (&dtmVert, 0, rChainage [wFromTo], rZ [wFromTo],
                        SECTZVAL_BELOW);
                    _dtmSects.SetEnd (&dtmVert, 1, rChainage [wFromTo],
                        rZ [wFromTo] - SECTVLINE_INITLEN, SECTZVAL_BELOW);
                    _dtmSects.AddNear (&dtmVert, FUZZFACTOR);
                }
                if (pdtmNode->wType & NODE_HILOPOINT) {
                    _dtmHiLoPoints.Set (&dtmPoint, rChainage [wFromTo], rZ [wFromTo],
                        SECTZVAL_HILOPOINT);
                    dtmPoint.wColour = PENCOLOUR_HILOPOINTS;
                    _dtmHiLoPoints.AddNear (&dtmPoint, FUZZFACTOR);
                }
            }
            if (pdtmPath->fCurved) {
                DWORD dwCountdown;
                DOUBLE rAngleInc, rChainageInc, rCurAngle, rCurChainage;

                if (fabs (rChainage [1] - rChainage [0]) <= MAX_ARC_STEPINC) {
                    dwCountdown = 1L;
                    rAngleInc = 0.0;
                    rChainageInc = 0.0;
                }
                else {
                    DOUBLE rArcLen, rFraction, rHowMany;

                    rArcLen = rChainage [1] - rChainage [0];
                    rFraction = modf (fabs (rArcLen) / MAX_ARC_STEPINC, &rHowMany);
                    if (rFraction != 0.0) {
                        rHowMany += 1.0;
                    }
                    dwCountdown = (DWORD) (rHowMany + FUZZFACTOR);
                    rAngleInc = (rAngle [1] - rAngle [0]) / rHowMany;
                    rChainageInc = rArcLen / rHowMany;
                }
                rCurAngle = rAngle [0];
                rCurChainage = rChainage [0];
                _dtmSects.SetEnd (&dtmSect, 0, rChainage [0], rZ [0], SECTZVAL_SECTLINE);
```

```
            while (dwCountdown > 0L) {
                BOOL fErrorGettingZ;

                dwCountdown --;
                fErrorGettingZ = FALSE;
                if (dwCountdown > 0L) {
                    DOUBLE rAngleRads, rX, rY, rZ;

                    rCurAngle += rAngleInc;
                    rCurChainage += rChainageInc;
                    rAngleRads = rCurAngle * PI / 180.0;
                    rX = pdtmPath->cdCentre.rX + pdtmPath->rRadius * cos (rAngleRads);
                    rY = pdtmPath->cdCentre.rY + pdtmPath->rRadius * sin (rAngleRads);
                    if (_dtmTrias.GetZ (pdtmTria, rX, rY, &rZ)) {
                        _dtmSects.SetEnd (&dtmSect, 1, rCurChainage, rZ,
                            SECTZVAL_SECTLINE);
                        if (fWithCurvePoints) {
                            DTMPOINT dtmPoint;

                            _dtmPlanPoints.Set (&dtmPoint, rX, rY, rZ);
                            dtmPoint.wColour = PENCOLOUR_PLANPOINTS;
                            _dtmPlanPoints.Add (&dtmPoint);
                        }
                    }
                    else {
                        fErrorGettingZ = TRUE;
                    }
                }
                else {
                    _dtmSects.SetEnd (&dtmSect, 1, rChainage [1], rZ [1],
                        SECTZVAL_SECTLINE);
                }
                if (!fErrorGettingZ) {
                    _dtmSects.AddNear (&dtmSect, FUZZFACTOR);
                    CopyCoords (&(dtmSect.cdEnd [0]), &(dtmSect.cdEnd [1]));
                }
            }
        }
        else {
            _dtmSects.SetEnd (&dtmSect, 0, rChainage [0], rZ [0], SECTZVAL_SECTLINE);
            _dtmSects.SetEnd (&dtmSect, 1, rChainage [1], rZ [1], SECTZVAL_SECTLINE);
            _dtmSects.AddNear (&dtmSect, FUZZFACTOR);
        }
        wNode ++;
    }
    return TRUE;
}

void GetCoordsAtMouse (void) {
    DTMCOORD dtmMouse;

    dtmMouse.rX = _dtmDisplay.GetSelFromX ();
    dtmMouse.rY = _dtmDisplay.GetSelFromY ();
    if (_dtmDisplay.GetModelID () == MODEL_PLAN) {
        DOUBLE rZvalue, rChainage, rOffset;

        if (_dtmTrias.GetZ (&dtmMouse, &rZvalue)) {
            _dtmText.Output (TEXT ("x, y, z: %.3f, %.3f, %.3f\r\n"),
                dtmMouse.rX, dtmMouse.rY, rZvalue);
        }
        else {
```

```
        _dtmText.Output (TEXT ("x, y, z: %.3f, %.3f, n/a\r\n"),
            dtmMouse.rX, dtmMouse.rY);
    }
    if (_dtmPaths.GetChainageAndOffset (&dtmMouse, &rChainage, &rOffset)) {
        _dtmText.Output (TEXT ("chainage, offset: %.3f, %.3f\r\n"),
            rChainage, rOffset);
    }
    else {
        _dtmText.Output (TEXT ("chainage, offset: n/a, n/a\r\n"));
    }
}
else {
    _dtmText.Output (TEXT ("chainage, z: %.3f, %.3f\r\n"),
        dtmMouse.rX, dtmMouse.rY);
}
}
```

**Chapter14.cpp** has the same layout as source code files in earlier chapters in this book. It starts with the header files, including <math.h> for the function *fabs, cos, sin, sqrt, pow* and *modf*, followed by child window IDs, task IDs, model IDs for identifying each model (like Chapter 2 in Book One), the task batch size constant GETSECTIONS_ STEPSIZE which is used when creating the section, and coloured pen numbers. There are then a further thirteen constants:

VERTICAL_EXAG is the vertical exaggeration applied to the section model when it is viewed in the graphics window.

NODE_MAX_COUNT is the maximum number of nodes that can be created per path element. A node is a location with special significance on a path element, such as (i) the start of a path element, (ii) the end of a path element, (iii) where a path element crosses the edge of a triangle, (iv) the high point (maximum z value) on a path arc element, and (v) the low point (minimum z value) on a path arc element. The following diagram shows how it is possible to obtain ten nodes when an arc crosses a triangle. Normally, the number of nodes created per path element is less than this maximum value.

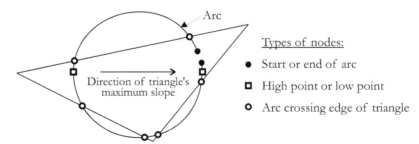

Types of nodes:

● Start or end of arc

□ High point or low point

○ Arc crossing edge of triangle

NODE_EMPTY, NODE_STARTOREND, NODE_HILOPOINT and NODE_ ATEDGE are types of nodes. Types include (i) empty or not defined, (ii) at the start or end of a path element, (iii) at a high or low point on a path arc element or (iv) where a path element crosses or touches the edge of a triangle. These constants (except NODE_EMPTY) can be combined as it is possible for a node to be, for example, at the start of an arc, at a high or low point and also crossing the edge of a triangle, all at the same location. Therefore these constants cannot be declared as an enumerated group.

SECTZVAL_SECTLINE, SECTZVAL_ABOVE, SECTZVAL_BELOW and SECTZVAL_HILOPOINT are z values that are applied to shapes in the section model depending on what the shape represents. They are applied (i) to lines that make the section, (ii) to vertical lines above the section, (iii) to vertical lines below the section and (iv) to high and low points. Different z values make it easier to differentiate between different types of shapes. For example you can sort data by z value in a spreadsheet program to group data together by type. Or when importing CAD script files into your CAD program you can use your CAD program's filter to select only drawing objects with a particular z value to group them together or change other properties like colour or line type. Different z values also prevent lines from different groups accidentally being joined together when exporting data.

In this program the section model includes vertical lines above the section at the ends of individual path elements. Vertical lines are included below the section where the path crosses edges of triangles in the DTM. The section model also includes high and low points on arc elements if these points are between each end of the arc.

SECTVLINE_INITLEN is the initial length of section vertical lines. This value is arbitrary, but cannot be zero. SECTVLINE_BEYONDMINMAX is by how much to extend vertical lines above or below the maximum and minimum z values in the section model. This value will be multiplied by the vertical exaggeration.

MAX_ARC_STEPINC is the maximum distance along an arc between intermediate points. If this number is increased, the number of nodes created along arcs is reduced and the section will look less smooth.

---

You might wish to experiment with the values of SECTVLINE_ BEYONDMINMAX and MAX_ARC_STEPINC depending on the units scale of your DTM. Alternatively you could change them from constants to static or global variables, maybe called *rSectVLineBeyondMinMax* and *rMaxArcStepInc*, that the user can change via custom dialog boxes while running your program.

---

Next, Chapter14.cpp declares the structure DTMNODE. This structure contains four member variables: *cdPoint* is the x,y,z coordinates of the node in the DTM. *rAlong* is the measure along the path element to the node. For arcs, *rAlong* is an angle between the start and end angles. For lines, *rAlong* is a fraction of the line's length from the line's start. *rChainage* is the change of the node along the section. *wType* is the node type. *wType* can be a combination of the NODE_ constants defined earlier in Chapter14.cpp. Nodes are used when calculating the section along each path element, and converted to x,y,z points in the plan model and 2D lines and points in the section model.

Chapter14.cpp then defines twelve global variables, most of which are the same as in earlier chapters. *_dtmTrias* contains the DTM triangles, *_dtmPaths* contains the path elements, *_dtmSects* contains the section lines, *_dtmPlanPoints* contains x,y,z points along the path, and _dtmHiLoPoints_ contains 2D high and low points on the section. _dtmTrias_, _dtmPaths_ and _dtmPlanPoints_ are only displayed when the plan model is visible in the graphics window. _dtmSects_ and _dtmHiLoPoints_ are only displayed when the section model is visible in the graphics window.

Fifteen functions are then declared, followed by the C++ source code.

The functions _WinMain_, _WndProc_, _CarryOutTasks_, _DrawModel_, _InitShowDropdownMenu_ and _InitMouseDropdownMenu_ are similar to the equivalent functions in earlier chapters.

In the WM_CREATE message in _WndProc_, the graphics window _dtmDisplay_ is initialised with the model ID number for the plan model and _dtmModel_ is initialised with the model ID number for the section model. This is unlike _WndProc_ in Chapters 3 to 13 where Model ID numbers are not used because those programs each contain a single model. _dtmDisplay_ also sets a tangent size of 10.0, and an increased border width size of 11.0. In the WM_INITMENUPOP message there is an extra case-statement compared to previous chapters because this program contains an extra item in the menu bar. As well as importing triangles and paths, creating sections, and exporting sections and points data, the user can also switch views between the plan model and the section model.

In the TASK_COMPLETED if-statement near the end of _CarryOutTasks_ it is necessary to call the function _DTMDISPLAY::SetView_ before the function _AddShapeToDisplay_ to ensure that the shapes' minimum and maximum x,y,z values are applied to the correct models. _SetView_ has no effect if the model viewed is already the model required for the shape data.

What _DrawModel_ draws depends on whether the plan model or the section model is visible in the graphics window. For the plan model it draws the triangles first, followed by the path elements and then the section x,y,z points along the path. For the section model it draws the section lines first and then the high and low points. There are no shapes to draw for Stage 4 in the section model. So it moves on to the next stage.

The function _InitViewDropdownMenu_ is similar to the equivalent function in Chapter02.cpp. It adds ticks next to items in the view drop-down menu before the menu is displayed, depending on which model is visible in the graphics window.

The function _GetSectionsStart_ starts the task that creates a section through the DTM along a path. _hwnd_ is the handle of the parent window and _uTaskID_ and _uTaskIDwithCurvePoints_ are the task ID numbers. If there are no triangles in _dtmTrias_ or no path elements in _dtmPaths_, the function displays an error message. If the lines array _dtmSects_ or the two points arrays _dtmPlanPoints_ and _dtmHiLoPoints_ already contain some lines or points, the function asks the user if they want to discard this data. If the user selects 'Yes', any existing section lines and points are discarded. Finally, _GetSectionsStart_ asks the user if they wish to include intermediate points, in the plan model, along path elements that are arcs, and starts the task with the task ID number _uTaskID_ if the user selects 'No', or the task ID number _uTaskIDwithCurvePoints_ if the user selects 'Yes'. The function returns TRUE if successful, or FALSE if the user cancels the task or an error occurs.

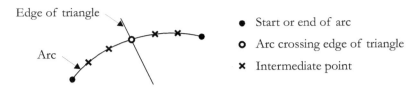

The chainage and z value of intermediate points along path arc elements are always included in the section model because they create a more accurate and smoother-looking section. However, adding intermediate points at their x,y,z values in the plan model, as in the diagram above, is optional. Intermediate points are not needed along path line elements because adding them would not improve the accuracy or overall appearance of the section.

The function *GetSectionsCont* carries out the task that creates a section through the DTM along a path. *fWithCurvePoints* is TRUE if intermediate points are to be calculated along path arc elements, or FALSE if they are not. *GetSectionsCont* follows the standard task manager template as discussed in Chapter 1, looking at each path element in *_dtmPaths* in batches. Within the main while-loop, the function enters a second while-loop that compares each path element with each triangle in *_dtmTrias*. It uses the break-statement to exit this second while-loop if the current triangle in *_dtmTrias* is to the right of the path element. This is because all subsequent triangles in *_dtmTrias* will also be to the right of the current path element, as the triangles are stored in ascending x-value order. Otherwise, if the current triangle and path element overlap, *GetSectionsCont* sets all the nodes in an array of nodes as empty, or undefined, and then calls the functions *GetNodesAlongArc* or *GetNodesAlongLine*, depending on whether the path element is an arc or a line. These functions fill the nodes array with data which is then used by the function *CreateSectionsFromNodes* to create section lines and points.

When the task is finished, *GetSectionsCont* then goes through the vertical lines in *_dtmSects*, extending lines above the section to just above the top of the sections model, and extending lines below the section to just below the bottom of the sections model. This process can mean some of the lines in *_dtmSects* are no longer in ascending x value order. Therefore *GetSectionsCont* calls the functions *DTMSHAPES::ReorderAll* and *DTMSHAPES::ResetLimits* to rearrange the lines back into ascending order, and to update the model's minimum and maximum x,y,z values. Finally, *GetSectionsCont* displays the number of section lines added to *_dtmSects*. The function returns the TASK_ constants as discussed in Chapter 1.

The function *GetNodesAlongArc* calculates node data for an individual path arc element relative to an individual triangle. *pdtmPath* points to the path element, *pdtmTria* points to the triangle, and *pdtmNodes* points to the nodes array that will hold the data when the function ends. The function starts by getting the start and end angles and chainages for the arc, swapping them around if necessary so that the start angle is always less than the end angle, and adding 360° to the values if necessary to ensure that they are positive. It also gets the x,y coordinates at each end of the arc. The z values of the path element are ignored.

Next, *GetNodesAlongArc* adds x,y,z data and angle and chainage data to the nodes array if the start and/or end of the arc are inside the triangle. Then it gets the angle of the maximum slope for the triangle and, if the triangle is not flat, converts the angle to radians to check if any high or low points are on the arc and also inside the triangle. It uses a for-loop to calculate the x,y coordinates of the low point and then the high point. If the point is inside the triangle and its angle is between the arc's start and end angles, *GetNodesAlongArc* calculates the point's chainage and adds x,y,z data and angle and chainage data to the nodes array. When adding 180° to the angle, it also checks that the angle is still between zero and 360°.

*GetNodesAlongArc* then checks if the arc crosses or touches any of the triangle's edges. It uses a for-loop to look at each edge of the triangle in turn, and calls the function *DoLineAndCircleCross* to determine if and where along the triangle edge the arc and the edge cross. *DoLineAndCircleCross* fills two 'along' values because a line can cross a circle in two locations. A second for-loop looks at each 'along' value in turn. The edge and arc cross between or on the ends of the edge if the following conditions are met:

```
rAlong >= 0 and rAlong <= 1
```

which when using FUZZFACTOR becomes:

```
rAlong > -FUZZFACTOR and (rAlong - 1) < FUZZFACTOR
```

Then *GetNodesAlongArc* calculates the x,y,z values at the intersection position along the edge, and also the angle, or bearing, from the centre of the arc to the intersection point. If the angle is between the start and end angles of the arc, the chainage of the intersection point is calculated and the x,y,z data and angle and chainage data are added to the nodes array. If the arc touches, or 'nudges', an edge of the triangle, there will be just one solution returned by *DoLineAndCircleCross* and the two 'along' values will be the same. In this situation a break-statement exits the inner for-loop. *GetNodesAlongArc* returns TRUE if successful, or FALSE if an error occurs.

The function *IsAngleBetween* checks if an angle is between two other angles. The function also checks the angle plus 360° to see if it is between the two other angles, and adds 360° to the angle if it is. *prAngle* points to a DOUBLE variable containing the angle. *rAngleFrom* and *rAngleTo* are the two other angles. *rAngleFrom* must be less than *rAngleTo*. Angles up to 720° are assumed, for example if the arc's start angle and sweep angle are both 359°, then *rAngleTo* will equal 718°. The function returns TRUE if successful, or FALSE if an error occurs.

The function *AddNode* adds data for a new node to a nodes array. *pdtmNodes* points to the nodes array, *rAlong* is the amount along the path element to the new node, *rChainage* is the new node's chainage, *rX*, *rY* and *rZ* are the new node's x,y,z values, and *wNodeType* is the new node's type. *wNodeType*'s value is one of the NODE_ constants discussed earlier in this chapter. *AddNode* uses a while-loop to step through the nodes array. If it finds an empty node, the new node is stored in that empty node's position. If it finds a node with the same 'along' value, the new node's type is combined with the existing node's type. FUZZFACTOR is used to compare 'along' values to accommodate any rounding errors. If *AddNode* finds an existing node with an 'along' value that is greater than the new node's 'along' value, it checks that the nodes array is not full, moves nodes at and beyond the current position one space forward to create an empty node at the current position, and copies the new node's data into that empty node. The function returns TRUE if successful, or FALSE if the nodes array is already full or if an error occurs.

Because the node's array size is set to the maximum theoretical size (see NODE_MAX_COUNT discussed earlier), *AddNote* should never return FALSE from an already-full array. However, the function still checks that the array is not already full in order to be safe.

The function *DoLineAndCircleCross* checks if a line and a circle cross, and calculates where they cross if they do. *rX1*, *rY1*, *rX2* and *rY2* are the x,y coordinates at each end of the line, *rXc* and *rYc* are the x,y coordinates at the centre of the circle, and *rRadius* is the circle's radius. *prAlong1* and *prAlong2* point to two DOUBLE variables which contain the fractions of the distance along the line to the intersection points if the line and circle do cross. The function returns TRUE if the line and circle cross, or FALSE if they do not cross or if an error occurs.

*DoLineAndCircleCross* uses the following equations:

$$m = \frac{-b \pm \sqrt{b^2 - 4ac}}{2a}$$

$$a = (x_2 - x_1)^2 + (y_2 - y_1)^2$$

$$b = 2(x_1 - x_c)(x_2 - x_1) + 2(y_1 - y_c)(y_2 - y_1)$$

$$c = (x_1 - x_c)^2 + (y_1 - y_c)^2 - r^2$$

where $x_1\, y_1$ and $x_2\, y_2$ are the coordinates at each end of the line, $x_c\, y_c$ are the coordinates at the centre of the circle, $r$ is the circle's radius, and $m$ is the fraction of the distance along the line to the intersection points. Refer to "Intersection of a 2D Line and a 2D Circle" in Appendix C for the derivation of these equations. *a*, *b* and *c* are stored in *rQuadA*, *rQuadB* and *rQuadC*. *m* is stored in *prAlong1* and *prAlong2*. *rB24AC* equals $b^2 - 4ac$. If *rB24AC* is negative, the line does not cross the circle. If it is zero, the line crosses the circle at one location and *prAlong1* and *prAlong2* have the same value. Otherwise the line crosses the circle in two locations and *prAlong1* and *prAlong2* have different values.

The function *GetNodesAlongLine* calculates node data for an individual path line element relative to an individual triangle. *pdtmPath* points to the path element, *pdtmTria* points to the triangle, and *pdtmNodes* points to the nodes array that will hold the data when the function ends. This function is the equivalent of *GetNodesAlongArc* except that it processes path elements that are lines instead of arcs.

*GetNodesAlongLine* starts by getting the chainages and x,y coordinates for each end of the line. The z values of the path element are ignored. Then *GetNodesAlongLine* adds x,y,z data and 'along' and chainage data to the nodes array if the start and/or end of the line are inside the triangle, the z value coming from the triangle. This function's 'along' values are fractions of the line's length, instead of angles like *GetNodesAlongArc*. The 'along' value at the start of the line is 0.0. At the far end of the line, the 'along' value is 1.0. *GetNodesAlongLine* then uses a for-loop to see if the line crosses any of the triangle's edges. The line and edge cross when the following conditions are met:

```
rAlong1 >= 0, rAlong1 <= 1 and rAlong2 >= 0, rAlong2 <= 1
```

which when using FUZZFACTOR becomes:

```
rAlong1 > -FUZZFACTOR, (rAlong1 - 1) < FUZZFACTOR and
rAlong2 > -FUZZFACTOR, (rAlong2 - 1) < FUZZFACTOR
```

If they cross, the x,y,z coordinates where they cross are calculated based on the triangle's edge (*rAlong2*), rather than the path line element (*rAlong1*), because the triangle's edge has valid z values and the path line element does not. However, the chainage at the intersection is calculated along the path line element. The node data is then added to the nodes array. *GetNodesAlongLine* does not add information about high or low points along a line because any high or low points will be at either end of the line, and will depend on adjacent sections which are not yet known. The function returns TRUE if successful, or FALSE if an error occurs.

The function *CreateSectionsFromNodes* creates section lines based on a path element, a triangle, and data in a nodes array. *pdtmPath* points to the path element, *pdtmTria* points to the triangle, and *pdtmNodes* points to the nodes array. *fWithCurvePoints* is TRUE if intermediate points along a path arc element are to be added to the plan model, or FALSE if they are not. The function starts by checking that the nodes array contains at least two nodes, as otherwise it is not possible to create any section lines. It then uses a while-loop to look through the nodes array, processing the current node and next node together each time. The while-loop exits one before the end of the nodes array because the final node cannot be processed on its own. Within the while-loop, *CreateSectionsFromNodes* stores angles for the current and next node and, if the path element is an arc, creates a point midway along the arc between the two nodes in order to check if this section of arc is inside the triangle. If it is not, the function uses the continue-statement to return to the start of the while-loop to look at the next pair of nodes. Otherwise, it adds a new point to *_dtmPlanPoints* at the nodes' x,y,z coordinates with a colour depending on whether the point is a high or low point, or not. It then adds a vertical line to *_dtmSects* above the section if the node is at the start or end of a path element, and a vertical line to *_dtmSects* below the section if the node is at the edge of a triangle. Else-if-statements are not used here because it is possible for a node to be both at the start or end of a path element and also on the edge of a triangle. If the node is a high or low point, a point is also added to *_dtmHiLoPoints*. Because this for-loop adds identical points and lines (for example when the 'next node' becomes the 'current node') *CreateSectionsFromNodes* calls *AddNear* functions with FUZZFACTOR so that duplicated points and lines are ignored. This marginally slows the function down, but makes the code simpler.

Next, *CreateSectionsFromNodes* adds section lines between the pair of nodes. If the path is an arc, the function calculates how many shorter lines to fit to the arc in order to create a smooth-looking section. If the arc's length is less than MAX_ARC_STEPINC, it uses one line. Otherwise it uses the function *modf* to calculate the number of shorter lines so that the length of the shorter line will always be MAX_ARC_STEPINC or less. For example, if the arc length *rArcLen* is 3.0 units and MAX_ARC_STEPINC equals 1.0, the following code:

```
rFraction = modf (rArcLen / MAX_ARC_STEPINC, &rHowMany);
rShorterLineLen = rArcLen / rHowMany;
```

makes *rFraction* = 0.0, *rHowMany* = 3.0, and *rShorterLineLen* = 1.0 units. If *rFraction* is not zero, 1.0 is added to *rHowMany* to ensure that *rShorterLineLen* remains at or below MAX_ARC_STEPINC. So if, for example, *rArcLen* is 3.5 units, the following code:

```
rFraction = modf (rArcLen / MAX_ARC_STEPINC, &rHowMany);
if (rFraction != 0.0) {
    rHowMany += 1.0;
}
rShorterLineLen = rArcLen / rHowMany;
```

makes *rFraction* = 0.5, *rHowMany* = 4.0, and *rShorterLineLen* = 0.875 units. When *rHowMany* is converted to a DWORD integer, FUZZFACTOR is added to the number to accommodate any rounding errors. The angle increment and the chainage increment, which is the same as the shorter line length, are calculated. Then *CreateSectionsFromNodes* prepares variables, including setting one end of the section line *dtmSect* to the start of the arc, before it enters a while-loop. In the while-loop it calculates the x,y,z values for each shorter line and adds shorter lines to _*dtmSects*. If *fWithCurvePoints* is TRUE it also adds intermediate points to _*dtmPlanPoints* which will be displayed in the plan model. The x,y values are calculated along the arc. The z values are obtained from the triangle. The function skips points along the arc if it fails to get z values, although this should never occur as earlier in the function it checks that the arc is inside the triangle. When the shorter lines reach the end of the arc, *CreateSectionsFromNodes* uses the node's coordinates, rather than calculate x,y,z values, as this avoids any compounded rounding errors in *rCurAngle* and *rCurChainage*, and will draw a line even if *fErrorGettingZ* is TRUE. Towards the end of the while-loop the end of the current shorter line becomes the start of the next shorter line. The final else-statement in *CreateSectionsFromNodes* adds a section line to _*dtmSects* for path line elements. *CreateSectionsFromNodes* returns TRUE if successful, or FALSE if an error occurs.

The function *GetCoordsAtMouse* displays x,y,z, chainage and offset values if the plan model is visible in the graphics window, or chainage and z values if the section model is visible in the graphics window. If any of the values cannot be calculated, for example because the user left-clicked the mouse outside the DTM in the plan model, then 'n/a' is displayed. Z values obtained from the plan model are stored as y values in the section model because the section model is at right angles to the plan model. Chainages along the section are stored as x values in the section model.

## Running Chapter14

Before you can compile and run your program, you need to add the following twenty-two source files to your Chapter14 project. Refer to Chapter 1 for how to do this:

| | | |
|---|---|---|
| **TextWnd.h** | **TextWnd.cpp** | |
| **FileInOut.h** | **FileInOut.cpp** | |
| **BigTask.h** | **BigTask.cpp** | |
| **Graphics.h** | **Graphics.cpp** | |
| **Colours.h** | **Colours.cpp** | |
| **Shapes.h** | **Shapes.cpp** | |
| **Points.cpp** | **Lines.cpp** | **Triangles.cpp** |
| **Paths.cpp** | **Circles.cpp** | |
| **Common.h** | **Common.cpp** | |
| **Chapter14.h** | **Chapter14.cpp** | **Chapter14.rc** |

You also need to add the Gdiplus.lib library file as an 'additional dependency' in your project's linker/input settings. Refer to Chapter 2 for how to do this. Finally, don't forget to set Chapter14 as your start-up project.

Otherwise, assuming you have compiled the code for Chapter14 successfully, and it is running, you can now test it out.

Start by importing your DTM of 3D triangles. Click on 'File' in the menu bar, then select 'Import' from the drop-down menu, and finally click on 'Triangles'. Next, select a file containing the triangles data. You can use the sample file Triangles.txt. Then import your path, again clicking on 'File', then 'Import' and 'Paths'. You can use the sample file Path.txt. You may also need to change the display scale via 'Show', 'Zoom extents' to display all of the path. If successful, the program's window should look something like this:

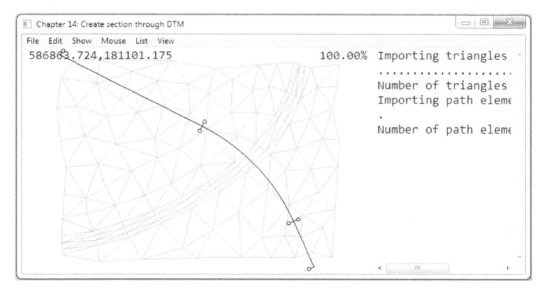

Next, to create your section through the DTM along the route of the path, click on 'Edit' in the menu bar and then select 'Calculate section' from the drop-down menu. A dialog box will appear asking if you wish to 'include intermediate plan points along curves'. If you select 'Yes', points will be added to the plan model along the parts of the path that are arcs. If you select 'No' points will only be placed at the ends of each path element (if inside the DTM), where path elements cross the edges of triangles in the DTM, and high and low points on path arc elements.

If you select 'Yes', the program will create a section and the program's window should look something like this:

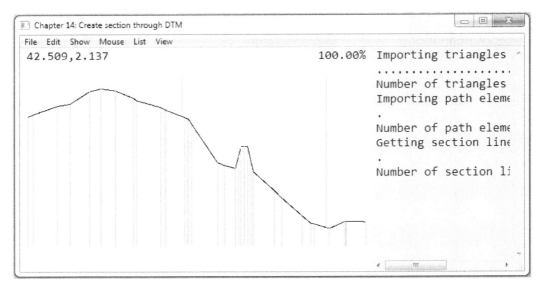

If you click on 'View' in the menu bar and then select 'Plan' from the drop-down menu, this will return you to the plan model. Notice that points have been added along the path, including close together along the part of the path that is an arc. Your program's window should now look something like this:

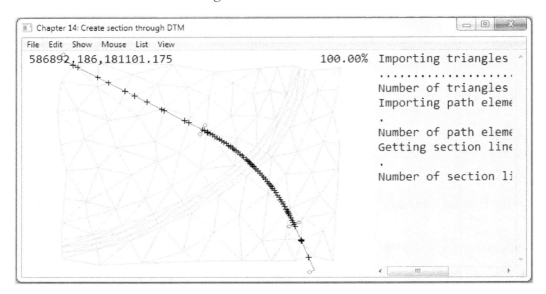

If you click on 'Edit' and 'Calculate section' again (answering 'Yes' when it asks if you wish to discard sections and points already created), and this time select 'No' when it asks if you want to include intermediate plan points along curves, the same section will be recreated and fewer points will be added to the path in the plan model (select 'View', 'Plan' to switch to the plan model).

You can export section lines, plan points, and high and low points (to be discussed shortly) by clicking on 'File' in the menu bar, selecting 'Export' from the drop-down menu and then selecting 'Sections', 'Plan points' or 'High/low points'. The data can be exported as CAD script files, as text files or as JPEG files.

It is also possible to create sections through multiple DTMs along the same path, and to display them in the same section model. To do this, import a new DTM via 'File', 'Import', 'Triangles'. For this example you can use the sample file TrianglesA_Ch13.txt used in Chapter 13. Select 'Yes' when the program asks if you wish to discard existing triangles. Next, create a new section via 'Edit', 'Calculate section'. Make sure you select 'No' when it asks if you wish to discard existing sections and points otherwise you will lose the existing section data. Select 'Yes' or 'No' when the program asks if you wish to include intermediate plan points, as this does not affect the section view. You program's window should look something like this:

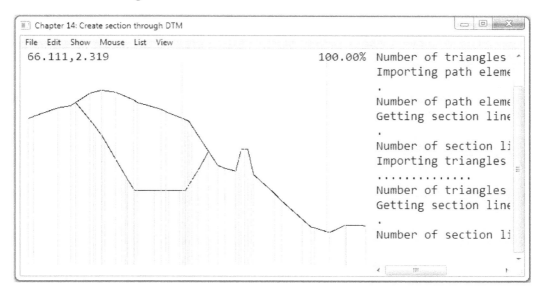

The DTM used in Chapter 13 is a flat-bottomed hole with sloping sides that tie into the DTM in Triangles.txt. The image above shows the flat and sloping sections of this hole.

Note that the section model includes just two vertical lines above the section, despite the path containing three elements (two lines and an arc). The reason only two vertical lines are shown above the section is that the start of the first element and the end of the final element are outside the extents of the DTM. Therefore they are not included in the section model. The vertical lines below the section are where the path crosses edges of triangles in the DTM. No extra vertical lines are created if you include intermediate points in your section. Intermediate points only affect the plan model.

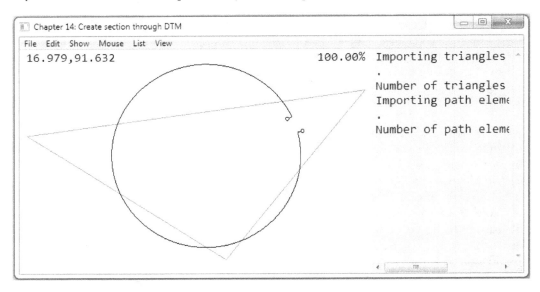

In the previous examples there are no high or low points shown on the arc. This is because the triangles are relatively small compared to the arc which is much larger. If you restart the program, and this time select the sample file Triangle_Ch14.txt via 'File', 'Import', 'Triangles' and the sample file Path_Ch14.txt via 'File', 'Import', 'Paths' you will see a single triangle and a path containing a single arc, as in the image above. This is similar to the earlier diagram shown when discussing NODE_MAX_COUNT.

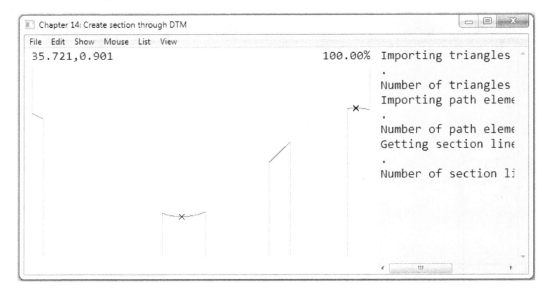

Next, create the section via 'Edit', 'Calculate section' (and 'No' to intermediate points so points are only added at the start/end, high/low and edge-crossing points) and you should see high and low points coloured red in the plan model on the path's arc and also on the section model. Your program's window should look like the image at the bottom of the previous page. You will also see, in the section model, that parts of the section are missing. This is because the path's arc crosses in and out of the DTM.

If you click on 'Mouse' in the menu bar and select 'Coordinates' from the drop-down menu, then when you left-click your mouse in the graphics window, x,y,z coordinates and chainage and offset values (when the plan model is visible) or chainage and z values (when the section model is visible) at the mouse's position are displayed in the text window.

As in previous chapters, to exit the program click on 'File' in the menu bar, select 'Exit' and then choose 'Yes' in the message box that appears.

---

This program is a very useful tool for working with a DTM. There are many ways in which you could add to your code to improve your version of this program.

For example, you could replace the constants VERTICAL_EXAG and MAX_ARC_STEPINC with global variables that the user could set via custom dialog boxes, and therefore change the vertical exaggeration in the section model and the spacing between intermediate points in the plan model while the program is running.

Another improvement could be to mark high and low points on the plan model and section model where the ends of path line elements form high or low points. This could be achieved by adding code near the end of *GetSectionsCont* to scan through the section lines to identify high and low points. It could then add points to *_dtmHiLoPoints* and change the colour of existing points at these locations in *_dtmPlanPoints*.

A more complicated improvement could be to process multiple paths. Currently, this program can only handle a single path. To handle multiple paths, you would need to adapt the path import function in the DTMPATHS class in Chapter 3 to identify a break between paths (similar to the DTMLINES class). You also need to consider how to display multiple paths in the section model. Options include displaying them side-by-side, one above the other, or in a grid pattern in a single section model. Alternatively you could create multiple section models, one per path. Each option has its advantages and disadvantages.

Other useful additions include (i) displaying a grid in the section model, with the grid spacing either calculated from the section's data or set by the user via custom dialog boxes, (ii) displaying chainage and z values as text along the side and bottom of the section model either next to grid lines, at section vertical lines, or both, and (iii) to include chainage and z values, as CAD text objects, when exporting the section as a CAD script file. It is relatively easy to display text in the graphics window using GDI+. However, it can be more difficult to include CAD commands for creating text objects in script files, depending on the CAD program you use.

# Conclusion

I hope that the programs in Book One and in this book have inspired you to create your own personalised digital terrain modelling program, or suite of programs. The programs in these two books show the basic steps and processes needed to create DTMs and to work with DTMs. As discussed in both books, there is plenty of scope to improve these programs with additional features. It is also possible to make the programs work faster and more efficiently, particularly for larger datasets.

Don't forget to check out my website (see the end of Chapter 3 in Book One) where you can download the latest version of the source files and the sample data files.

Giles Darling
December 2020.

# Appendix A – Lisp Files

Appendix A contains lisp files that define functions to extract point, line, path and triangle data from objects in CAD drawings. The final lisp file contains a function to add points at each end of selected lines or paths/polylines.

Not all CAD programs can process lisp files, but for those that can, lisp files are typically loaded by typing in a command such as APPLOAD or LOADAPPLICATION on the command line and then selecting a lisp file from a dialog box. Alternatively you can type (LOAD "xxx.lsp") where xxx.lsp is the filename, on the command line to load a lisp file directly. To run a function defined in a lisp file, you type the function's name on the command line. A single lisp file can contain multiple functions. However, all the lisp files in this appendix contain one function each.

The data extracted by these functions can then be imported into the DTM programs detailed in Book One and in this book.

## Extract Point Data

The following lisp file defines a single function called EXTRACTPOINTS that extracts x,y,z data from selected POINT objects in a CAD drawing.

**EXTRACTPOINTS.LSP**

```
(defun C:EXTRACTPOINTS ( / s1 n1 f1 c1 d1 p1 t1)
 (princ "\nSelect POINT objects...")
 (if (= (setq s1 (ssget (list (cons 0 "POINT")))) nil)
  (princ "\nNo POINTs selected. Command terminating")
  (if (= (setq n1 (getfiled "Enter destination filename" "" "txt" 5)) nil)
   (princ "\nNo filename entered. Command terminating")
   (if (= (setq f1 (open n1 "w")) nil)
    (princ "\nUnable to open file to save data to. Command terminating")
    (progn
     (write-line "*X, Y, Z" f1)
     (setq c1 0)
     (repeat (sslength s1)
      (setq d1 (entget (ssname s1 c1)))
      (setq p1 (cdr (assoc 10 d1)))
      (setq t1 (strcat (rtos (car p1) 2 3) ", "
                       (rtos (cadr p1) 2 3) ", "
                       (rtos (caddr p1) 2 3)))
      (write-line t1 f1)
      (setq c1 (1+ c1))
     )
     (close f1)
     (princ (strcat "\nData for " (rtos c1 2 0) " point(s) saved to file"))
    )
   )
  )
 )
 (princ)
)
```

```
(princ "\nType EXTRACTPOINTS to use\n")
(princ)
```

**ExtractPoints.lsp** starts by asking the user to select some POINT objects in their CAD drawing. It uses a filter to ensure that only POINT objects can be selected. If successful, it then asks the user for a filename to write the data to. Next, it creates the file, overwriting any previous version that already exists. If any errors occur, for example the user failed to select any POINT objects, no filename was entered, or the file could not be created, an appropriate error message is displayed.

If there are no errors, the function writes a header comment line to the output file. It then uses a counter in a repeat-loop to extract the insertion point of each selected POINT in turn. The insertion point is then converted to a text string which is written to the output file. When the repeat-loop is finished, the function closes the output file and displays a message saying how many insertion points have been extracted.

The following example of an output file shows the format of some extracted data:

```
*X, Y, Z
500, 150, 30.4
600, 150, 35.3
500, 250, 27.8
600, 250, 31.2
```

Each line contains the x,y,z coordinates of a single point. The values are stored as comma-separated numbers. In this example there are four points that form a square shape with each side of the square being 100 units long in the x,y plane.

## Extract Line Data for Chapter 2

The following lisp file defines a single function called EXTRACTLINES4PT that extracts x,y,x,y data from selected LINE objects in a CAD drawing. The data extracted by this function can only be used in the program detailed in Chapter 2.

**EXTRACTLINES4PT.LSP**

```
(defun C:EXTRACTLINES4PT ( / s1 n1 f1 c1 d1 p1 p2 t1)
 (princ "\nSelect LINE objects...")
 (if (= (setq s1 (ssget (list (cons 0 "LINE")))) nil)
  (princ "\nNo LINEs selected. Command terminating")
  (if (= (setq n1 (getfiled "Enter destination filename" "" "txt" 5)) nil)
   (princ "\nNo filename entered. Command terminating")
   (if (= (setq f1 (open n1 "w")) nil)
    (princ "\nUnable to open file to save data to. Command terminating")
    (progn
     (write-line "*X1, Y1, X2, Y2" f1)
     (setq c1 0)
     (repeat (sslength s1)
      (setq d1 (entget (ssname s1 c1)))
      (setq p1 (cdr (assoc 10 d1)) p2 (cdr (assoc 11 d1)))
      (setq t1 (strcat (rtos (car p1) 2 3) ", " (rtos (cadr p1) 2 3) ", "
                       (rtos (car p2) 2 3) ", " (rtos (cadr p2) 2 3)))
      (write-line t1 f1)
      (setq c1 (1+ c1))
```

```
        )
        (close f1)
        (princ (strcat "\nData for " (rtos c1 2 0) " line(s) saved to file"))
      )
     )
    )
  )
 (princ)
)
(princ "\nType EXTRACTLINES4PT to use\n")
(princ)
```

**ExtractLines4pt.lsp** is very similar to ExtractPoints.lsp. The primary differences are that the user selects LINE objects instead of POINT objects, and the x,y coordinates at each end of each LINE object are written to the output file. The z values of the coordinates are ignored.

The following example of an output file shows the format of some extracted data:

```
*X1, Y1, X2, Y2
350, 70, 350, 120
310, 120, 350, 180
350, 180, 390, 120
390, 120, 310, 120
```

Each line of data contains the x,y coordinates of each end of a single line. The values are stored as comma-separated numbers. In this example there are four lines that form an arrow pointing upwards.

## Extract Line Data for Chapters 3 and Beyond

The following lisp file defines a single function called EXTRACTLINES that extracts x,y,z data from selected LINE objects and lightweight polylines in a CAD drawing. The data extracted by this function can be used in the programs in Chapters 3 and beyond.

**EXTRACTLINES.LSP**

```
(defun C:EXTRACTLINES ( / s1 n1 f1 c1 c2 z1 d1 p1 t1 c3 c4 d2 z2)
 (princ "\nSelect LINE and/or LIGHTWEIGHT POLYLINE objects...")
 (if (= (setq s1 (ssget (list (cons -4 "<OR")
                              (cons 0 "LINE") (cons 0 "LWPOLYLINE")
                              (cons -4 "OR>")))) nil)
  (princ "\nNo LINEs or LWPOLYLINEs selected. Command terminating")
  (if (= (setq n1 (getfiled "Enter destination filename" "" "txt" 5)) nil)
   (princ "\nNo filename entered. Command terminating")
   (if (= (setq f1 (open n1 "w")) nil)
    (princ "\nUnable to open file to save data to. Command terminating")
    (progn
     (write-line "*X, Y, Z" f1)
     (setq c1 0 c2 0 z1 0.0)
     (repeat (sslength s1)
      (setq d1 (entget (ssname s1 c1)))
      (if (= (cdr (assoc 0 d1)) "LINE")
       (progn
        (setq p1 (cdr (assoc 10 d1)))
        (setq t1 (strcat (rtos (car p1) 2 3) ", "
```

```
                                 (rtos (cadr p1) 2 3) ", "
                                 (rtos (caddr p1) 2 3)))
          (write-line t1 f1)
          (setq p1 (cdr (assoc 11 d1)))
          (setq t1 (strcat (rtos (car p1) 2 3) ", "
                           (rtos (cadr p1) 2 3) ", "
                           (rtos (caddr p1) 2 3)))
          (write-line t1 f1)
          (write-line "-1" f1)
          (setq c2 (1+ c2))
        )
        ; code for lightweight polylines:
        (progn
          (setq c3 0 c4 -1)
          (repeat (length d1)
            (setq d2 (nth c3 d1))
            (if (= (car d2) 38)
              ; found polyline's Z value
              (setq z1 (cdr d2))
              (if (= (car d2) 10)
                ; found insertion point
                (progn
                  (setq p1 (cdr d2))
                  (if (= (caddr p1) nil)
                    (setq z2 z1)
                    (setq z2 (caddr p1))
                  )
                  (setq t1 (strcat (rtos (car p1) 2 3) ", "
                                   (rtos (cadr p1) 2 3) ", "
                                   (rtos z2 2 3)))
                  (write-line t1 f1)
                  (setq c4 (1+ c4))
                )
              )
            )
            (setq c3 (1+ c3))
          )
          (write-line "-1" f1)
          (if (> c4 -1)
            (setq c2 (+ c2 c4))
          )
        )
      )
      (setq c1 (1+ c1))
    )
    (close f1)
    (princ (strcat "\nData for " (rtos c2 2 0) " line segment(s) saved to file"))
  )
 )
 )
)
(princ)
)
(princ "\nType EXTRACTLINES to use\n")
(princ)
```

**ExtractLines.lsp** is more complicated than the previous two lisp files. Its filter allows the user to select LINE objects and/or lightweight polyline LWPOLYLINE objects, and it includes a second counter in the repeat-loop that counts how many line or line segments have been written to the output file. This second counter is needed because a single polyline object can contain multiple line segments. The function also sets a default z value to zero. This z value is used when lightweight polylines contain 2D data.

> Because a lightweight polyline is a 2D object in the x,y plane, the ends of all its segments will have the same z value. Some CAD programs store lightweight polylines using 2D x,y coordinates with an extra single data item that sets the z value. Other CAD programs store lightweight polylines using 3D x,y,z coordinates, each with the same z value. EXTRACTLINES can handle both types of lightweight polyline data.

Inside the repeat-loop, the function handles each selected object differently, depending on its type:

If it's a LINE object, the x,y,z coordinates at each end of the line are written to the output file, creating two separate lines of data. A single -1 is then written to the output file to indicate that any following data will be the start of a new line or line segment.

If it's a lightweight polyline LWPOLYLINE object, two new counters are used: one to step through the polyline's data items, the second to count how many line segments the polyline contains. The second counter starts at -1 because the number of segments is always one less than the number of insertion points. For example, a polyline containing a single line segment is defined by two insertion points. A second repeat-loop then looks at each data item in the lightweight polyline in turn. If the polyline's z value is found, the value is stored as the default z value. If an insertion point is found, the default z value is only used if the point is 2D. The insertion point's coordinates are then converted to a text string which is written to the output file. When the repeat-loop is finished, a single -1 is written to the output file to indicate the end of a polyline, and the number of line segments is added to the overall line counter. This function assumes all the polyline's segments are lines. Any arcs are treated as straight lines.

When all the selected objects have been processed, a message displays how many lines or line segments have been extracted.

The following example of an output file shows the format of some extracted data:

```
*X, Y, Z
300, 820, 17.6
340, 860, 24.2
-1
370, 810, 15.9
410, 850, 20.7
-1
260, 840, 31.2
290, 790, 29.0
350, 770, 25.5
410, 790, 18.8
440, 840, 12.3
-1
```

Each line of data contains either the x,y,z coordinates of one end of a line or line segment, or a single number (in this example -1) to indicate the end of a line or polyline object. Any data after the single number is the start of a new line object. The x,y,z values are stored as comma-separated numbers. In this example there are two separate diagonal lines followed by a sequence of four lines that form an approximate arc when viewed in the x,y plane. The final -1 can be omitted because there is no more data after it.

## Extract Path Data

The following lisp file defines a single function called EXTRACTPATH that extracts path data, including arcs, from a single lightweight polyline object in a CAD drawing.

**EXTRACTPATH.LSP**

```
(defun C:EXTRACTPATH ( / e1 d1 n1 f1 c1 t1 b1 p1 p2 c2 d2 n2 x1 y1 x2 y2 x3 y3 x4 y4)
 (if (= (setq e1 (entsel "\nSelect LIGHTWEIGHT POLYLINE: ")) nil)
  (princ "\nNo object selected. Command terminating")
  (progn
   (setq d1 (entget (car e1)))
   (if (/= (cdr (assoc 0 d1)) "LWPOLYLINE")
    (princ "\nObject selected is not a LWPLINE. Command terminating")
    (if (= (setq n1 (getfiled "Enter destination filename" "" "txt" 5)) nil)
     (princ "\nNo filename entered. Command terminating")
     (if (= (setq f1 (open n1 "w")) nil)
      (princ "\nUnable to open file to save data to. Command terminating")
      (progn
       (if (/= (setq c1 (getreal "\nEnter chainage at start: <0> ")) nil)
        (progn
         (write-line "*Ch" f1)
         (setq t1 (rtos c1 2 3))
         (write-line t1 f1)
        )
       )
       (write-line "*X, Y, arcX, arcY" f1)
       (setq c1 0 b1 0.0 p1 nil p2 nil c2 0)
       (repeat (length d1)
        (setq d2 (nth c1 d1))
        (setq n2 (car d2))
        (if (= n2 42)
         ; store bulge factor
         (setq b1 (cdr d2)))
        (if (= n2 10)
         ; found insertion point
         (if (= p1 nil)
          ; at start of polyline
          (setq p1 (cdr d2))
          (progn
           ; defines line or arc
           (setq p2 (cdr d2))
           (setq t1 (strcat (rtos (car p1) 2 3) ", " (rtos (cadr p1) 2 3)))
           (if (/= b1 0.0)
            ; calculate and output midpoint along arc
            (progn
             (setq x1 (car p1) y1 (cadr p1) x2 (car p2) y2 (cadr p2))
             (setq x3 (/ (+ x1 x2) 2.0) y3 (/ (+ y1 y2) 2.0))
             (setq x4 (+ x3 (* b1 (- y3 y1))) y4 (- y3 (* b1 (- x3 x1))))
             (setq t1 (strcat t1 ", " (rtos x4 2 3) ", " (rtos y4 2 3)))
            )
```

```
              )
              (write-line t1 f1)
              (setq p1 p2 b1 0.0 c2 (1+ c2))
            )
          )
        )
      )
      (setq c1 (1+ c1))
    )
    (if (/= p2 nil)
      (progn
        (setq t1 (strcat (rtos (car p2) 2 3) ", " (rtos (cadr p2) 2 3)))
        (write-line t1 f1)
      )
    )
    (close f1)
    (princ (strcat "\nData for " (rtos c2 2 0) " pline segment(s) saved to file"))
  )
      )
    )
   )
  )
 )
 (princ)
)
(princ "\nType EXTRACTPATH to use\n")
(princ)
```

**ExtractPath.lsp** starts by asking the user to select a single lightweight polyline object in their CAD drawing. Unlike the previous lisp files, here the user can only select a single object, not a group or selection of objects. If the object selected is not a lightweight polyline an error message is displayed. Otherwise the function asks the user for a filename to write the data to, and then creates the file, overwriting any previous version that already exists. If no errors have occurred, the function asks the user to enter the chainage at the start of the path. If the user enters a non-zero value, that value is converted to a text string and written, after a 'chainage' comment line, to the output file.

The function then writes a header comment line to the output file and initialises a counter that will look through the lightweight polyline's data. It also sets the bulge factor to zero to indicate a line rather than an arc, and sets two point variables to nil to indicate that they are both undefined. A second counter of line or arc segments written to the output file is also initialised to zero. Next, the function uses a repeat-loop to look through the lightweight polyline's data. If it finds a bulge factor (see the diagram on the next page), the value is stored. If it finds a point, it either stores the point if at the start of the polyline, or it combines the point with the previous point to define a line or an arc.

If defining a line or an arc, the previous point is converted to a text string. If the bulge factor is non-zero, the mid-point along the arc is calculated and appended to the text string. The text string is then written to the output file, and the newest point overwrites the previous point, the bulge factor is reset to zero, and the segment counter is increased by one.

The following diagram shows how the mid-point $x_4$ $y_4$ along the arc relates to the start $x_1$ $y_1$ and end $x_2$ $y_2$ of the arc, the half-way point $x_3$ $y_3$ between the start and end of arc, and the bulge factor $b$. The perpendicular line $x_3$ $y_3$ to $x_4$ $y_4$ is created by flipping the horizontal and vertical offsets $dx$ and $dy$, and swapping the sign of $dx$. A negative bulge factor creates an arc to the left of the line (looking from $x_1$ $y_1$ to $x_2$ $y_2$). A positive bulge factor creates an arc to the right of the line. A bulge factor of -1 or 1 will create a semi-circle.

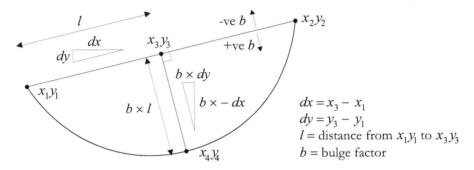

$$dx = x_3 - x_1$$
$$dy = y_3 - y_1$$
$$l = \text{distance from } x_1 y_1 \text{ to } x_3 y_3$$
$$b = \text{bulge factor}$$

When the end of the polyline's data is reached, the coordinates of the last point found are converted to a text string and written to the output file.

When the repeat-loop is finished, the output file is closed and a message displays how many line and/or arc segments have been extracted.

The following example of an output file shows the format of some extracted data:

```
*Ch
250
*X, Y, arcX, arcY
80, 90
200, 90, 230, 60
200, 30
50, 30, 25, 55
50, 80
160, 80, 180, 60
160, 40
100, 40
```

The first line of data contains the initial chainage. If this value is missing, the initial chainage is assumed to be zero. The chainage cannot be defined after any x,y data. The first two numbers of each subsequent line of data contain the x,y coordinates of one end of a line or arc segment. If there are two further numbers, they contain the x,y coordinates of a point on an arc between the current end-of-segment x,y coordinates and the end-of-segment x,y coordinates in the next line of data. In EXTRACTPATH the point on the arc is always the mid-point. However, it can be anywhere along the arc if you're creating your output file by hand. The x,y values are stored as comma-separated numbers. In this example there is sequence: line, arc, line, arc, line, arc, line that forms a shape that resembles a paperclip. The first line goes from 80,90 to 200,90. The first arc goes from

200,90 to 200,30 with a mid-point along the arc at 230,60. The second line goes from 200,30 to 50,30 and so on.

## Extract Triangle Data

The following lisp file defines a single function called EXTRACTTRIAS that extracts triangle data from 3D POLYLINE objects in a CAD drawing.

This function might be useful if you have created your own 3D triangles in your CAD drawing, rather than using the program in Chapter 4, and you want to obtain or calculate other data, such as contours or volumes, using the programs from later chapters in this book.

**EXTRACTTRIAS.LSP**

```
(defun C:EXTRACTTRIAS ( / s1 n1 f1 c1 c2 d1 e1 l1 c3 p1 t1)
 (princ "\nSelect 3D POLYLINE objects...")
 (if (= (setq s1 (ssget (list (cons 0 "POLYLINE")))) nil)
  (princ "\nNo 3D POLYLINEs selected. Command terminating")
  (if (= (setq n1 (getfiled "Enter destination filename" "" "txt" 5)) nil)
   (princ "\nNo filename entered. Command terminating")
   (if (= (setq f1 (open n1 "w")) nil)
    (princ "\nUnable to open file to save data to. Command terminating")
    (progn
     (write-line "*X1, Y1, Z1, X2, Y2, Z2, X3, Y3, Z3" f1)
     (setq c1 0 c2 0)
     (repeat (sslength s1)
      (setq d1 (entget (setq e1 (entnext (ssname s1 c1)))) l1 nil c3 0)
      (while (and (= (cdr (assoc 0 d1)) "VERTEX") (< c3 4))
       (setq p1 (cdr (assoc 10 d1)))
       (if (= l1 nil)
        (setq l1 (list p1))
        (setq l1 (append l1 (list p1)))
       )
       (setq d1 (entget (setq e1 (entnext e1)))) c3 (1+ c3))
      )
      (if (= c3 3)
       (progn
        (setq c3 0 t1 "")
        (repeat (length l1)
         (setq p1 (nth c3 l1))
         (setq t1 (strcat t1 (rtos (car p1) 2 3) ", "
                             (rtos (cadr p1) 2 3) ", "
                             (rtos (caddr p1) 2 3)))
         (if (< c3 2)
          (setq t1 (strcat t1 ", "))
         )
         (setq c3 (1+ c3))
        )
        (write-line t1 f1)
        (setq c2 (1+ c2))
       )
      )
      (setq c1 (1+ c1))
     )
     (close f1)
     (princ (strcat "\nData for " (rtos c2 2 0) " triangle(s) saved to file"))
    )
```

```
   )
  )
 )
 (princ)
)
(princ "\nType EXTRACTTRIAS to use\n")
(princ)
```

**ExtractTrias.lsp** starts the same as ExtractPoints.lsp and ExtractLines4pt.lsp except that the user selects 3D polyline objects instead of POINT or LINE objects. The code inside the repeat-loop is more complicated because the data for each 3D polyline is stored across multiple consecutive data items, unlike POINTs, LINEs or lightweight polylines where the data for each object is stored in a single data item. The first data item for a 3D polyline has the description "POLYLINE". It is followed by data items with the description "VERTEX" that define the polyline's shape. The number of "VERTEX" items matches the number of points in the polyline. The final data item for a 3D polyline has the description "SEQEND" although this is not searched for explicitly in ExtractTrias.lsp.

In the outer repeat-loop the function uses a while-loop to add each "VERTEX" point to a list of points. The while-loop exits when a non-"VERTEX" data item is found (i.e. "SEQEND") or when the list of points is more than three items long. After the while-loop, if the list of points is three items long the 3D polyline represents a triangle. In the inner repeat-loop, the points are converted to a text string which is then written to the output file. Three counters are used in the two repeat-loops: The first looks at each selected 3D polyline, the second counts how many 3D triangles have been written to the output file, and the third converts the list of points to a text string.

When the outer repeat-loop is finished, the output file is closed and a message displays how many 3D triangles have been extracted.

The following example of an output file shows the format of some extracted data:

```
*X1, Y1, Z1, X2, Y2, Z2, X3, Y3, Z3
520, 640, 57.7, 480, 700, 49.8, 560, 730, 46.8
590, 660, 50.2, 520, 640, 57.7, 560, 730, 46.8
610, 670, 35.0, 650, 740, 31.6, 680, 610, 33.7
```

Each line of data contains three sets of x,y,z coordinates that define the three corners of a single triangle. The values are stored as comma-separated numbers. In this example there are three triangles, two of which share an edge, and one which is separate from the others.

## Add Points to Lines and Paths

The following lisp file defines a single function called POINTSONLINES that adds 3D points to a CAD drawing at each end of selected lines and/or at each end of elements in selected 3D polylines.

## POINTSONLINES.LSP

```
(defun C:POINTSONLINES ( / s1 c1 c2 d1 e1)
 (princ "\nSelect LINE and/or 3D POLYLINE objects...")
 (if (= (setq s1 (ssget (list (cons -4 "<OR")
                              (cons 0 "LINE") (cons 0 "POLYLINE")
                              (cons -4 "OR>")))) nil)
  (princ "\nNo LINEs or 3D POLYLINEs selected. Command terminating")
  (progn
   (setq c1 0 c2 0)
   (repeat (sslength s1)
    (setq d1 (entget (setq e1 (ssname s1 c1))))
    (if (= (cdr (assoc 0 d1)) "LINE")
     (progn
      (entmake (list (cons 0 "POINT") (assoc 10 d1)))
      (entmake (list (cons 0 "POINT") (list 10 (cdr (assoc 11 d1)))))
      (setq c2 (+ c2 2))
     )
     (progn
      (setq d1 (entget (setq e1 (entnext e1))))
      (while (= (cdr (assoc 0 d1)) "VERTEX")
       (entmake (list (cons 0 "POINT") (assoc 10 d1)))
       (setq c2 (1+ c2))
       (setq d1 (entget (setq e1 (entnext e1))))
      )
     )
    )
    (setq c1 (1+ c1))
   )
   (princ (strcat "\n" (rtos c2 2 0) " points created"))
  )
 )
 (princ)
)
(princ "\nType POINTSONLINES to use\n")
(princ)
```

**PointsOnLines.lsp** starts by asking the user to select some LINE and/or 3D POLYLINE objects in their CAD drawing. It uses a filter to ensure that only these two types of objects can be selected. If successful, it then uses a counter in a repeat-loop to look at each selected object in turn.

For lines, it adds new 3D points at each end of each line to the CAD drawing. If two lines end at the same position, two identical 3D points will be created. For 3D polylines, it enters a while-loop that adds new 3D points at each vertex in the polyline to the CAD drawing. It also keeps a counter of how many points have been created, and displays the total when the function ends.

If any errors occur, for example if the user fails to select any LINE or 3D POLYLINE objects, an error message is displayed.

# Appendix B – CAD commands

Appendix B lists the generic CAD script file CAD commands used in Book One and in this book. Some of these commands may not be recognised by your CAD program. Therefore potential equivalent commands are also included in this appendix. When testing equivalent commands you need to find the version that takes its data from the command line and not from dialog boxes, otherwise your CAD script file will pause when it displays a dialog box and it will not complete automatically. Command line versions of CAD commands typically, but not always, start with a hyphen or an underscore character.

Once you have determined which commands or equivalent commands are recognised by your CAD program you can adapt your version of the source code in Book One and in this book to create CAD script files using these commands. Alternatively, you can use a text editor like Windows Notepad to find and replace the generic commands in the CAD script files with the equivalent commands recognised by your CAD program.

In addition to equivalent commands, some commands in your CAD program may require an additional new-line character at the end of the command, creating a blank line in your text file. For example, in my CAD program I had to include an additional new-line character after -3DPOLY data when the 3D polyline was not closed. However, if the -3DPOLY command ended with a C (for a closed 3D polyline) it was not necessary to include an additional new-line character. It was also necessary, for my CAD program, to include an additional empty line at the end of the CAD script file irrespective of the script file's contents. You might find that you need to make similar adjustments so that your CAD script files function correctly in your CAD program.

The format of the data that follows each command listed below may also differ depending on your CAD program's requirements.

## -3DPOLY

The command -3DPOLY draws a 3D polyline in your CAD drawing. The format used in Book One and in this book is:

```
-3DPOLY x,y,z x,y,z x,y,z C
```

where *x,y,z* are the coordinates at the end of each 3D line in the polyline and *C* creates a closed 3D polyline. The example above would create a 3D triangle. The number of x,y,z coordinates can be two to create a 3D line, or higher to create other shapes. The *C* is optional. If it is omitted the 3D polyline created will not be closed and it can have different start and end points.

Equivalent commands include 3DPOLY, _3DPOLY, 3DPLINE, PLINE3D and POLYLINE3D.

# -BLOCK

The command -BLOCK groups together existing object(s) in your CAD drawing that can then be inserted later as a 'block' using the -INSERT command (see below). The format used in Book One and in this book is:

```
-BLOCK name x,y,z L
```

where *name* is a unique name for the block, $x,y,z$ are the coordinates that will form the block's insertion point, and $L$ selects the last object that was created. The example above only selects the last object created.

If a block with the same name already exists, an error message will be displayed and the example above will fail to complete.

Equivalent commands include BLOCK, _BLOCK, MAKEBLOCK, DEFBLOCK and BMAKE.

# -COLOR

The command -COLOR sets the colour of the next and subsequent objects drawn in your CAD program. The format used in Book One and in this book is:

```
-COLOR n
```

where $n$ is the pen number with the range $1 \leq n \leq 255$.

Equivalent commands include COLOR, _COLOR and SETCOLOR.

# -INSERT

The command -INSERT inserts a block previously created using the -BLOCK command (see above) into your CAD drawing. The format used in Book One and in this book is:

```
-INSERT name x,y,z h v r
```

where *name* is the block's name, $x,y,z$ are the insertion point's coordinates, $h$ and $v$ are the horizontal and vertical scale factors (values of 1.0 maintain the original size) and $r$ is the rotation angle, measured in degrees in an anti-clockwise direction from the positive x axis.

Equivalent commands include INSERT, _INSERT and INSERTBLOCK.

# -PLINE

The command -PLINE draws a lightweight 2D polyline in your CAD drawing. The format used in Book One and in this book is:

```
-PLINE x,y W 0.0 n x,y W 0.0 0.0 x,y
```

where $x,y$ are the coordinates at the end of each line in the polyline, and $W$, followed by two numbers, specifies the line width for the next line. In the example above a polyline containing two lines is created. The first line forms an arrow-head shape with the line width increasing from 0 up to $n$ along the line. The second line has zero line width.

Lightweight polylines can also include arcs, but as the programs in Book One and in this book do not create polylines containing arcs, this is not shown in the example above.

Equivalent commands include PLINE, _PLINE, LWPOLYLINE and POLYLINE.

# -POINT

The command -POINT draws a 3D point in your CAD drawing. The format used in Book One and in this book is:

```
-POINT x,y,z
```

where $x,y,z$ are the point's coordinates.

Equivalent commands include POINT and _POINT.

# Appendix C – Mathematical Equations

Appendix C contains derivations of the equations used in Book One and in this book.

## Intersection of Two 2D Lines

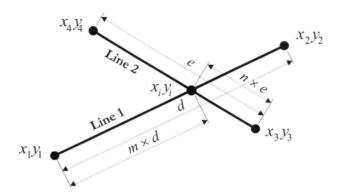

(i) Known variables:

$x_1\ y_1$ and $x_2\ y_2$ are the coordinates at each end of Line 1

$x_3\ y_3$ and $x_4\ y_4$ are the coordinates at each end of Line 2

(ii) Unknown variables:

$d$ is the length of Line 1

$e$ is the length of Line 2

$x_i\ y_i$ are the coordinates at the intersection of the two lines

$m$ is the distance along Line 1, expressed as a fraction of $d$

$n$ is the distance along Line 2, expressed as a fraction of $e$

(iii) Initial equations:

$$x_i = x_1 + m(x_2 - x_1)$$
$$y_i = y_1 + m(y_2 - y_1)$$
$$x_i = x_3 + n(x_4 - x_3)$$
$$y_i = y_3 + n(y_4 - y_3)$$

(iv) To find $m$ first equate the $x_i$'s and rearrange so that $n$ is alone:

$$x_i = x_1 + m(x_2 - x_1) = x_3 + n(x_4 - x_3)$$

$$\therefore x_1 - x_3 + m(x_2 - x_1) = n(x_4 - x_3)$$

$$\therefore n = \frac{(x_1 - x_3) + m(x_2 - x_1)}{(x_4 - x_3)}$$

(v) Then equate the $y_i$'s from (iii) and rearrange so that $n$ is alone:

$$y_i = y_1 + m(y_2 - y_1) = y_3 + n(y_4 - y_3)$$

$$\therefore y_1 - y_3 + m(y_2 - y_1) = n(y_4 - y_3)$$

$$\therefore n = \frac{(y_1 - y_3) + m(y_2 - y_1)}{(y_4 - y_3)}$$

(vi) Next, equate the $n$'s from (iv) and (v) and rearrange so that $m$ is alone:

$$n = \frac{(x_1 - x_3) + m(x_2 - x_1)}{(x_4 - x_3)} = \frac{(y_1 - y_3) + m(y_2 - y_1)}{(y_4 - y_3)}$$

$$\therefore (x_1 - x_3)(y_4 - y_3) + m(x_2 - x_1)(y_4 - y_3)$$
$$= (x_4 - x_3)(y_1 - y_3) + m(x_4 - x_3)(y_2 - y_1)$$

$$\therefore m(x_2 - x_1)(y_4 - y_3) - m(x_4 - x_3)(y_2 - y_1)$$
$$= (x_4 - x_3)(y_1 - y_3) - (x_1 - x_3)(y_4 - y_3)$$

$$\boxed{\therefore m = \frac{(x_4 - x_3)(y_1 - y_3) - (x_1 - x_3)(y_4 - y_3)}{(x_2 - x_1)(y_4 - y_3) - (x_4 - x_3)(y_2 - y_1)}}$$

(vii) Similarly, to find $n$ first equate the $x_i$'s from (iii) and rearrange so that $m$ is alone:

$$x_i = x_1 + m(x_2 - x_1) = x_3 + n(x_4 - x_3)$$

$$\therefore m(x_2 - x_1) = (x_3 - x_1) + n(x_4 - x_3)$$

$$\therefore m = \frac{(x_3 - x_1) + n(x_4 - x_3)}{(x_2 - x_1)}$$

(viii) Then equate the $y_i$'s from (iii) and rearrange so that $m$ is alone:

$$y_i = y_1 + m(y_2 - y_1) = y_3 + n(y_4 - y_3)$$

$$\therefore m(y_2 - y_1) = (y_3 - y_1) + n(y_4 - y_3)$$

$$\therefore m = \frac{(y_3 - y_1) + n(y_4 - y_3)}{(y_2 - y_1)}$$

(ix) Next, equate the $m$'s from (vii) and (viii) and rearrange so that $n$ is alone:

$$m = \frac{(x_3 - x_1) + n(x_4 - x_3)}{(x_2 - x_1)} = \frac{(y_3 - y_1) + n(y_4 - y_3)}{(y_2 - y_1)}$$

$$\therefore (x_3 - x_1)(y_2 - y_1) + n(x_4 - x_3)(y_2 - y_1)$$
$$= (x_2 - x_1)(y_3 - y_1) + n(x_2 - x_1)(y_4 - y_3)$$

$$\therefore n(x_4 - x_3)(y_2 - y_1) - n(x_2 - x_1)(y_4 - y_3)$$
$$= (x_2 - x_1)(y_3 - y_1) - (x_3 - x_1)(y_2 - y_1)$$

$$\therefore n = \frac{(x_2 - x_1)(y_3 - y_1) - (x_3 - x_1)(y_2 - y_1)}{(x_4 - x_3)(y_2 - y_1) - (x_2 - x_1)(y_4 - y_3)}$$

(x) Finally, multiply top and bottom by -1 to make the denominator the same as the equation to calculate $m$ in (vi):

$$n = \frac{(x_3 - x_1)(y_2 - y_1) - (x_2 - x_1)(y_3 - y_1)}{(x_2 - x_1)(y_4 - y_3) - (x_4 - x_3)(y_2 - y_1)}$$

This reduces the number of calculations required because $m$ and $n$ now share the same denominator.

(xi) The lines are parallel and therefore do not intersect if the denominator is zero:

$$(x_2 - x_1)(y_4 - y_3) - (x_4 - x_3)(y_2 - y_1) = 0$$

(xii) Otherwise the lines intersect within the extents of both lines when:

$$0 \le m \le 1 \ \text{ and } \ 0 \le n \le 1$$

## Location of a 2D Point Relative to a 2D Line

The following equations calculate the shortest distance from a 2D point to a 2D line, and identify which side of the line the point is on.

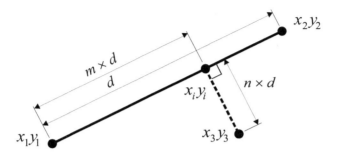

(i) Known variables:

$x_1\,y_1$ and $x_2\,y_2$ are the coordinates at each end of the line

$x_3\,y_3$ are the coordinates of the point

(ii) Unknown variables:

$d$ is the length of the line

$x_i\,y_i$ are the coordinates on the line that are closest to the point

$m$ is the distance along the line, expressed as a fraction of $d$

$n$ is the distance from the line to the point, expressed as a fraction of $d$

(iii) Initial equations:

$$x_i = x_1 + m(x_2 - x_1)$$

$$y_i = y_1 + m(y_2 - y_1)$$

$$x_i = x_3 - n(y_2 - y_1)$$

$$y_i = y_3 + n(x_2 - x_1)$$

(iv) To find $m$ first equate the $x_i$'s and rearrange so that $n$ is alone:

$$x_i = x_1 + m(x_2 - x_1) = x_3 - n(y_2 - y_1)$$

$$\therefore n(y_2 - y_1) = (x_3 - x_1) - m(x_2 - x_1)$$

$$\therefore n = \frac{(x_3 - x_1) - m(x_2 - x_1)}{(y_2 - y_1)}$$

(v) Then equate the $y_i$'s from (iii) and rearrange so that $n$ is alone:

$$y_i = y_1 + m(y_2 - y_1) = y_3 + n(x_2 - x_1)$$

$$\therefore y_1 - y_3 + m(y_2 - y_1) = n(x_2 - x_1)$$

$$\therefore n = \frac{(y_1 - y_3) + m(y_2 - y_1)}{(x_2 - x_1)}$$

(vi) Then switch the order of $(y_1 - y_3)$ to match the order of other coordinate pairs:

$$n = \frac{-(y_3 - y_1) + m(y_2 - y_1)}{(x_2 - x_1)}$$

(vii) Next, equate the $n$'s from (iv) and (vi) and rearrange so that $m$ is alone:

$$n = \frac{(x_3 - x_1) - m(x_2 - x_1)}{(y_2 - y_1)} = \frac{-(y_3 - y_1) + m(y_2 - y_1)}{(x_2 - x_1)}$$

$$\therefore (x_3 - x_1)(x_2 - x_1) - m(x_2 - x_1)^2 = -(y_3 - y_1)(y_2 - y_1) + m(y_2 - y_1)^2$$

$$\therefore (x_3 - x_1)(x_2 - x_1) + (y_3 - y_1)(y_2 - y_1) = m(x_2 - x_1)^2 + m(y_2 - y_1)^2$$

$$\boxed{\therefore m = \frac{(x_3 - x_1)(x_2 - x_1) + (y_3 - y_1)(y_2 - y_1)}{(x_2 - x_1)^2 + (y_2 - y_1)^2}}$$

(viii) Similarly, to find $n$ first equate the $x_i$'s from (iii) and rearrange so that $m$ is alone:

$$x_i = x_1 + m(x_2 - x_1) = x_3 - n(y_2 - y_1)$$

$$\therefore m(x_2 - x_1) = (x_3 - x_1) - n(y_2 - y_1)$$

$$\therefore m = \frac{(x_3 - x_1) - n(y_2 - y_1)}{(x_2 - x_1)}$$

(ix) Then equate the $y_i$'s from (iii) and rearrange so that $m$ is alone:

$$y_i = y_1 + m(y_2 - y_1) = y_3 + n(x_2 - x_1)$$

$$\therefore m(y_2 - y_1) = (y_3 - y_1) + n(x_2 - x_1)$$

$$\therefore m = \frac{(y_3 - y_1) + n(x_2 - x_1)}{(y_2 - y_1)}$$

(x) Next, equate the $m$'s from (viii) and (ix) and rearrange so that $n$ is alone:

$$m = \frac{(x_3 - x_1) - n(y_2 - y_1)}{(x_2 - x_1)} = \frac{(y_3 - y_1) + n(x_2 - x_1)}{(y_2 - y_1)}$$

$$\therefore (x_3 - x_1)(y_2 - y_1) - n(y_2 - y_1)^2 = (x_2 - x_1)(y_3 - y_1) + n(x_2 - x_1)^2$$

$$\therefore (x_3 - x_1)(y_2 - y_1) - (x_2 - x_1)(y_3 - y_1) = n(x_2 - x_1)^2 + n(y_2 - y_1)^2$$

$$\therefore n = \frac{(x_3 - x_1)(y_2 - y_1) - (x_2 - x_1)(y_3 - y_1)}{(x_2 - x_1)^2 + (y_2 - y_1)^2}$$

(xi) If the ends of the line have the same coordinates, the line has no length and the denominator is zero. In this situation it's not possible to find the closest point on the line:

$$(x_2 - x_1)^2 + (y_2 - y_1)^2 = 0$$

(xii) Otherwise the sign of $n$ indicates which side of the line the point is on:

| | |
|---|---|
| $n < 0$ | the point is to the left of the line |
| $n = 0$ | the point is on the line |
| $n > 0$ | the point is to the right of the line |

where 'left' and 'right' assume that you are at $x_1\,y_1$ and looking towards $x_2\,y_2$

(xiii) $x_i\,y_i$ is on or between the ends of the line when:

$$0 \leq m \leq 1$$

# Defining a 3D Plane from Three 3D Points

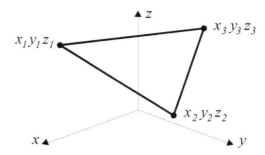

(i) Known variables:

$x_1\ y_1\ z_1$ , $x_2\ y_2\ z_2$ and $x_3\ y_3\ z_3$ are coordinates of the three 3D points

(ii) Initial equations:

$$z_1 = a + bx_1 + cy_1$$

$$z_2 = a + bx_2 + cy_2$$

$$z_3 = a + bx_3 + cy_3$$

(iii) Unknown variables:

$a$ is where the plane crosses the z axis when $x$ and $y$ are both zero

$b$ is the slope of the line when the 3D plane crosses the x,z plane when $y = 0$

$c$ is the slope of the line when the 3D plane crosses the y,z plane when $x = 0$

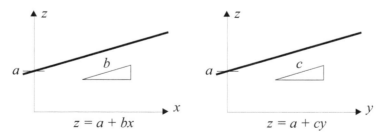

(iv) To find $b$ first equate the $a$'s and rearrange so that $c$ is in terms of $b$:

$$a = z_1 - bx_1 - cy_1 = z_2 - bx_2 - cy_2$$

$$\therefore -cy_1 + cy_2 = -z_1 + z_2 + bx_1 - bx_2$$

$$\therefore -c(y_1 - y_2) = -(z_1 - z_2) + b(x_1 - x_2)$$

$$\therefore c(y_1 - y_2) = (z_1 - z_2) - b(x_1 - x_2)$$

$$\therefore c = \frac{(z_1 - z_2) - b(x_1 - x_2)}{(y_1 - y_2)}$$

$$a = z_1 - bx_1 - cy_1 = z_3 - bx_3 - cy_3$$

$$\therefore c = \frac{(z_1 - z_3) - b(x_1 - x_3)}{(y_1 - y_3)}$$

Then equate the $c$'s to find $b$:

$$\therefore c = \frac{(z_1 - z_2) - b(x_1 - x_2)}{(y_1 - y_2)} = \frac{(z_1 - z_3) - b(x_1 - x_3)}{(y_1 - y_3)}$$

$$\therefore (y_1 - y_3)(z_1 - z_2) - b(x_1 - x_2)(y_1 - y_3)$$
$$= (y_1 - y_2)(z_1 - z_3) - b(x_1 - x_3)(y_1 - y_2)$$

$$\therefore (y_1 - y_3)(z_1 - z_2) - (y_1 - y_2)(z_1 - z_3)$$
$$= b(x_1 - x_2)(y_1 - y_3) - b(x_1 - x_3)(y_1 - y_2)$$

$$\therefore b = \frac{(y_1 - y_3)(z_1 - z_2) - (y_1 - y_2)(z_1 - z_3)}{(x_1 - x_2)(y_1 - y_3) - (x_1 - x_3)(y_1 - y_2)}$$

(v) Similarly, to find $c$ first equate the $a$'s and rearrange so that $b$ is in terms of $c$:

$$a = z_1 - bx_1 - cy_1 = z_2 - bx_2 - cy_2$$

$$\therefore -bx_1 + bx_2 = -z_1 + z_2 + cy_1 - cy_2$$

$$\therefore -b(x_1 - x_2) = -(z_1 - z_2) + c(y_1 - y_2)$$

$$\therefore b(x_1 - x_2) = (z_1 - z_2) - c(y_1 - y_2)$$

$$\therefore b = \frac{(z_1 - z_2) - c(y_1 - y_2)}{(x_1 - x_2)}$$

$$a = z_1 - bx_1 - cy_1 = z_3 - bx_3 - cy_3$$

$$\therefore b = \frac{(z_1 - z_3) - c(y_1 - y_3)}{(x_1 - x_3)}$$

Then equate the $b$'s to find $c$:

$$\therefore b = \frac{(z_1 - z_2) - c(y_1 - y_2)}{(x_1 - x_2)} = \frac{(z_1 - z_3) - c(y_1 - y_3)}{(x_1 - x_3)}$$

$$\therefore (x_1 - x_3)(z_1 - z_2) - c(x_1 - x_3)(y_1 - y_2)$$
$$= (x_1 - x_2)(z_1 - z_3) - c(x_1 - x_2)(y_1 - y_3)$$

$$\therefore c(x_1 - x_2)(y_1 - y_3) - c(x_1 - x_3)(y_1 - y_2)$$
$$= (x_1 - x_2)(z_1 - z_3) - (x_1 - x_3)(z_1 - z_2)$$

$$\therefore c = \frac{(x_1 - x_2)(z_1 - z_3) - (x_1 - x_3)(z_1 - z_2)}{(x_1 - x_2)(y_1 - y_3) - (x_1 - x_3)(y_1 - y_2)}$$

(vi) To find $a$ rearrange any of the equations from (ii):

$$a = z_1 - bx_1 - cy_1$$

(vii) The following equation finds the direction of maximum slope of a 3D plane:

$$\theta_{max} = tan^{-1}\left(\frac{c}{b}\right)$$

where $\theta_{max}$ is the angle of maximum slope, anti-clockwise from the positive x axis

(viii) The following equation finds the magnitude of the maximum slope:

$$s_{max} = \sqrt{(b^2 + c^2)}$$

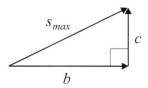

where $s_{max}$ is the maximum slope. It is the sum of adding two vectors at right angles formed from $b$ and $c$ and it equals the change in the z axis divided by the distance in the x,y plane. For example, if the change in the z axis is 1 unit, and the distance in the x,y plane is 40 units, then:

$$s_{max} = \frac{1}{40} = 0.025 = 2.5\%$$

$s_{max}$ can be multiplied by 100 to express the slope as a percentage.

## Calculating the Area and Volume of a Triangle from Three 3D Points

(i) The standard equation for calculating the area of a triangle is:

$$A = \frac{l \times h}{2}$$

where $A$ is the area, $l$ is the length of one edge, and $h$ is the perpendicular distance from that edge to the opposite corner. The edge $l$ can be any edge of the triangle. It does not have to be the longest edge.

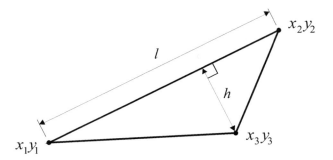

From the section "Location of a 2D Point Relative to a 2D Line" earlier in this appendix we can express $l$ and $h$ as follows:

$$l = \sqrt{(x_2 - x_1)^2 + (y_2 - y_1)^2}$$

$$h = |n \times l|$$

where:

$$n = \frac{(x_3 - x_1)(y_2 - y_1) - (x_2 - x_1)(y_3 - y_1)}{(x_2 - x_1)^2 + (y_2 - y_1)^2}$$

$$\therefore A = \frac{l \times h}{2} = \frac{l \times |n \times l|}{2} = \frac{|n| l^2}{2}$$

$$\therefore A = \frac{|(x_3 - x_1)(y_2 - y_1) - (x_2 - x_1)(y_3 - y_1)|}{(x_2 - x_1)^2 + (y_2 - y_1)^2} \times \frac{(x_2 - x_1)^2 + (y_2 - y_1)^2}{2}$$

$$\boxed{\therefore A = \frac{|(x_3 - x_1)(y_2 - y_1) - (x_2 - x_1)(y_3 - y_1)|}{2}}$$

This area is in the x,y plane only: z values at the corners of the triangle are ignored.

(ii) To calculate the volume between the 3D triangle and the x,y plane where $z = 0$, the area calculated in (i) is multiplied by the z value at the triangle's centroid:

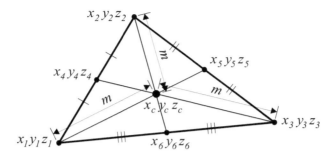

where $x_1\ y_1\ z_1$ , $x_2\ y_2\ z_2$ and $x_3\ y_3\ z_3$ are the coordinates of the triangle's corners, and $x_4\ y_4\ z_4$ , $x_5\ y_5\ z_5$ and $x_6\ y_6\ z_6$ are the coordinates at the mid-points of the opposite edges:

$$x_4 = \frac{x_1 + x_2}{2} \qquad y_4 = \frac{y_1 + y_2}{2} \qquad z_4 = \frac{z_1 + z_2}{2}$$

$$x_5 = \frac{x_2 + x_3}{2} \qquad y_5 = \frac{y_2 + y_3}{2} \qquad z_5 = \frac{z_2 + z_3}{2}$$

$$x_6 = \frac{x_1 + x_3}{2} \qquad y_6 = \frac{y_1 + y_3}{2} \qquad z_6 = \frac{z_1 + z_3}{2}$$

and $x_c\ y_c\ z_c$ are the coordinates of the triangle's centroid:

$$x_c = x_1 + m(x_5 - x_1) = x_2 + m(x_6 - x_2) = x_3 + m(x_4 - x_3)$$

$$y_c = y_1 + m(y_5 - y_1) = y_2 + m(y_6 - y_2) = y_3 + m(y_4 - y_3)$$

$$z_c = z_1 + m(z_5 - z_1) = z_2 + m(z_6 - z_2) = z_3 + m(z_4 - z_3)$$

where $m$ is the distance from the corner to the centroid, expressed as a fraction of the distance from the corner to the mid-point of the opposite side.

To calculate $m$ equate two of the $x_c$ equations above and rearrange so that $m$ is alone:

$$x_c = x_1 + m(x_5 - x_1) = x_2 + m(x_6 - x_2)$$

$$\therefore (x_1 - x_2) = m\{(x_6 - x_2) - (x_5 - x_1)\}$$

$$\therefore (x_1 - x_2) = m\left\{\left(\frac{x_1 + x_3}{2} - x_2\right) - \left(\frac{x_2 + x_3}{2} - x_1\right)\right\}$$

$$\therefore (x_1 - x_2) = m\left\{\frac{x_1}{2} + \frac{x_3}{2} - \frac{2x_2}{2} - \frac{x_2}{2} - \frac{x_3}{2} + \frac{2x_1}{2}\right\}$$

$$\therefore (x_1 - x_2) = m\left\{\frac{3x_1}{2} - \frac{3x_2}{2}\right\}$$

$$\therefore m = \frac{(x_1 - x_2)}{\frac{3}{2}(x_1 - x_2)} = \frac{2}{3}$$

Now reapply to the $x_c$ equations above to replace $m$:

$$x_c = x_1 + m(x_5 - x_1) = x_1 + \frac{2}{3}(x_5 - x_1)$$

$$\therefore x_c = x_1 + \frac{2}{3}\left(\frac{x_2 + x_3}{2} - x_1\right)$$

$$\therefore x_c = x_1 + \frac{x_2}{3} + \frac{x_3}{3} - \frac{2x_1}{3} = \frac{x_1}{3} + \frac{x_2}{3} + \frac{x_3}{3}$$

$$\therefore x_c = \frac{x_1 + x_2 + x_3}{3}$$

The same process can be used to similarly derive $y_c$ and $z_c$:

$$y_c = \frac{y_1 + y_2 + y_3}{3} \qquad\qquad z_c = \frac{z_1 + z_2 + z_3}{3}$$

Finally, multiply $z_c$ by $A$ from (i) above to obtain the triangle's volume:

$$V = A \times z_c = \frac{|(x_3 - x_1)(y_2 - y_1) - (x_2 - x_1)(y_3 - y_1)|}{2} \times \frac{z_1 + z_2 + z_3}{3}$$

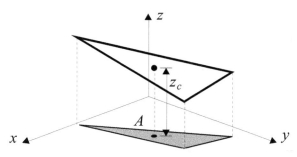

$$V = A \times \left(\frac{z_1 + z_2 + z_3}{3}\right)$$

## Defining a 2D Circle from Three 2D Points

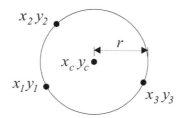

(i) Known variables:

$x_1\,y_1$ , $x_2\,y_2$ and $x_3\,y_3$ are the coordinates of the three 2D points

(ii) Initial equations:

$$r^2 = (x_1 - x_c)^2 + (y_1 - y_c)^2$$

$$r^2 = (x_2 - x_c)^2 + (y_2 - y_c)^2$$

$$r^2 = (x_3 - x_c)^2 + (y_3 - y_c)^2$$

(iii) Unknown variables:

$r$ is the circle's radius

$x_c\,y_c$ are the coordinates at the centre of the circle

(iv) Equate the first two equations, expand, and rearrange to find $y_c$ in terms of $x_c$:

$$(x_1 - x_c)^2 + (y_1 - y_c)^2 = (x_2 - x_c)^2 + (y_2 - y_c)^2$$

$$\therefore x_1^2 - 2x_1 x_c + x_c^2 + y_1^2 - 2y_1 y_c + y_c^2 = x_2^2 - 2x_2 x_c + x_c^2 + y_2^2 - 2y_2 y_c + y_c^2$$

$$\therefore x_1^2 - 2x_1 x_c + y_1^2 - 2y_1 y_c = x_2^2 - 2x_2 x_c + y_2^2 - 2y_2 y_c$$

$$\therefore x_1^2 - x_2^2 + y_1^2 - y_2^2 = 2x_1 x_c - 2x_2 x_c + 2y_1 y_c - 2y_2 y_c$$

$$\therefore x_1^2 - x_2^2 + y_1^2 - y_2^2 = 2x_c(x_1 - x_2) + 2y_c(y_1 - y_2)$$

$$\therefore y_c = \frac{x_1^2 - x_2^2 + y_1^2 - y_2^2 - 2x_c(x_1 - x_2)}{2(y_1 - y_2)}$$

(v) Create a similar equation for the first and third equations using the same steps:

$$y_c = \frac{x_1^2 - x_3^2 + y_1^2 - y_3^2 - 2x_c(x_1 - x_3)}{2(y_1 - y_3)}$$

(vi) Equate the equations in (iv) and (v) and rearrange to find $x_c$:

$$\frac{x_1^2 - x_2^2 + y_1^2 - y_2^2 - 2x_c(x_1 - x_2)}{2(y_1 - y_2)} = \frac{x_1^2 - x_3^2 + y_1^2 - y_3^2 - 2x_c(x_1 - x_3)}{2(y_1 - y_3)}$$

$$\therefore (x_1^2 - x_2^2 + y_1^2 - y_2^2)(y_1 - y_3) - 2x_c(x_1 - x_2)(y_1 - y_3)$$
$$= (x_1^2 - x_3^2 + y_1^2 - y_3^2)(y_1 - y_2) - 2x_c(x_1 - x_3)(y_1 - y_2)$$

$$\therefore (x_1^2 - x_2^2 + y_1^2 - y_2^2)(y_1 - y_3) - (x_1^2 - x_3^2 + y_1^2 - y_3^2)(y_1 - y_2)$$
$$= 2x_c(x_1 - x_2)(y_1 - y_3) - 2x_c(x_1 - x_3)(y_1 - y_2)$$

$$\therefore x_c = \frac{(x_1^2 - x_2^2 + y_1^2 - y_2^2)(y_1 - y_3) - (x_1^2 - x_3^2 + y_1^2 - y_3^2)(y_1 - y_2)}{2[(x_1 - x_2)(y_1 - y_3) - (x_1 - x_3)(y_1 - y_2)]}$$

(vii) Repeat (iv) to find $x_c$ in terms of $y_c$:

$$(x_1 - x_c)^2 + (y_1 - y_c)^2 = (x_2 - x_c)^2 + (y_2 - y_c)^2$$

$$\therefore x_1^2 - x_2^2 + y_1^2 - y_2^2 = 2x_c(x_1 - x_2) + 2y_c(y_1 - y_2)$$

$$\therefore x_c = \frac{x_1^2 - x_2^2 + y_1^2 - y_2^2 - 2y_c(y_1 - y_2)}{2(x_1 - x_2)}$$

(viii) Repeat (v) to find $x_c$ in terms of $y_c$:

$$x_c = \frac{x_1^2 - x_3^2 + y_1^2 - y_3^2 - 2y_c(y_1 - y_3)}{2(x_1 - x_3)}$$

(ix) Equate the equations in (vii) and (viii) and rearrange to find $y_c$:

$$\frac{x_1^2 - x_2^2 + y_1^2 - y_2^2 - 2y_c(y_1 - y_2)}{2(x_1 - x_2)} = \frac{x_1^2 - x_3^2 + y_1^2 - y_3^2 - 2y_c(y_1 - y_3)}{2(x_1 - x_3)}$$

$$\therefore (x_1^2 - x_2^2 + y_1^2 - y_2^2)(x_1 - x_3) - 2y_c(x_1 - x_3)(y_1 - y_2)$$
$$= (x_1^2 - x_3^2 + y_1^2 - y_3^2)(x_1 - x_2) - 2y_c(x_1 - x_2)(y_1 - y_3)$$

$$\therefore (x_1^2 - x_3^2 + y_1^2 - y_3^2)(x_1 - x_2) - (x_1^2 - x_2^2 + y_1^2 - y_2^2)(x_1 - x_3)$$
$$= 2y_c(x_1 - x_2)(y_1 - y_3) - 2y_c(x_1 - x_3)(y_1 - y_2)$$

$$\therefore y_c = \frac{(x_1^2 - x_3^2 + y_1^2 - y_3^2)(x_1 - x_2) - (x_1^2 - x_2^2 + y_1^2 - y_2^2)(x_1 - x_3)}{2[(x_1 - x_2)(y_1 - y_3) - (x_1 - x_3)(y_1 - y_2)]}$$

(x) The equations in (vi) and (ix) share coefficients and can therefore be simplified:

$$C_1 = (x_1^2 - x_2^2 + y_1^2 - y_2^2)$$

$$C_2 = (x_1^2 - x_3^2 + y_1^2 - y_3^2)$$

$$C_3 = 2[(x_1 - x_2)(y_1 - y_3) - (x_1 - x_3)(y_1 - y_2)]$$

$$\therefore x_c = \frac{[C_1(y_1 - y_3) - C_2(y_1 - y_2)]}{C_3}$$

and

$$y_c = \frac{[C_2(x_1 - x_2) - C_1(x_1 - x_3)]}{C_3}$$

(xi) No circle can be found when:

$C_1 = 0$          The first and second points are identical

$C_2 = 0$          The first and third points are identical

$C_3 = 0$          The three points are collinear or any of the points are identical

(xii) Note that $C_1$ and $C_2$ can also be rewritten in similar terms to $C_3$:

$$C_1 = (x_1 + x_2)(x_1 - x_2) + (y_1 + y_2)(y_1 - y_2)$$

and

$$C_2 = (x_1 + x_3)(x_1 - x_3) + (y_1 + y_3)(y_1 - y_3)$$

When these equations are multiplied out they are the same equations as in (x) above.

## Intersection of Two 3D Planes

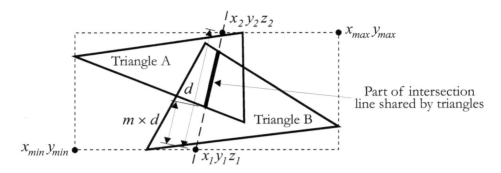

(i) Known variables:

$a_1$ $b_1$ $c_1$ and $a_2$ $b_2$ $c_2$ are 3D plane coefficients for the two planes

Refer to "Defining a 3D Plane from Three 3D Points" earlier in this appendix for how to obtain these coefficients from a 3D triangle.

$x_{min}$ $y_{min}$ and $x_{max}$ $y_{max}$ and are the minimum and maximum x,y values of the rectangle that surrounds the two triangles that define the two planes

(ii) Unknown variables:

$x_1$ $y_1$ $z_1$ and $x_2$ $y_2$ $z_2$ are two points on the intersection line of the two planes

$d$ is the distance between $x_1$ $y_1$ $z_1$ and $x_2$ $y_2$ $z_2$

$m$ is a fraction of the distance $d$ along the line between $x_1$ $y_1$ $z_1$ and $x_2$ $y_2$ $z_2$

(iii) Initial 3D plane equations:

$$z = a_1 + b_1 x + c_1 y$$

$$z = a_2 + b_2 x + c_2 y$$

(iv) Initial 3D intersection line equations:

$$x = x_1 + m(x_2 - x_1)$$

$$y = y_1 + m(y_2 - y_1)$$

$$z = z_1 + m(z_2 - z_1)$$

(v) Equate the z values in the two equations in (iii):

$$a_1 + b_1 x + c_1 y = a_2 + b_2 x + c_2 y$$

(vi) Then rearrange to get $x$ in terms of $y$ and $y$ in terms of $x$:

$$x = \frac{(a_2 - a_1) + (c_2 - c_1)y}{(b_1 - b_2)}$$

$$y = \frac{(a_2 - a_1) + (b_2 - b_1)x}{(c_1 - c_2)}$$

(vii) Set x or y to the minimum and maximum x or y values and calculate y or x, and z:

| If $(c_1 - c_2) \neq 0$ then: | If $(b_1 - b_2) \neq 0$ then: |
|---|---|
| $x_1 = x_{min}$ | $y_1 = y_{min}$ |
| $y_1 = \dfrac{(a_2 - a_1) + (b_2 - b_1)x_1}{(c_1 - c_2)}$ | $x_1 = \dfrac{(a_2 - a_1) + (c_2 - c_1)y_1}{(b_1 - b_2)}$ |
| $z_1 = a_1 + b_1 x_1 + c_1 y_1$ | $z_1 = a_1 + b_1 x_1 + c_1 y_1$ |
| $x_2 = x_{max}$ | $y_2 = y_{max}$ |
| $y_2 = \dfrac{(a_2 - a_1) + (b_2 - b_1)x_2}{(c_1 - c_2)}$ | $x_2 = \dfrac{(a_2 - a_1) + (c_2 - c_1)y_2}{(b_1 - b_2)}$ |
| $z_2 = a_1 + b_1 x_2 + c_1 y_2$ | $z_2 = a_1 + b_1 x_2 + c_1 y_2$ |

If $(b_1 - b_2) = 0$ and $(c_1 - c_2) = 0$ then the two planes are coplanar and there is no intersection line.

(viii) To determine the part of the intersection line that is shared by both triangles, calculate where the line crosses the edges of the triangles (refer to "Intersection of Two 2D Lines" earlier in this appendix), to obtain values for $m$.

# Intersection of a 2D Line and a 2D Circle

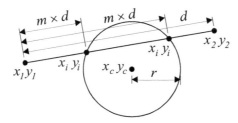

(i) Known variables:

$x_1\ y_1$ and $x_2\ y_2$ are the coordinates at each end of the line

$x_c\ y_c$ are the coordinates at the centre of the circle

$r$ is the circle's radius

$d$ is the line's length

(ii) Initial equations:

$$x_i = x_1 + m(x_2 - x_1)$$

$$y_i = y_1 + m(y_2 - y_1)$$

$$r^2 = (x_i - x_c)^2 + (y_i - y_c)^2$$

(iii) Unknown variables:

$m$ is the fraction of the distance along the line to the intersection points

$x_i\ y_i$ are the coordinates at the intersection points

There are zero, one or two solutions for $m$ and $x_i\ y_i$

(iv) To find $m$, substitute $x_i\ y_i$ in the first two equations in (ii) into the third equation:

$$r^2 = (x_1 + m(x_2 - x_1) - x_c)^2 + (y_1 + m(y_2 - y_1) - y_c)^2$$

then rearrange to pair $x$ and $y$:

$$r^2 = [(x_1 - x_c) + m(x_2 - x_1)]^2 + [(y_1 - y_c) + m(y_2 - y_1)]^2$$

then expand the contents of each square-brackets:

$$r^2 = (x_1 - x_c)^2 + 2m(x_1 - x_c)(x_2 - x_1) + m^2(x_2 - x_1)^2 + (y_1 - y_c)^2$$
$$+ 2m(y_1 - y_c)(y_2 - y_1) + m^2(y_2 - y_1)^2$$

Next, rearrange to group $m$ by their power to form a quadratic equation:

$$[(x_2 - x_1)^2 + (y_2 - y_1)^2]m^2 + [2(x_1 - x_c)(x_2 - x_1) + 2(y_1 - y_c)(y_2 - y_1)]m$$
$$+ [(x_1 - x_c)^2 + (y_1 - y_c)^2 - r^2] = 0$$

(v) Substitute this equation for a standard quadratic equation:

$$ax^2 + bx + c = 0$$

where:

$$a = (x_2 - x_1)^2 + (y_2 - y_1)^2$$

$$b = 2(x_1 - x_c)(x_2 - x_1) + 2(y_1 - y_c)(y_2 - y_1)$$

$$c = (x_1 - x_c)^2 + (y_1 - y_c)^2 - r^2$$

$$x = m$$

(vi) Use the standard equation to solve $m$:

$$x = \frac{-b \pm \sqrt{b^2 - 4ac}}{2a}$$

where:

$$x = m$$

(vii) There are zero, one or two solutions depending on the values of $a$, $b$ and $c$:

If:

$$2a = 0$$

then there is no solution because the line has no length.

If:

$$(b^2 - 4ac) < 0$$

then there is no solution because the line and circle do not cross.

If:

$$(b^2 - 4ac) = 0$$

then there is one solution because the line intersects the circle at one point only (see the diagram over the page):

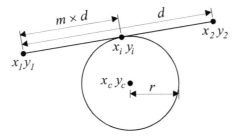

If:

$$(b^2 - 4ac) > 0$$

then there are two solutions:

$$m = \frac{-b + \sqrt{b^2 - 4ac}}{2a} \qquad\qquad m = \frac{-b - \sqrt{b^2 - 4ac}}{2a}$$

(viii) Finally, put $m$ into the first two equations in (ii) to get $x_i\, y_i$

# Index

# D

Delete key, 81, 90, 93
*DeleteFlowPaths* function: Ch.10, **87**, 90
*DeleteSelectedTriangles*: Ch.4, 90
*DIFF_PROXIMITY* constant: Ch.13, **128**, 136
Ditch, 92, 93
*DoLineAndCircleCross* function: Ch.14, **159**, 167, 168
Downhill, slope arrows, 52
*DrawModel* function: Ch.10, **86**, 90; Ch.11, **101**, 103;
    Ch.12, **114**, 118; Ch.13, **132**, 136; Ch.14, **153**,
    165; Ch.5, **9**, 15; Ch.6, **30**, 33; Ch.7, **45**, 50; Ch.8,
    **60**, 62; Ch.9, **72**, 76
*DTMFLOWPATH* structure: Ch.10, **82**, 89
*DTMNODE* structure: Ch.14, **147**, 164
*dwTria* variable: DTMFLOWPATH, 89

# E

Escape key, 35
Exit program, 21
*ExtractLines.lsp* file, **181**, 182
*ExtractLines4pt.lsp* file, **180**, 181
*ExtractPath.lsp* file, **184**, 185
*ExtractPoints* lisp routine, 124
*ExtractPoints.lsp* file, **179**, 180
*ExtractTrias* lisp routine, 1, 141
*ExtractTrias.lsp* file, **187**, 188

# F

*fabs* function, 14, 118, 163
Fill colour, 37, 49
Fill, cut and, 123, 140
Filter, CAD, 164
*FINDPOINTS_STEPSIZE* constant: Ch.9, **68**, 76
*FindPointsCont* function: Ch.9, **74**, 76
*FindPointsStart* function: Ch.9, **73**, 76
Flat points, 65, 76, 78
Flat triangle, 16
*floor* function, 14, 16
Flow paths, 79, 90, 91, 93
*FUZZFACTOR* constant, 16, 91, 120, 138, 167, 169,
    170

# G

GDI+, 36
*Gdiplus.lib* library file, 18, 34, 52, 63, 78, 92, 105,
    121, 138, 171
*GETBOUNDARIES_STEPSIZE* constant: Ch.11, **97**,
    103
*GetBoundariesCont* function: Ch.11, **102**, 104
*GetBoundariesStart* function: Ch.11, **102**, 103
*GetContourAtMousePosition* function: Ch.5, **14**, 17

*GetCoordsAtMouse* function: Ch.14, **162**, 170
*GETDIFFERENCE_STEPSIZE* constant: Ch.13, **127**,
    136
*GetDifferenceAtCorners* function: Ch.13, **134**, 137
*GetDifferenceAtCrossingEdges* function: Ch.13, **135**,
    137
*GetDifferenceAtMouse* function: Ch.13, **136**, 138
*GetDifferenceCont* function: Ch.13, **133**, 137
*GetDifferenceStart* function: Ch.13, **133**, 136
*GETINTERSECTION_STEPSIZE* constant: Ch.12,
    **109**, 118
*GetIntersectionCont* function: Ch.12, **115**, 119
*GetIntersectionLine* function: Ch.12, **116**, 119
*GetIntersectionStart* function: Ch.12, **115**, 118
*GetNodesAlongArc* function: Ch.14, **156**, 166
*GetNodesAlongLine* function: Ch.14, **159**, 166, 168
*GETSECTIONS_STEPSIZE* constant: Ch.14, **146**,
    163
*GetSectionsCont* function: Ch.14, **155**, 166
*GetSectionsStart* function: Ch.14, **154**, 165
*GetSlopeAtMousePosition* function: Ch.7, **49**, 51
*GETSLOPES_STEPSIZE* constant: Ch.7, **40**, 49
*GetSlopesCont* function: Ch.7, **46**, 50
*GetSlopesStart* function: Ch.7, **46**, 50
*GetZValueAtMousePosition* function: Ch.6, **32**, 33
*GETZVALUES_STEPSIZE* constant: Ch.6, **26**, 32
*GetZValuesCont* function: Ch.6, **32**, 33
*GetZValuesStart* function: Ch.6, **31**, 33
Grid, section, 175

# H

Hide, 53
High points, 65, 76, 78, 143, 163, 169, 174, 175

# I

*InitMouseDropdownMenu* function: Ch.10, **87**, 90;
    Ch.11, **102**, 103; Ch.12, **114**, 118; Ch.13, **133**,
    136; Ch.14, **154**, 165; Ch.5, **10**, 15; Ch.6, **31**, 33;
    Ch.7, **46**, 50; Ch.8, **61**, 62; Ch.9, **73**, 76
*InitShowDropdownMenu* function: Ch.10, **87**, 90;
    Ch.11, **102**, 103; Ch.12, **114**, 118; Ch.13, **133**,
    136; Ch.14, **153**, 165; Ch.5, **10**, 15; Ch.6, **31**, 33;
    Ch.7, **45**, 50; Ch.8, **61**, 62; Ch.9, **73**, 76
*InitViewDropdownMenu* function: Ch.14, **154**, 165
*-INSERT* command, **192**
Intermediate points, section, 164, 166, 170, 174
Intersection, 107, 118, 122, 210
*IsAngleBetween* function: Ch.14, **158**, 167

# J

JPEG file, 1, 21, 23, 36, 37, 54, 65, 78, 79, 93, 95,
    106, 107, 125, 143, 173